Departure and Consolation

Supplements to Novum Testamentum

VOLUME 117

Departure and Consolation

The Johannine Farewell Discourses in Light of Greco-Roman Literature

by

George L. Parsenios

BRILL

LEIDEN • BOSTON

2005

This book is printed on acid-free paper.

Library of Congress Cataloging-in-Publication Data

Parsenios, George L.
  Departure and consolation: the Johannine farewell discourses in light of Greco-Roman literature / by George L. Parsenios.
    p. cm. — (Supplements to Novum Testamentum, ISSN 0167-9732; v. 117)
  Includes bibliographical references and indexes.
  ISBN 90-04-14278-9 (alk. paper)
    1. Bible, N.T. John XIII–XVII—Language, style. 2. Farewells in the Bible.
3. Greek Literature, Hellenistic—History and criticism. 4. Farewells in literature.
I. Title. II. Series.

  BS2615.6.F35P37 2005
  226.5'066—dc22

                                                        2004062544

100430655T
ISSN 0167-9732
ISBN 90 04 14278 9

PRINTED IN THE NETHERLANDS

For Maureen

CONTENTS

ACKNOWLEDGEMENTS

This monograph is a revised version of a doctoral dissertation accepted by the Graduate School of Yale University in December, 2002. It is appropriate, therefore, to begin by expressing my great esteem and gratitude to Harold W. Attridge for his careful oversight of the dissertation, as well as for his invaluable support and advice in initiating my academic career. It also gives me great pleasure to thank warmly the official readers of the dissertation, Dale B. Martin, Adela Yarbro Collins, and David L. Bartlett. They offered generous and helpful criticism of my work, and also provided essential advice and encouragement in the opening stages of my professional life. Remaining errors of style or substance in what follows are, of course, my own.

For illuminating conversations, advice and support along the way, I would like to thank Wayne A. Meeks, Leander E. Keck, Nicholas P. Constas, Jürgen Zangenberg, and all of the participants in the Yale New Testament/Ancient Christianity Dissertation Colloquium and the Princeton Theological Seminary New Testament Colloquium. Special appreciation goes to both John T. Fitzgerald and Paul Holloway, not only for their kind encouragement, but also and more especially for generously sharing their important work on the Farewell Discourses even before it had gone to press.

The Yale University Graduate School, The Holy Cross Greek Orthodox School of Theology and The Greek Orthodox Archdiocese of America supported my doctoral study and I am grateful for their assistance.

I am deeply honored that this study is included in Novum Testamentum Supplements, and express sincere thanks to the series editors, Margaret M. Mitchell and David Moessner, for agreeing to publish my work. First Regine Reincke and finally Ivo Romein from Brill worked industriously to bring the study to press. To the anonymous reader of the manuscript, I offer public thanks for clear, helpful criticism.

Revisions of the dissertation are minimal, with each chapter being streamlined but not substantially altered. Aspects of chapters 1 and 3 of the dissertation have since been incorporated into the essay "Παραμυθητικὸς Χριστός: John Chrysostom interprets the Johannine Farewell

Discourses," which was delivered in November, 2003 at the conference *Sacred Text and Interpretation: Perspectives in Orthodox Biblical Studies, A Conference in Honor of Professor Savas Agourides*. The conference papers are being published in a forthcoming commemorative volume of the *Greek Orthodox Theological Review*, and the relevant sections are published here by permission. Chapter 2 has been changed slightly in light of further reflection on the delayed exit in Greek and Latin drama.

The publication of my dissertation is not only a professional milestone, but a personal one as well, and I would like here to acknowledge with deep affection all that I owe to my grandparents, my parents, my brother Nicholas and my children Nicholas and Julia. This monograph is dedicated to my wife, Maureen.

ABBREVIATIONS

AION (archeol.)	*Annali dell' istituto Orientale di Napoli* (Sezione di Archeologia e Storia Antica)
AJP	American Journal of Philology
ANF	*Ante-Nicene Fathers*
ANRW	Aufstieg und Niedergang der Römischen Welt, ed. H. Temporini and W. Haase (Berlin and New York: De Gruyter, 1972–)
ATR	*Anglican Theological Review*
CBQ	*Catholic Biblical Quarterly*
CP	*Classical Philology*
EphTheolLov	*Ephemerides Theological Lovanienses*
ET	*Expository Times*
EtudTheolRel	*Études Théologiques et Religeuses*
FRLANT	Forschungen zur Religion und Literatur des Alten und Neuen Testaments
Goggin	Saint John Chrysostom, *Commentary on Saint John the Apostle and Evangelist* (trans. Sister Thomas Aquinas Goggin, S.C.H.; New York: Fathers of the Church, 1960)
GOTR	*Greek Orthodox Theological Review*
GRBS	Greek, Roman and Byzantine Studies
HSCP	*Harvard Studies in Classical Philology*
HTR	*Harvard Theological Review*
JBL	*Journal of Biblical Literature*
JDAI	*Jahrbuch, Deutschen Archäologischen Instituts*
JSNT	*Journal for the Study of the New Testament*
JSNTSS	Journal for the Study of the New Testament Supplement Series
MDAI (A)	Mitteilungen des Deutschen archäologischen Instituts, Athener Abteilung
NovT	*Novum Testamentum*
NPNF	*Nicene and Post-Nicene Fathers*
NTS	*New Testament Studies*
PG	Patrologia Graeca. Ed. J.-P. Migne
RAC	*Reallexikon für Antike und Christentum*, ed. T. Klauser, E. Dassman, et al. (Stuttgart: Hiersemann, 1950–)
SANT	Studien zum Alten und Neuen Testaments
SBLDS	Society of Biblical Literature Dissertation Series
SBLSymS	Society of Biblical Literature Symposium Series
SGKA	Studien zur Geschichte und Kultur des Altertums
SNTSMS	Society for New Testament Studies Monograph Series
TAPA	*Transactions of the American Philological Association*
ThPh	*Theologie und Philosophie*
TJT	*Toronto Journal of Theology*
TrierTheolZeit	*Trierer Theologische Zeitschrift*
Tru	*Theologische Rundschau*
ZNW	*Zeitschrift für die neutestamentliche Wissenschaft*
ZTK	*Zeitschrift für Theologie und Kirche*

CHAPTER ONE

THE ONE AND THE MANY

Consensus is rare in New Testament interpretation, but not impossible. Much current Johannine study, for instance, reflects a common opinion regarding the origins and historical context of the Gospel of John. Gone are the days when Bultmann and Dodd could confidently claim a Mandaean or a Hermetic framework for the Logos theology and the cosmic dualism that underlie the thought of the Gospel.[1] Current trends place the Gospel of John against the backdrop of the Dead Sea Scrolls and other contemporary Judaisms, rather than against the broader Greco-Roman world.[2] Interestingly, W.D. Davies traces the origins of this shift in emphasis to the very work of Dodd himself.[3] Dodd's *Interpretation of the Fourth Gospel* is at one and the same time the high water mark of Greek approaches to the Gospel of John as well as a harbinger of Semitic theories.[4] The shift from Hellenism to Judaism has, of course, not been total. Studies still appear in which John's Gospel is compared to contemporary Greek and Latin literature.[5] Unlike the work of Bultmann

---

[1] Rudolf Bultmann, *The Gospel of John: A Commentary* (trans. G.R. Beasley-Murray et al.; Philadelphia: Westminster, 1971) 7–9 and passim; idem, "Die Bedeutung der neuerschlossenen mandäischen und manichäischen Quellen fur das Verständnis des Johannesevangeliums," *ZNW* 24 (1925) 100–146; C.H. Dodd, *The Interpretation of the Fourth Gospel* (Cambridge: Cambridge University Press, 1970) 10–53 and passim. But see recently, Andreas Dettwiler, *Die Gegenwart des Erhöhten: Eine Exegetische Studie zu den johanneischen Abschiedsreden (Joh 13:31–16:33) unter besonderer Berückstigung ihres Relecture-Charakters* (FRLANT 169; Göttingen: Vandenhoeck and Ruprecht, 1995) 21–33, where the Gnostic genre "Dialog des Erlösers" is compared to the Farewell Discourses in order to illuminate their synchronic and phenomenological character.

[2] See, for just one example, John Ashton, *Understanding the Fourth Gospel* (Oxford: Clarendon Press, 1993) 205, who counters Bultmann's claim that John was a Gnostic with the argument that he is better understood as a former Essene.

[3] W.D. Davies, "Reflections on Aspects of the Jewish Background of the Gospel of John," in *Exploring the Gospel of John in Honor of D. Moody Smith* (ed. R. Alan Culpepper and C. Clifton Black; Louisville: Westminster John Knox Press, 1996) 43.

[4] Ibid., 43.

[5] For a broad sketch of arguments about the use of both "Jewish" and "Greek" literature in the study of John, see most recently, Harold W. Attridge, "Genre Bending in the Fourth Gospel," *JBL* 121 (2002) 3–21. For a more elaborate study, with particular attention to the Farewell Discourses, see John T. Fitzgerald, *Jesus'*

and Dodd, however, these recent studies focus more on literary, rhetorical and cultural matters and less on the theological and philosophical influences behind the Gospel. The present work will also address literary and narrative concerns in the Gospel of John with the help of classical literature. Such literary questions inevitably lead to theological matters, given the character and purpose of the Gospel of John, but the following arguments are not rooted in classical philosophy as much as they are in classical philology.

Even so, one ancient philosophical dilemma provides a helpful framework for the concerns of the present study. The pre-Socratics were the first to ponder the alternate poles of the One and the Many. Although the world appeared to them to be a collection of random, separate items (trees, humans, snakes), thinkers like Thales (ca. 585 BC) hoped to see an underlying unity to the world's diversity. For Thales, everything in the universe was actually comprised of water, though in different forms. What appeared, therefore, to be Many (trees, humans, snakes) was actually One (water).

Last Will and Testament: Wills, Friendship and the Fourth Gospel (Atlanta: Scholars Press, forthcoming), which is a comparison of the discourses with Greek and Latin wills. For the application of classical rhetorical categories to the Farewell Discourses, see both George Kennedy, *New Testament Interpretation through Rhetorical Criticism* (Chapel Hill: University of North Carolina Press, 1984) 73–85, and C. Clifton Black, "The Words That You Have Given to Me I Have Given to Them: The Grandeur of Johannine Rhetoric," in *Exploring the Gospel of John*, 220–39. It is misleading, of course, to suggest that the terms "Judaism" and "Greco-Roman" correspond to utterly distinct realities in the study of 1st century Christianity or Judaism. But previous work has not adequately brought classical literature to bear on the Gospel of John generally, and on the Farewell Discourses in particular, based on the assumption that the Gospel is more "Jewish" than "Greek." It is to fill this lack that the present study will focus particularly on Greco-Roman literature. See also, Mark Stibbe, *John as Storyteller: Narrative Criticism and the Fourth Gospel* (SNTSMS 73; Cambridge: Cambridge University Press, 1992) 129–30. For a recent discussion on the history of this problem, as well as efforts at a new way forward, see the essays in Troels Engberg-Pedersen, ed., *Paul Beyond the Judaism/Hellenism Divide* (Louisville: Westminster/John Knox, 2001). Finally, a comment of Paul Holloway, "Left Behind: Jesus' Consolation of His Disciples in John 13,31–17,26," *ZNW* (forthcoming: January, 2005) 35 n. 6, deserves repeating here. After insisting that the Gospel of John can be profitably read in light of classical literature Holloway writes,

> The distinction here between "Jewish" and "Greco-Roman" is not altogether satisfactory, since first-century Judaism was by definition a Greco-Roman religion. Indeed, the Jewish testament derives its unique generic form not from the fact that it is "Jewish" versus "Greco-Roman," but from the fact that it draws almost exclusively on earlier "biblical" models. I do not mean to imply that by following Greco-Roman models the author of John has consciously turned his back on Jewish traditions, or for that matter that he was even aware of employing one type of death scene versus another.

This study will understand the terminology of the One and the Many in a slightly different sense, assigning to the categories of One-ness and Many-ness two questions critical to interpreting the Farewell Discourses. One-ness refers to the common assumption that only one literary genre, the testament, defines the shape and content of the Farewell Discourses.[6] Although there have been, and continue to be, scholars who read these chapters through other generic lenses, the thoroughgoing belief in the testament quality of the discourses continues.[7] In the testament, venerable figures follow a usual pattern of speech and actions on the brink of death. Moses' speech to the assembled Israelites in Deuteronomy 34 represents the paradigmatic

---

[6] The term testament covers the body of literature that is alternately called either the farewell speech (Abschiedsrede, Discours d' adieu) or testament. See Fitzgerald, *Jesus' Last Will*, pp. 62–63 for a distinction between the terms, as well as an explanation for their being used without distinction. Brown (*Gospel of John*, 2.598f.) uses the English "farewell speech" in keeping with the French and German terminology of Johannes Munck, "Discours d'adieu dans le Nouveau Testament et dans la littérature biblique," in *Aux sources de la tradition chrétienne*, Mélanges M. Goguel (Neuchatel: Delachaux, 1950) 155–70, and Ethelbert Stauffer, "Abschiedsreden," *RAC* (1950) 29–35. Francis Moloney uses the terms farewell speech and testament interchangeably, *Glory Not Dishonor: Reading John 13–21* (Minneapolis: Fortress Press, 1998) 4ff. D. Moody Smith compromises and uses the phrase "testament of farewell" in *John* (Nashville: Abingdon, 1999) 264. Fernando Segovia refers to "the testament or farewell of a dying hero," *The Farewell of the Word: The Johannine Call to Abide* (Minneapolis: Fortress, 1991) 5.

[7] Even when Ashton and Winter examine biblical and early Jewish literature in important ways that transcend the typical arguments made about the testament, they are not pushing too far into new literature. Ashton, *Understanding*, 443–484, distinguishes in these chapters a type closely related to the testament – the commission form. The commission is actually a composite form, combining the elements of the later testaments (e.g., *Testaments of the Twelve Patriarchs*) with the features of the commission, e.g. Deut. 34. Ashton follows the delineation of the genre as outlined by N. Lohfink, "Die deuteronomistische Darstellung des Übergangs der Führung Israels von Mose auf Josue," *Scholastik* 37 (1962) 32–44 in order to argue that John has twisted both the commission and the testament form in producing the Farewell Discourses. A similar operation is performed by Martin Winter, *Das Vermächtnis Jesu und die Abschiedsworte der Väter. Gattungsgeschichtliche Untersuchung der Vermächtnisrede im Blick auf Joh. 13–17* (Göttingen: Vandenhoeck and Ruprecht, 1994). Winter isolates a form that he calls the *Vermächtnis*, ("will," "bequest," "legacy") which he distinguishes sharply from farewell speeches, as well as from the testament form (36ff.). Both scholars, however, base their arguments on the same Old Testament and Jewish texts, generally used to delineate the traditional testament form. To note this fact is not to critique their careful and important arguments, but to recognize that they have not necessarily brought new literature to bear on the problems, as much as they have looked anew at the same books, or at least different chapters of the same books. The goal of the present study is to bring new comparative material to the discussion of the Farewell Discourses.

example of the phenomenon in the Old Testament. The basic template appears in a variety of later Jewish texts, most notably the *Testaments of the Twelve Patriarchs*.

Investigations of this genre have led scholars to look beyond Jewish literature, however, and to notice similarities between the Jewish testaments and the farewell scenes from Greek and Latin texts.[8] In classical literature, the death of Socrates in Plato's *Phaedo* is the model farewell text, and, as in the case of Moses, Socrates' example is copied in numerous later texts.[9] As will become more obvious below in the discussion of consolation literature, however, the influence of Greco-Roman writings like the *Phaedo* is often only superficial. The limits and guidelines of analysis are still set by the boundaries of the biblical testaments and extra-biblical Jewish texts (which are largely based on biblical exemplars). This particular use of classical literature does not actually, then, open up new avenues of inquiry; it slightly extends well-traveled roads.[10] By One-ness, then, is meant the thoroughgoing assumption that the testament – particularly the biblical testament – is the single most important literary influence on the Farewell Discourses.

This sense of unity on formal questions sits surprisingly alongside ideas about the Many-ness of the discourses, and belief in the Many-ness of John 13–17 has been equally persistent and widely assumed. Although the farewell scene of Jesus appears to be an extended, single discourse stretching from 13:1 to 18:1, various seams have been discovered in the literary flow of these chapters.[11] The discovery of these aporias has inspired claims that the unity of the discourses is only apparent and is the result of several stages of redaction. As in the case of One-ness, there have been notable deviations from the

---

[8] See, for example, William Kurz, "Luke 22:14–38 and Greco-Roman and Biblical Farewell Addresses," *JBL* 104 (1985) 251–68. For the relationship between classical and Jewish farewell scenes, see Segovia, *Farewell of the Word*, 5–20.

[9] See Ibid., 6.

[10] Fitzgerald, of course, works very differently in his forthcoming *Jesus' Last Will and Testament*, where he investigates with great precision and breadth Greek and Roman official procedures and cultural assumptions regarding last wills and testaments, particularly as they relate to the institution of friendship. His approach deviates dramatically from standard work and the present study will follow his lead in pursuing classical literature to explain aspects of the Farewell Discourses, as will be explained below.

[11] See, for instance, Raymond Brown, *The Gospel According to John* (2 vols.; Garden City, NY: Doubleday), 2.582ff.

scholarly consensus about the editorial history of the text. Recent narrative critics have made valuable contributions to the study of these discourses, and have demonstrated that the chapters are far more unified than has been traditionally thought.[12] However, because some aspects of the discourses defy efforts to see unity, the narrative critics themselves often stop short of marshalling a definitive defense of unity theories. They seem to concede that their pursuit of narrative unity is a contrived effort. In a footnote or a passing comment, even narrative critics are likely to refer to the redactional history of this or that verse, indicating that their own efforts do not come to grips with the actual editorial record of the text.[13] Thus, the core belief in the discourses' Many-ness persists.

The Farewell Discourses, then, are One and Many at the same time. But, for such a heavily edited text to maintain such rigid generic unity implies that each new editor remained true to the literary and generic purposes of the original author(s). This is certainly not hypothetically impossible, and Winter has argued that there are precedents for this practice.[14] Regardless, the apparent illogic of this scenario is rarely so pronounced in actual work on the discourses. Brown, for instance, is one who assumes that the discourses are both a testament and heavily edited. But for him, the editorial process begins with raw materials left behind by the original Evangelist.[15] He thus adequately explains the consistent prevalence of testament themes, while also allowing for editorial revision. Segovia takes Brown a step further and allows for the possibility that the original author of the Gospel himself could have been involved in the editorial process.[16]

---

[12] See Segovia, *Farewell of the Word*; Moloney, *Glory Not Dishonor*; David Tolmie, *Jesus' Farewell to the Disciples* (Leiden: E.J. Brill, 1995).

[13] This matter will be taken up at greater length in the latter half of this chapter.

[14] Winter, *Vermächtnis*, argues that John 13–17 is both an example of only one genre, the "legacy speech," as well as the product of heavy redaction. He offers several texts (Gen 47–50; Deut; Joshua 23–24; 1 Enoch) that are heavily edited, yet faithful to one genre, as similar to the Johannine material. (Ibid., loc. cit., 229). He does recognize, however, that some Johannine insertions do not follow the Old Testament and Jewish "Vermächtnis" form. Among the foreign features in John is the function of the Paraclete (316f., 319, 323). The present study will explain precisely those features of the discourses that cannot be explained by recourse to Jewish and Old Testament models – such as the function of the Paraclete.

[15] Brown, *Gospel of John*, 2.586ff., 598ff.

[16] Segovia, *Farewell of the Word*, 320 and passim. See also Moloney, *Glory not Dishonor*, 4 n. 13.

The One-ness and Many-ness of the discourses are thereby kept from coming into conflict with one another.

This brief review, however, intends not merely to point out other interpreters' ability or inability to reconcile the One and the Many, but rather to introduce the present argument. For, the following study will reverse the patterns of One and Many that currently dominate discussion of the Johannine Farewell Discourses. First, where the scholarly consensus has seen One-ness in questions of genre, the ensuing chapters will argue for greater generic variety. Rather than reading the Farewell Discourses solely as a testament, the present study will multiply the generic associations of the discourses. Certainly, as was noted above, this is not an entirely novel effort. Some have already noticed that one of these genres, the literary symposium, influences certain parts of the Farewell Discourses.[17] But, in addition to the literary symposium are the exit to death in ancient drama and certain aspects of ancient consolation literature. Thus, where scholarly consensus has typically seen only the testament genre as a template for the structure of these chapters, the following study will investigate various literary associations. To argue in the language of the pre-Socratics, the first concern is to see Many where others have seen One.

The second goal is the opposite, to see One where others have seen Many. Chapter 2 will focus particularly on this effort. The material from ancient drama surveyed in that chapter will provide a means for resolving long-standing questions about the curious narrative seam that separates John 14 and 15. At the close of chapter 14, Jesus announces a departure that he does not complete until 18:1. Interpreters have typically viewed the delayed departure as a

---

[17] Several interpreters have briefly proposed some connection between these chapters and the ancient symposium. See the following: Josef Martin, *Symposion: Die Geschichte einer literarischen Form* (Paderborn: Ferdinand Schöningh, 1931) 314ff.; David E. Aune, *The New Testament in its Literary Environment* (Philadelphia: Westminster, 1987) 122; Idem, "Septem Sapientum Convivium," in *Plutarch's Ethical Writings and Early Christian Literature*, (ed. Hans Dieter Betz. Leiden: E.J. Brill, 1978) passim; Joel C. Relihan, et al. "Rethinking the History of the Literary Symposium." *ICS* 17 (1992) 216, 241–2; Ben Witherington, *John's Wisdom: A Commentary on the Fourth Gospel* (Cambridge: Lutterworth Press, 1995) 232–3; Sjef Van Tilborg, *Imaginative Love in John* (Leiden: E.J. Brill, 1993) 133 and passim; Dennis Smith, *From Symposium to Eucharist: The Banquet in the Early Christian World* (Minneapolis: Fortress, 2003), especially chapter 8, "The Banquet in the Gospels;" Mary L. Coloe, "Welcome into the Household of God: The Footwashing in John 13," *CBQ* 66 (2004) 400–415.

sign of sloppy editing. In the history of research, this delay is one of the first features of the discourses suggesting to commentators that chapters 13–17 are not a united whole.[18] In defense of the discourses' literary coherence, chapter 2 will view the delay instead as a distinct feature of the Gospel's reliance on dramatic modes of narration, and a signal actually of literary unity, not disunity.

To summarize briefly, then, the following study will argue that the Johannine Farewell Discourses do not follow the model of the testament alone. The discourses are a composite of various literary forms, not One but Many. On another level, however, this generic variety supports narrative unity. When read only against the testament form, John 14:31 appears to upset the ordered flow of Jesus' departure and to justify redaction theories. When read in light of additional literary possibilities, however, such as the dramatic exit to death, the narrative coherence of the scene is more obvious. In at least this one case, then, the pursuit of Many-ness on the level of literary genres supports the pursuit of One-ness on the level of narrative coherence.

Presence in Absence

For now, however, questions about the One and the Many can recede temporarily in order to introduce an additional matter. Each of the following chapters will draw on a different generic category for illuminating the Farewell Discourses, giving the impression that each chapter will stand on its own, with no connection to the others. The chapters will be more interconnected than this situation suggests. A consistent red thread runs through the course of the study: the presence-in-absence of Jesus. The pursuit of generic problems illuminates the constellation of themes in the Farewell Discourses related to the continuing presence of Jesus after he has departed from his disciples and from the world.[19]

In the wake of thinkers like Lacan, it has become common for interpreters to seek out themes of presence-in-absence, wherein

---

[18] Ashton, *Understanding*, 30.

[19] For the theme of presence in absence in the Farewell Discourses, see especially Attridge, "Genre Bending," 17–18, and Ashton, *Understanding*, 443ff.

departed people survive in traces of their presence.[20] One needs no
high-powered critical lenses to discover such themes in John, however. With no recourse to post-modern theory, Ashton writes point-
edly as follows about Jesus in John 14:

> It follows that if the disciples' faith is to be securely grounded, his
> departure must be succeeded by some kind of presence-in-absence.
> This of course is what we do find: indeed it may be said to be *the*
> subject of the discourse.[21]

The motif of presence-in-absence will unite the various components
of this study. Each chapter is intended to shed new light on the
nature of Jesus' departure as well as his continuing presence in spite
of that departure. To clarify how this is so, it is necessary to return
to discussions of genre.

A. *Turning One into Many: Questions of Literary Influence*

In multiplying the literary associations in the Farewell Discourses,
this study will not assume an either-or posture. The intention is not
to suggest that these chapters are not a testament. They are indeed
a testament, but they are other things as well, and at the same time.
A variety of literary options exist in ancient literature for depicting
a person's departure to death. The goal is to bring several of these
options to bear on the Johannine Farewell Discourses. The testament is certainly an important literary influence, but this study will
argue that other literary options exist in antiquity, and the Gospel's
author (or authors) takes advantage of them for the furtherance of
theological and narrative designs.[22] Following John's typical patterns,

---

[20] Cf. James Davidson, "Pleasure and Pedantry in Athenaeus," in *Athenaeus and
his World: Reading Greek Culture in the Roman Empire* (eds. David Braund and John
Wilkins; Exeter: University of Exeter Press, 2000) 292.

[21] Ashton, *Understanding*, 456. For his views on contemporary literary theory, particularly narrative criticism and post-modern literary theory, see John Ashton, *Studying
John* (Oxford: Clarendon Press, 1994), especially chapter 6 ("Narrative Criticism")
and chapter 8 ("Studying John"). See also Dettwiler, *Gegenwart*, 33 and passim, who
insists that the central problem of the departure of Christ (*Entzogenheit Christi*) is
resolved by the presence of the Paraclete and the command to love.

[22] This study will make no creative claims about the specific identify of the author
of the Gospel of John, but, for the sake of clear prose, will refer to the author(s)
in a variety of ways, such as "John", the "Evangelist", "the author(s)" or "the
composers."

the Farewell Discourses are not faithful to any single genre, even the testament.[23] The Gospel's purpose is to narrate the story and the significance of Jesus. To do this, it makes use of several different literary forms depicting death and responses to death and departure.

Multiplicity is not an end in and of itself, however. Discovering generic Many-ness serves a larger purpose. If the testament could have succeeded in explaining every literary move in the Fourth Gospel, then there would be no need to explore other literary genres. But there are several aspects of the Johannine Farewell that the testament does not cover. Additional literary styles will fill the voids that the testament exposes.

The viability of this effort is strengthened by the fact that it is not entirely unique. The Farewell Discourses have already benefited from being read against the backdrop of multiple genres simultaneously, most recently by John Ashton.[24] The following study will build upon many of Ashton's important arguments about John 13–17, but in somewhat different directions. Especially helpful is Ashton's dissatisfaction with the one-dimensional assumption that the testament is the only literary backdrop of the Farewell Discourses. For him, merely to assemble lists of parallels between John and the testament is not helpful. When scholars rely on such parallels alone,

> they do nothing more than confirm what is obvious even to an untrained eye: that in taking a formal farewell from his disciples before his death, Jesus is preparing them for the future they will have to face without him.[25]

For Ashton, to identify the form of a text is essential, but merely noting the similarities with a larger genre is not the most important feature of genre identification. The dissimilarities tell much more.

---

[23] Cf. Attridge, "Genre Bending."

[24] See also use of multiple genres in Dettwiler, *Gegenwart*, 17–33. He opens his analysis with an attempt to assign the discourses to a generic category. He opts for two genres, one to express the synchronic dimensions of the text, the other the diachronic. The synchronic/phenomenological dimension is put into perspective by comparison with the gnostic "Dialogue of the Savior." The diachronic quality of the discourses is explained by reference to M. Winter's category, the Vermächtnis (legacy/will), among other reasons, because texts that fit this form, such as Gen 47–50, are often sites of editing and addition. Thus, the final form of the text is helpfully compared to the Gnostic dialogue, while the historical development of the discourses resembles other examples of the Vermächtnis form. Generic classification reconciles the synchronic and diachronic features of the text.

[25] Ashton, *Understanding*, 445.

"The points at which the form is bent or twisted out of its usual shape are those which give some clue to the particular pressures to which it has been subjected."[26] It is one thing to say that these chapters are a testament, but merely saying so does not explain John's particular use of the testament. Ashton argues that John 14 is a combination of the testament and the related commission form, in order to show the particular way in which the testament has been twisted to fit the Gospel's larger interests. But, where Ashton sees only Jewish literature at work, the present study is more interested in John's associations with classical literature. Davies' term "bilingualism" is instructive.[27] While he believes that the Gospel operates in a primarily Semitic framework linguistically and theologically, Davies still recognizes in John the language of the *Hermetica* to which Dodd was so attuned.[28] The Farewell Discourses reflect "bilingualism", in that they share similarities with the testament, and yet they also speak in several other ancient idioms of departure. Whether or not the composer(s) of the Gospel consciously shifted from biblical and Jewish models to Greco-Roman ones is impossible to determine, and really not important. What is important is to see how the Gospel bends and twists the various raw materials that existed in ancient literature.

Furthermore, the effort to multiply generic associations beyond the testament is intimately connected to the theme of presence in absence. A typical testament is primarily about the departure of a dying figure, emphasizing absence and loss. But, in a variety of ways, the Johannine Farewell Discourses emphasize, not the lack of Jesus' presence, but his abundantly continued presence. Harold Attridge insists that, by emphasizing Jesus' abiding presence, the Fourth Gospel has "bent" the expectations of the testament genre.[29] The present study will argue that this "bending" is the effect of blending various literary forms. To this end, the material from dramatic exits (chapter 2) will emphasize Jesus' departure, but consolation literature (chapter 3) and the literary symposium (chapter 4) will accentuate Jesus' continuing presence, and thereby transcend the usual expectations of the testament. The multiplication of comparative genres in this study, therefore, is designed to illustrate how John bends and twists the testament form.

---

[26] Ibid., 445.
[27] Davies, "Reflections," 44.
[28] Ibid., 45.
[29] Attridge, "Genre Bending," 17–18.

Having clarified this posture, the remainder of the introduction
will have two purposes. The immediately following section will introduce the additional genres that will be brought to bear on the discourses, and suggest how they will compensate for the deficiencies
of the testament. The final section will address questions of the literary unity of the discourses, in order to prepare especially for discussing in chapter 2 the puzzling exit of Jesus at John 14:31. First,
then, in what ways will additional literary forms surpass the testament in solving some of the interpretive difficulties in the Farewell
Discourses?

The Testament and the Fourth Gospel

Before looking beyond the testament, some clarification is needed
regarding how the present study views the testament quality of the
Farewell Discourses. First, to define John 13–17 as a testament sug-
gests that scholars have a clear idea of what constitutes a testament.
At the most general level, there is unanimity, expressed neatly in
Brown's definition of the genre:

> The common situation is that of a great man who gathers together
> his followers (his children, his disciples or the people) on the eve of his
> death to give them instructions that will help them after his departure.[30]

Beyond this general notion, however, lies diversity in details. Segovia
very neatly outlines the several features of the ensuing debates.[31] For
instance, interpreters differ in whether or not to include classical literature with Jewish and biblical texts in defining the genre.[32] Or,
some interpreters define the genre according to very specific elements, while others operate within very broad, general parameters.[33]

---

[30] Brown, *Gospel of John*, 2.598.
[31] *Farewell of the Word*, 5–20.
[32] Those who employ classical and Jewish/OT texts in concert are, for example,
Kurz, "Luke 22:14–38;" Stauffer, *New Testament Theology* (transl. John Marsh; London,
SCM Press, 1955) and E. Cortés, *Los Discursos de adiós de Gn 49 a Jn 13–17: Pistas para
la historia de un género literario en la antigua literatura judía* (Barcelona, 1976). Munck, "Discours d' adiieu," on the other hand, focuses solely on biblical material in both Old
and New Testaments, and on early Jewish material. Cf. Segovia, *Farewell of the Word*,
5–19. More recently, Winter also focuses solely on OT and Jewish material, *Vermächtnis*.
[33] Compare the very lengthy, specific categories of Kurz, "Luke 22:14–38," who
finds twenty different features of the farewell address, with the work of Cortés, who
defines the genre according to only three broadly construed constitutive motifs. See
Segovia, *Farewell of the Word*, 5–19.

But, the Farewell Discourses can be argued to intersect with the testament form no matter how it is defined. Brown sees 13 points of contact between John and biblical and extra-biblical testaments. Some of these are the following:

> A speaker will pronounce that death is imminent, as in Jub 36.1 and John 13:33, 36; 14:2–3. This announcement can produce sorrow, and some words of comfort will assuage the sorrow, as in Jub 22.23 and John 14:1, 27; 16:6–7, 22.
>
> In the classic Old Testament examples, a speaker recalls what God has done for Israel; in later Jewish examples, a speaker recalls his own deeds. For instance, Mattathias reminds his sons of what he has done for Israel, and urges them to emulate his deeds (Josephus, *AJ*, 12.6.3). In John, Jesus recalls his words and works (14:10; 15:3; 17:4–8).
>
> A speaker will either tell his disciples to keep the commands of God (Abraham in Jub 21.5), or the speaker's own commands (1 Enoch 94.5). Jesus repeatedly urges the disciples to keep his commandments (14:15, 21, 23; 15:10, 14). In the testaments, there is sometimes a command to love one another (Abraham in Jub 20.2). Jesus insists on this as well (13:34; 15:12).

Given even this brief list, Johannine parallels to the testament form are obvious, and the list of parallels could be expanded considerably. Since this study does not dispute the broad connections between John 13–17 and the testament, however, there is no need to demonstrate every point of association between the Farewell Discourses and the testament form. The question arises, however, as to whether or not the testament classification can explain all of the generic influences that sit behind the Farewell Discourses. The purpose of the present work is to demonstrate that the testament cannot adequately do so, and that other literary springs flow into these chapters of the Gospel.

Exits in Ancient Drama

The first point at which John differs from the standard testament scene is in the reliance on dynamic movement. The entire scene, stretching from 13:1 to 18:1 is centered around two dynamic deeds, or rather, two dynamic exits: that of Jesus, announced at 14:31 and executed at 18:1, and that of Judas at 13:30.[34] There are no such

---

[34] Unrelated to the exits of Judas and Jesus is yet another way in which the scene is made more "dramatic" in a non-technical sense, meaning that it is ren-

exits in the farewell scenes in the testaments. People who die in them typically wait for death to come to them on a deathbed.[35] The exits of Judas and Jesus add a dimension to the Johannine scene, therefore, that differs markedly from the typical testament. These exits are readily recognizable in ancient drama, however, where exits and entrances profoundly effect narrative development.

Classicists have endeavored in recent decades to establish what one eminent scholar has dubbed a "grammar of dramatic technique."[36] Their research has especially clarified the structural function of exits and entrances in dramatic narrative.[37] Exits and entrances work in concert with various shifts in mode of expression (i.e., from spoken dialogue to lyric songs) to open and close the acts of a Greek tragedy.[38]

---

dered more vivid. Note the use of the verb νεύει by Peter when he motions to the Beloved Disciple at 13:24. To Bultmann, the use of the verb "shows that Peter is acting secretly," *Gospel of John*, 481n. A recent study on gestures in Greek literature suggests that Bultmann is correct to see in the term a great deal of significance. Alan L. Boegehold, *When a Gesture Was Expected: A Selection of Examples from Archaic and Classical Greek Literature* (Princeton: Princeton University Press, 1999) tries to read, literally, between the lines of Greek literature in order to account as much as possible for those places where a gesture might be expected and implied. Νεύει and its compounds ἀνανεύει, διανεύει, ἐπινεύει and κατανεύει are used in authors ranging from Homer to Plato and beyond to enliven a scene, Ibid., 61. In Sophocles' *Antigone*, it is argued that paying attention to the use of this verb in line 270 indicates that Antigone does not cower to Creon, but stands boldly before him, Ibid., 61–2. The context of John's gesture, where the other disciples seem oblivious to the event (13:28–29), suggests that the motion is indeed meant to be secretive, but also that it is meant to animate the interaction of Peter and the Beloved Disciple. Bultmann's attention is not misplaced.

[35] See, for instance, the death of Jacob at Genesis 49:33: "When Jacob ended his charge to his sons, he drew up his feet into the bed, breathed his last, and was gathered to his people." The same pattern is followed with minor variation throughout the *Testaments of the Twelve Patriarchs*. For the most part, Greco-Roman literature is the same. In the case of Plato's *Phaedo*, Socrates reclines into death, 117bff.

[36] Eduard Fraenkel, *Aeschylus, Agamemnon* (Oxford: Clarendon Press, 1950) 3.305. This approach, of course, relies on "reading" tragedy and may not attend thoroughly enough to the experience of a tragic play as a live event. For a critique of the text-centered study of Greek tragedy, see recently Rush Rehm, *The Play of Space: Spatial Transformation in Greek Tragedy* (Princeton: Princeton University Press, 2002).

[37] Oliver Taplin, *The Stagecraft of Aeschylus: The Dramatic Use of Exits and Entrances in Greek Tragedy* (Clarendon Press: Oxford, 1977); Michael R. Halleran, *Stagecraft in Euripides* (Totowa, New Jersey: Barnes and Noble, 1985); David Bain, *Masters, Servants and Orders in Greek Tragedy: Some Aspects of Dramatic Technique and Convention* (Manchester: Manchester University Press, 1981). Joe Park Poe, "The Determination of Episodes in Greek Tragedy," *AJP* 114 (1993) 343–396.

[38] For a helpful outline of how a tragedy moves from song to spoken lines, and from characters entering to exiting, see Mark Griffith's introduction to his text and commentary on the *Antigone* in *Sophocles, Antigone* (Cambridge: Cambridge University Press, 1999) 12ff. Prior to Taplin, the role of exits and entrances was not so obvious,

The following outline displays how dramatic narrative proceeds through alternating vocal deliveries, exits and entrances:[39]

> – enter actor (s)
>> – actors' dialogue
> – exeunt actor (s)
>> – choral strophic song
> – enter new actor (s)
> – et cetera . . .

For the sake of the present work, the different forms of vocal delivery are not important. No claim is made here that the Gospel of John in any way exemplifies the shifts in meter and style that characterize verses spoken and sung. What this study will claim, however, is that attention to the critical function of exits and entrances in Greek tragedy can illuminate the Fourth Gospel. The ground pattern outlined above is not immediately obvious in every Greek tragedy, and can be modified in a variety of ways.[40] But each play is structurally oriented around the exits and entrances of its characters. Any deviation from the norm serves a dramatic purpose. Exits and entrances are equally significant for the dramatic flow of ancient comedy, both Greek and Latin.[41]

The exit of Judas in John 13:30 provides a suggestive example of the likely gains to be had from comparing exits in John to ancient dramatic technique. For, Judas does not leave the supper of his own accord. Jesus orders him to exit, very much like masters and superiors in ancient drama order servants or messengers offstage to perform any number of errands. Such departures carry the labels "involuntary" and "forced" exits.[42] These exits can be critical for the

---

as attempts were made to define the shift in acts as solely dependent on the appearance of strophic choral odes, Taplin, *Stagecraft*, 49ff. For an effort to define more sharply Taplin's insights, or rather, an attempt to keep his work from being too rigidly enforced, see Poe, "Determination of Episodes." See also the highly regarded Donald J. Mastronarde, *Contact and Discontinuity* (University of California Publications in Classical Studies, 21; Berkeley and Los Angeles: University of California, 1979).

[39] Adapted from Taplin, *Stagecraft*, 55.

[40] Ibid., 55f.

[41] For a study of the techniques of exit and entrance in Menander, see K.B. Frost, *Exits and Entrances in Menander* (Oxford: Clarendon Press, 1988). For both Greek and Roman comedy, see Kathryn Bennet, *The Motivation of Exits in Greek and Latin Comedy* (Ann Arbor: University of Michigan Press, 1932). For exit commands delivered by superiors to their underlings in classical tragedy, in comparison to comedy, see Bain, *Master and Servants*.

[42] Bennet, *Motivation*, 7.

proper development of the plot, serving at least two functions.

First, such an exit sends someone offstage in order to prepare for future action.[43] If some deed needs to be accomplished in order for the tension of the play to properly resolve itself, a master will send an underling to carry out the necessary activities. In the *Lysistrata* (244), Lysistrata commands Lampito to enlist the aid of Spartan women in ending the Peloponnesian War. The success of Lysistrata's plan depends on this errand. Likewise, in the *Hecyra* (720) Laches sends a servant to call on Bacchis. Only after the servant discharges his duties is Bacchis able to clear up the mystery of a wife's mishap. In each case, the progress of the plot depends on the departure of the servant.

Second, these involuntary exits remove from the stage a character whose presence would disrupt the natural flow of a scene.[44] For instance, in the *Casina* of Plautus, Lysidamus orders his servant Chalinus out of his sight (line 302). This allows Lysidamus to meet secretly with Olympio, Chalinus' rival. In the same way, in Plautus' *Captivi* (953) Hegio orders Philopolemus and Philocrates to the bath, thereby leaving him alone with Stalagmus. Hegio is thus able to learn the fate of his kidnapped son.

The departure of Judas at 13:30 is ordered by Jesus at 13:27 and serves both of the dramatic functions outlined above.[45] In the first place, Judas' departure sets in motion the events culminating in Jesus' crucifixion. When Judas exits, the reader knows to expect trouble soon.

Judas' departure also fulfills the other common function of mid-scene exits. The exit keeps Judas from interrupting the present conversation between Jesus and his disciples. Immediately after Judas' departure in 13:30, the narrator transitions with the phrase, "Therefore, when he left, Jesus said . . ." (13:31). Only after Judas departs can Jesus begin his speech to the disciples. Up to this point, Jesus has said nothing about his departure or his continuing presence with the disciples. Rather, from 13:18 until Judas' departure in 13:30, the

---

[43] The following examples are culled from ibid., 6ff.

[44] Ibid., 7, 9.

[45] Jesus' command also fits well into the Gospel's Christology: even his betrayal occurs at his own command and Jesus is in complete control of the events surrounding his passion. In this case, the christological point is scored through recourse to a device that parallels ancient dramatic art. On this common christological characteristic of the Gospel of John, see, for instance, Moloney, *Glory not Dishonor*, 52.

topic of conversation is Judas' betrayal. Jesus' testament to his disciples cannot proceed until Judas has left. Jesus' expressions of love
and intimacy and insight are not fit for the betrayer.[46]

Thus, Judas' exit is a lynch pin in the scene.[47] It removes from
the stage a character whose continuing presence would interfere with
Jesus' intimacy with his disciples. And, in addition, it pushes the plot
along, since this character has gone to prepare for future action, the
arrest of Jesus. By performing these two functions, the exit draws a
sharp line between the scene of the dinner (13:1–29) and the discourses that follow the dinner until 18:1.[48]

Even more than Judas' exit, Jesus' exit operates according to dramatic principles. Chapter 2 will compare Jesus' exit from the farewell
discourses to exits to death in ancient drama, in order to cast light
especially on the confusing delay of the exit at 14:31.

At this point, however, other types of confusion must be resolved.
To compare the Gospel of John to ancient tragedy requires some
explanation. Clearly, as was said above, the Gospel of John is a
prose work and in no way seems to mimic the poetic format of
Greek tragedy. Further, the fact that the Gospel concludes after the
Resurrection indicates that there is nothing "tragic" about the fate
of Jesus. Out of the sadness surrounding his death develops the joy
of his rising from the dead.[49] Insisting that tragedy can illuminate
the Gospel of John, therefore, implies neither that the Gospel of
John is a tragic poem, nor that it is a tragic story ending in tragic
defeat. But the exit of Judas shows that dramatic material can illumine
aspects of the Gospel of John. Precisely how, then, does the Gospel
depend, or not, on ancient dramatic models?

---

[46] Ibid., 23–24.

[47] The significance of Judas' exit in v. 31 for Jesus' comments in vv. 31b–32 is
often ignored, as commentators view v. 31a ("Therefore, when he had left . . .") as
a redactional link. Moloney attempts to correct this oversight, *The Gospel of John*
(Sacra Pagina 4; Collegeville, MN: Liturgical Press, 1998) 385, 388.

[48] The structural relevance of Judas' departure will be emphasized even further
in chapter 4.

[49] In this, the Gospel of John actually follows tragedies like Euripides' *Alcestis*.
The *Alcestis* opens with the sad death of Alcestis, and dwells at length on the grief
of her husband, Admetus. In a strange twist at the end of the play, however, Alcestis
returns from the dead. This sequence reverses the standard tragic progression from
glory to grief, and has led one commentator to refer to the *Alcestis* as an "inverted
tragedy" because "the progress of the play is from ruin to safety, reversing what
might be considered the normal course of tragedy," Richmond Lattimore, *The
Complete Greek Tragedies* (3 vols.; Chicago: University of Chicago Press, 1955) 3.4. See
also Stibbe, *John as Storyteller*, 129.

To begin with, this study is not the first to draw comparisons between the Gospel of John and dramatic modes of narration. Previous studies tend toward one of two poles. Some use the term dramatic too specifically, and claim that the Gospel of John is, in fact, a tragic drama in the same way that *Oedipus Rex* is a tragedy. For one scholar, this assertion is supported by the fact that John meets the basic criteria of a tragedy as Aristotle defines them in Book 12 of the *Poetics*.[50] But the belief that the Fourth Gospel is a tragedy, strictly speaking, is as indefensible as the claim that the Gospel of John is a sonnet. The Gospel does not look anything like ancient – or modern – dramatic works. Again, the Gospel does not follow a metrical scheme; there is no shift from speech to song; the text (obviously) gives no hint that it was supposed to be performed on the stage; etc.

On the opposite pole are those interpreters who employ the term "dramatic" strictly as an adjective. In this sense, the Gospel of John is dramatic in the same way that a thunderbolt is dramatic. The term "dramatic" is roughly synonymous with words like "arresting" or "moving." No attempt is made to see in John any actual interface with ancient dramatic techniques.[51]

---

[50] F.R.M. Hitchcock, "Is the Fourth Gospel a Drama?" in *The Gospel of John as Literature: An Anthology of Twentieth Century Perspectives* (ed. M. Stibbe; Leiden: E.J. Brill, 1993) 15–24. The same use of Aristotle's *Poetics* is aimed at the Gospel of Mark in Martin Hengel, *Studies in the Gospel of Mark* (transl. John Bowden; Philadelphia: Fortress, 1985) 34f. See, for a more thorough attempt to read Mark dramatically, Gilbert G. Bilezikian, *The Liberated Gospel: A Comparison of the Gospel of Mark and Greek Tragedy* (Grand Rapids: Baker, 1977). In regard to Hengel and Hitchcock's use of Aristotle, however, it is important to note that some classicists have recognized that Aristotle is not entirely helpful in determining the limits and character of tragedy. Oliver Taplin writes, "Aristotle's *Poetics* is the most influential critical work on Tragedy ever written, and with good reason. But its influence has not been wholly for good. The over-emphasis on plausibility and consistency, for example, has wasted a lot of disciples' time on insignificant trifles, the teleological framework has led to an overemphasis on the primitive in Aeschylus, and the failure to appreciate complex plots has hindered the understanding of Euripides," Taplin, *Stagecraft*, 25. But, even where Aristotle is correct, relying solely on Aristotle's theoretical comments on tragedy, as opposed to actual tragedies, is similar to the now outdated practice of assessing Paul's connection to ancient rhetoric through reference to rhetorical handbooks, but not to actual speeches. For the importance of using actual speeches in rhetorical analysis, and not just handbooks, see Margaret M. Mitchell, *Paul and the Rhetoric of Reconciliation: An Exegetical Investigation of the Language and Composition of 1 Corinthians* (Tübingen: Mohr [Siebeck], 1991; repr. Louisville: Westminster/John Knox, 1993) especially 8–11.

[51] R.H. Strachan, *The Fourth Evangelist: Dramatist or Historian?* (London: Hodder and Stoughton, 1925); James Muilenberg, "Literary Form in the Fourth Gospel," *JBL* 51 (1932) 40–3. C. Milo Connick, "The Dramatic Character of the Fourth

The following analysis stands at the midpoint between these two poles. While it is clearly a mistake to read John as a thoroughgoing Greek tragedy, the Gospel is dramatic in more than an adjectival sense. Other scholars have already recognized this fact, and have benefited from reading John as a prose work that employs devices from ancient drama.[52] John's use of a prologue, for instance, has been compared to the use of the prologue in ancient dramas.[53] Further, the dramatic structure of John 9 is compared to devices regarding stage management in ancient drama.[54] Investigations of Johannine irony have also devoted a great deal of attention to dramatic irony.[55]

Such studies provide the model followed herein. To compare the exit of Jesus in John 14 to exits in ancient drama is not to say that the Gospel of John is in fact a drama, but only that it employs a dramatic device. Schenke has similarly argued that John 7–10 is a dramatic scene, not in the sense that it is to be performed on a stage, but in the sense that the author thinks in dramatic categories.[56]

Gospel," *JBL* (1948) 159–170. Brown, *Gospel of John*, refers to the "dramatic" quality of the Gospel regularly, as in 2.843ff. in his treatment of Jesus' trial before Pilate.

[52] See, for example, a suggestive but brief article by William Domeris, "The Johannine Drama," *Journal for Theology for Southern Africa* 42 (1983) 29–35.

[53] Elizabeth Harris, *Prologue and Gospel: The Theology of the Fourth Evangelist* (JSNTS 107; Sheffield: Sheffield Academic Press, 1994).

[54] J.L. Martyn, *History and Theology in the Fourth Gospel* (New York: Harper and Row, 1979) 26. In response to Martyn's historical reconstructions of the Johannine community, in which the Gospel is portrayed as a "Two-Level Drama," see recently Tobias Hägerland, "John's Gospel: A Two-Level Drama?" *JSNT* 25 (2003) 309–22, as well as Colleen Conway, "The Production of the Johannine Community: A New Historicist Perspective," *JBL* 121 (2002) 479–95.

[55] See, for example, George W. MacRae, "Theology and Irony in the Fourth Gospel," in *The Word in the World: Essays in Honor of F.L. Moriarty* (Cambridge, MA: Weston College, 1973) 83–96; repr. pages 103–113 in *The Gospel of John as Literature* (ed. M. Stibbe; Leiden: E.J. Brill, 1993); Paul D. Duke, *Irony in the Fourth Gospel* (Atlanta: John Knox Press, 1985). For an insightful article that uses ancient drama in the way that the present article would like to proceed, see J. Albert Harrill, "The Dramatic Function of the Running Slave Rhoda (Acts 12:13–16): A Piece of Greco-Roman Comedy," *NTS* 46 (2000) 150–57.

[56] Ludger Schenke, "Joh 7–10: Eine dramatische Szene," ZNW 80 (1989) 188: "Der Autor denkt in Kategorien des 'Dramas'..." See also, for a study of the entire Gospel with loose recourse to dramatic concerns, Schenke's *Johannes Kommentar* (Dusseldorf: Patmos, 1998), and his *Das Johannesevangelium: Einführung, Text, dramatische Gestalt* (Stuttgart: Verlag W. Kohlhammer, 1992), especially pages 211ff., which address the question, "Ist das JohEv ein Drama?" 211. While Schenke, however, does not rely exclusively on Aristotle's *Poetics* to determine to what extent the Gospel of John is or is not a drama, he relies much on Aristotle, which is not an entirely

To argue this is no different from claiming that the Gospel borrows structural and thematic motifs from ancient biographical literature.[57]

A related concern arises with the use of texts so far removed in time and space from the Gospel of John. Some might find it hard to accept that a first or second century Jewish community, like that out of which the Gospel arose, would create a narrative on the basis of ancient dramatic techniques, especially since much of the argument in the present study is based on comparison with 5th century BC Athenian tragedy. In order to describe the dramatic possibilities as thickly as possible, the following study focuses on a device, the delayed exit, which is common in all types of drama, in all times and places.[58]

Our knowledge of Hellenistic and Roman tragedy is very slim, and gets even slimmer when we try to consider what sorts of productions took place in certain cities.[59] But if, as some believe, the Gospel of John was written in Ephesus, then the enormous Ephesian theatre would have been the home of many types of comedy and tragedy.[60] Further, it is not at all unreasonable to assume that a Jew living in the first two centuries could have employed the techniques of Greek drama. Two hundred or so years before the Gospel of John was written, Ezekiel the Tragic Poet wrote the *Exagoge*, a verse rendering of the Exodus of Moses that is heavily indebted to the

helpful way to determine to what extent the Gospel of John relies on ancient dramatic material (see above, note 50).

[57] R.A. Burridge, *What are the Gospels?: A Comparison with Graeco-Roman Biography* (Cambridge/New York: Cambridge University Press, 1992).

[58] In this sense, the use of dramatic materials here differs somewhat from the interesting work of Stibbe, who compares chapters 18 and 19 of John to the activity of a specific character in a specific text, Dionysus in Euripides' *Bacchae*, Stibbe, *John as Storyteller*, 140ff.

[59] The only complete surviving tragedies from antiquity are from the pens of Aeschylus, Sophocles, Euripides and Seneca. Tarrant writes, "What is known of tragedy between Euripides and Seneca – the tragedy of the fourth century and the Hellenistic age, of the Roman Republic and the time of Augustus – is at best fragmentary, at worst purely conjectural," R.J. Tarrant, "Senecan Drama and its Antecedents," *HSCP* 82 (1978) 214–15. See also G.M. Sifakis, *Studies in the History of Hellenistic Drama* (London: University of London, 1967), which focuses primarily on evidence for dramatic performances in Delos and Delphi.

[60] Brown writes, "Ephesus still remains the primary contender for identification as the place where John was composed," *Gospel of John*, 1.ciii. Theatres also existed throughout Palestine, if a Palestinian provenance for the Gospel is more acceptable. See, for instance, Arthur Segal, *Theatres in Roman Palestine and Provincia Arabia* (Mnemosyne Supplements 140; trans. N.H. Reisner; Leiden: E.J. Brill, 1995).

dramatic style of Euripides.[61] If Ezekiel, a Jew, can write a full-blown
poetic drama, then John's Gospel can employ dramatic devices.[62]

But there is an even deeper and broader justification for exploring the dramatic quality of the Fourth Gospel. P.E. Easterling has
recently coined the phrase "the theatricalization of ancient culture"
in order to describe the prevalence and influence of Greek drama
as it extended geographically far beyond the boundaries of Athens,
and chronologically well into late antiquity.[63] The survival of Greek
drama into the Roman world is superficially most obvious in the
fact that Roman drama developed much of its content from Greek
models, as authors like Seneca make clear.[64] The spread of Greek
drama, though, is easy to map neither on the basis of obvious manuscript production, nor in the continued production of classical plays.
We know that scribes and scholars continued to read and analyze
Greek dramas well beyond the classical era, but obvious evidence is
sparse. Dramatic terminology also becomes confused. By the first
century, even the pantomime (a ballet-like performance with musi-
cal accompaniment) could be described as a tragedy if a tragic theme
merely provided the mythical background for the interpretive dance.[65]
It is very difficult, then, to know what was actually performed when
ancient sources refer to tragic productions.

---

[61] The standard work on the *Exagoge* is H. Jacobson, *The Exagoge of Ezekiel*.
Cambridge: Cambridge University Press, 1983.

[62] Stibbe helpfully warns against overemphasizing John's Jewishness to the detri-
ment of seeing any possible interface with classical literature, *John as Storyteller*,
129–30.

[63] P.E. Easterling, "From Repertoire to Canon," in *The Cambridge Companion to
Greek Tragedy*, ed. P.E. Easterling (Cambridge: Cambridge University Press, 1997) 226.

[64] For Seneca's indebtedness to Greek models, see R.J. Tarrant, "Senecan Drama,"
213–263; Idem, "Greek and Roman in Seneca's Tragedies," *HSCP* 97 (1995) 215–230.
The use of Greek comedy by Romans like Plautus and Terrence is even more obvious in their announcement of the fact in the prologues of their plays. The prologue of Plautus' *Casina* says (30ff.): "I wish to give you the name of our comedy.
Its Greek title is *Clerumenoe*, in Latin, *Sortientes*. Diphilus wrote the play in Greek,
and later Plautus ... gave us a fresh version of it in Latin." More was involved in
adaptation than mere translation, however. Scafuro has shown how Plautus and
Terrence altered legal language and situations in order to be more suitable to the
Roman setting, Adele C. Scafuro, *The Forensic Stage: Settling Disputes in Graeco-Roman
New Comedy* (Cambridge: Cambridge University Press, 1997).

[65] Easterling, "Repertoire," 220–1. On the pantomime, see M. Kokolakis, "Pantomimus and the treatise περὶ ὀρχήσεως," *Platon* 11 (1959) 1–56; W.J. Slater, "Pantomime Riots," *Classical Antiquity* 13 (1994) 120–144; C.P. Jones, "Dinner Theatre,"
in *Dining in a Classical Context* (ed. W.J. Slater, Ann Arbor: University of Michigan,
1991) 185–98.

And yet, the influence of Greek tragedy extends well beyond the production of plays. The "theatricalization of ancient culture" is obvious in many places. The dramatization of Roman life is reflected in the grisly practice of staging public executions and punishments in the form of dramatic productions, as when Tertullian recalls seeing a person burned to death in the role of Hercules as a form of capital punishment.[66] But the legacy of classical drama, and especially of tragedy, is even more obvious in Greek prose authors of the Roman Empire. Continuing the literary tradition of Thucydides and Herodotus, both of whom employed tragic themes in their histories, Polybius is indebted to tragic models.[67] Even closer in time and place to the Gospel of John, Josephus also relies on dramatic models at great length for character development and the staging of scenes in the production of his *Bellum Judaicum*.[68] The same can be said about Greek and Roman novels.[69] Lucian[70] and Plutarch[71] also refer in many ways to tragic performances or themes, and structure their prose works around dramatic models. Thus, the legacy of tragic poetry shines brightly in later prose authors.[72] Easterling writes:

---

[66] *Apol.* 15.4. See, on the drama of Roman punishment, K.M. Coleman, "Fatal Charades: Roman Executions Staged as Mythological Enactments," *JRS* 80 (1990) 44–73.

[67] Charles Fornara, *The Nature of History in Ancient Greece and Rome* (Berkeley: University of California, 1983) 171. On Polybius, see F.W. Walbank, "History and Tragedy," *Historia* 9 (1960) 216–34.

[68] Jonathan Price, "Drama and History in Josephus' *BJ*" (paper presented at the annual meeting of the Society of Biblical Literature Josephus Seminar, Boston, MA, 1999); Louis Feldman, "The Influence of the Greek Tragedians on Josephus," in *Hellenic and Jewish Arts: Interaction, Tradition and Renewal* (ed. A. Ovadiah; Tel Aviv: Ramot Publ. House, Tel Aviv University, 1998) 51–80.

[69] See the following, for instance, in regard to the *Satyricon* of Petronius: Gerald N. Sandy, "Scaenica Petroniana," *TAPA* 104 (1974) 329–346; Gianpiero Rosati, "Trimalchio on Stage," in *Oxford Readings in the Roman Novel* (ed. S.J. Harrison; Oxford: Oxford University Press, 1999) 85–104.

[70] For the study of Lucian's writings, with an eye toward using them to determine theatre productions occurring in the 2nd century AD, see M. Kokolakis, "Lucian and the Tragic Performances in his Time," *Platon* 12 (1960) 67–106. See also for attention to the dramatic character of Lucian's writing, Diskin Clay, "Lucian of Samosata: Four Philosophical Lives (Nigrinus, Demonax, Peregrinus, Alexander Pseudomantis)" *ANRW* 36.5: 3414f., where Clay begins to speak of "The Mime of Philosophy."

[71] For an analysis of Plutarch's condemnation of tragedy, as well as the nevertheless very full use of tragic elements in the *Demetrios*, see Phillip de Lacy, "Biography and Tragedy in Plutarch," *AJP* 73 (1952) 159–71. More recently, see, J.M. Mossman, "Tragedy and Epic in Plutarch's *Alexander*," in *Essays on Plutarch's Lives* (ed. Barbara Scardigli; Oxford: Clarendon Press, 1995) 209–228.

[72] For further bibliography on the spread of Greek tragedy in late antiquity, see Easterling, "Repertoire," 226–7.

This intense penetration of the language and literature of antiquity gave tragedy a special imaginative status that did not ultimately depend on performance traditions for its survival. The task of capturing in detail the reverberations of tragedy in later antiquity is one of the most interesting challenges for contemporary critics.[73]

Chapter 2 will argue that John's Gospel is attuned to these "reverberations of tragedy," especially in the exit of Jesus from the Farewell Discourses.

The pursuit of dramatic qualities in the Farewell Discourses, however, is not an end in and of itself. This dramatic reading will attempt to reconcile competing methodological voices in the current study of the Fourth Gospel. In the language used above, the One-ness of these chapters will appear more clearly when the discourses are read through the lens of ancient drama. The comparison of Jesus' exit at 14:31/15:1 to ancient dramatic exits in chapter 2 will argue for seeing greater narrative unity in the Farewell Discourses.

Furthermore, highlighting Jesus' exit movement also draws to the fore the Gospel's concern for Jesus' presence-in-absence. The exit emphasizes his departure, and therefore, his absence. Other literary styles address the question of his continuing presence. The first of these is ancient consolation literature.

Ancient Consolation

This is not the first study to see in the Johannine Farewell Discourses some interaction with classical consolation literature. George Kennedy has taken steps in this direction by attending to the rhetoric of John 13–17.[74] He is most concerned to show that these chapters are an example of epideictic oratory.[75] Epideictic, of course, is the species of oratory that confirms a community or person's adherence to a particular set of beliefs or values. In the Farewell Discourses, then, Jesus encourages the disciples to respond to his departure with an appropriate set of emotions and beliefs.[76] Kennedy's rhetorical arguments focus on Menander Rhetor (ca. 300), who compiled two trea-

---

[73] Ibid., 226.
[74] Kennedy, *New Testament Interpretation*, 73–85. See as well the forthcoming important study of Paul Holloway, "Left Behind."
[75] See Kennedy, 73–85; Black, "Grandeur."
[76] Kennedy, *New Testament Interpretation*, 77.

tises listing the different forms of epideictic oration and the topics appropriate to each of the many sub-categories of epideictic speech.[77] Among the categories included in Menander's handbook, the two thought by Kennedy most closely to resemble John 13–17 are the "leave taking" or "syntactic"[78] speech and the "consolatory" or "paramythetic" speech.[79]

Kennedy decides for the consolation speech, in Greek the λόγος παραμυθητικός and in Latin the *consolatio*.[80] Almost as quickly as he allows for this possibility, however, Kennedy wonders, "[whether] or not a classical rhetorician would regard John 13–17 as a consolation . . ."[81] He seems to assume that this is merely a rhetorical question, but it need not be. John Chrysostom identifies several elaborate connections between Jesus' Farewell Discourses and the expectations of classical consolation.[82] Chrysostom repeatedly defines Jesus' teaching as an expression of παραμυθία,[83] or he insists that in whatever Jesus says to the disciples, he consoles them (παραμυθεῖται αὐτούς).[84] A more full quotation will indicate precisely how extensively Chrysostom sees consolatory tropes in these discourses:

> The tyranny exercised over us by despondency is a strong one. We need great courage if we are to persevere in resisting this emotion, and if, after deriving from it what profit we can, we are to refrain from indulging in it to excess . . . Therefore, as despondency was taking hold of the disciples, since they were not yet perfect, see how Christ set them right . . .[85]

---

[77] See *Menander Rhetor* (edited with translation and commentary by D.A. Russell, N.G. Wilson; Oxford: Clarendon Press, 1981).

[78] See Black, "Grandeur," 224 and passim for more on the syntactic speech.

[79] Kennedy, *New Testament Interpretation*, 76–7, 80–5.

[80] He writes of John's similarity to the paramythetic speech as follows: "Menander suggests, for example, that one should say that the deceased has enjoyed enough of life, that he has escaped its pains, that he is now living with the gods, and a speaker can even find fault with those who lament the deceased. He should be blessed as a god and placated as superhuman." Ibid., 76.

[81] Ibid., 78.

[82] For a study on Chrysostom's reading of the Farewell Discourses as a consolatory treatise, see George Parsenios, "Παραμυθητικὸς Χριστός: John Chrysostom interprets the Johannine Farewell Discourses," *GOTR* (forthcoming).

[83] See, for instance *Hom. Jo.* 72.2 (PG 59:398). He also uses the term παράκλησις to refer to the comfort or encouragement that Jesus gives to the disciples in, for instance *Hom. Jo.* 70.1 (PG 59:382).

[84] See, for instance, *Hom. Jo.* 72.3 (PG 59:393).

[85] All translations of Chrysostom's Homilies on John are taken from Saint John Chrysostom, *Commentary on Saint John the Apostle and Evangelist* (trans. Sister Thomas Aquinas Goggin, S.C.H.: New York; Fathers of the Church, 1960). Hereafter, texts

At least one ancient orator, then, sees these discourses as a consolatory treatise. Chapter 3 will follow Chrysostom's suggestions, but
not on the pattern of Kennedy's work. Kennedy relies exclusively
on Menander's rhetorical manual in determining what can or cannot be classified as consolatory.[86] This study will cast the net wider.
Before reviewing classical consolation, however, it is necessary to
review previous work that has connected the consolatory character
of the Farewell Discourses to the testament form.

Consolation is a familiar theme in discussions of the Farewell
Discourses, but any explanation of how the discourses are consolatory is characterized by the same conceptual confusion that typifies
the use of the term "dramatic" noted previously. "Consolation" comes
to mean several different things, depending on the interpreter.

At least two ways exist for determining the consolatory character
of the Farewell Discourses. Segovia's rich study, *Farewell of the Word*,
exemplifies one approach. In his discussion of the constituent elements of the testament genre, Segovia determines not to define the
genre simply by its composite features, but also by the function of
those features.[87] Therefore, Segovia generally determines the consolatory quality of a passage by ascribing to it a consolatory function,
broadly construed. The consolatory quality of the discourses is not
tied to any specific aspect of the discourses, but operates at a level
of abstraction beyond the various details of each example of the testament genre. There is no clear, consistent content for the label
"consolatory." What qualifies as consolation is limited only by the
interpreter's insight or perspective. Certainly, Segovia's reading is
helpfully suggestive, especially in regard to the consolatory quality
of the sending of the Paraclete, which will be the central concern
of chapter 3.[88] But this way of proceeding has no controls. No specific,
recurring trope or device is considered to be consolatory in every

---

will be cited by page numbers in the Goggin translation and from the PG volume.
The text cited here is *Hom. Jo.* 78.1 (PG 59:419/Goggin, 338).

[86] Paul Holloway has now significantly expanded Kennedy's insights by more
assiduously exploring the relations between Menander's epideictic categories of the
syntactic and the propemptic speech and the Johannine Farewell. His insights are
especially groundbreaking for the prayer in John 17. Interpreters have found this
prayer notoriously difficult to categorize, but Holloway compellingly illustrates essential connections between this prayer and the prayers that typically conclude Menander's
category of "Syntactic Speech." See Holloway, "Left Behind," 15–18, 28–32.

[87] *Farewell of the Word*, 19.

[88] Ibid., 316, passim.

testament document. It is simply asserted that one of the general
purposes of the testament is to console, and this, apparently, can
take place in an unlimited number of unspecified ways.

The problem comes to the surface in a comparison between
Segovia's view of consolation and that of any other commentator,
such as R. Schnackenburg. Schnackenburg, for instance, argues that
16:4b–33 is a "Consolatory Discourse."[89] In this, he and Segovia are
in agreement.[90] Unlike Segovia, however, Schnackenburg believes
that the consolatory quality of chapter 16 differentiates it from chapter 14. In chapter 14, Schnackenburg argues that the primary point
is "to indicate the way that the disciples' faith should follow in the
future, despite Jesus' passion and departure."[91] Thus, for Schnackenburg, chapter 14 is not intended to console, but to focus on the
need for faith in Jesus' promises. For Segovia, however, it is the disciples' faith in Jesus' promises that is the very basis for chapter 14's
consolatory quality. In his analysis of the section 13:31–14:31, for
instance, Segovia identifies a consolatory dimension in all of the
promises Jesus makes to the disciples: promises that he will return;
that the Paraclete will come to them; that the disciples will perform
works even greater than those of Jesus. All of these promises, for
Segovia, are consolatory.[92] What Schnackenburg sees as non-conso-
latory, therefore, Segovia sees as consolatory. In the end, this difference
of opinion is not a critical issue differentiating Schnackenburg and
Segovia. But this difference of identification does demonstrate why
their procedure for labeling something consolatory is problematic. It
relies only on their ability to see consolation at work, and is not tied
to specific tropes. The approach is a too general way to proceed.

The more specific procedure for identifying consolation in the testament genre is equally problematic. In this way of proceeding, it is
not the general tendency of the work that makes it consolatory, but
the presence of specific words or actions. Stauffer, Kurz, Michel and
Brown list passages from testament texts that are said to be comforting or consolatory, but in each case these examples are only partly
helpful for reading the Farewell Discourses.[93] One would expect a

---

[89] Rudolf Schnackenburg, *The Gospel According to Saint John* (trans. K. Smyth;
3 vols.; New York: Herder and Herder, 1968) 3.123ff.

[90] *Farewell of the Word*, 278ff.

[91] Schnackenburg, *Gospel of John*, 3.124.

[92] *Farewell of the Word*, 118–19.

[93] E. Stauffer, *New Testament Theology*, 345. H.J. Michel, *Die Abschiedsrede des Paulus*

departing leader to urge his followers or loved ones not to be saddened by his or her departure, and this is roughly what is found in some farewell texts, such as Jub 22:23. Other supposed examples of consolation in the testament, however, have a different tone. Although some testaments involve consolation, the grief they address and seek to assuage arises not from a leader's impending death, but from some other cause. In 1 Sam 12:20, for example, Samuel comforts his people with the phrase, "Do not be afraid . . ." Their fear, however, is not a response to his departure; it stems from the people's anxiety that they will be punished for their sin of calling for a king to rule them (1 Sam 12:19). The same could be said for Moses' injunction, "Be strong and bold, have no fear of them . . ." (Deut 31:6). Moses comforts his people, not in the face of his departure, but in anticipation of their coming struggles in Canaan (31:4–5). Other testament passages include a word of consolation, but only briefly, such as 1 Enoch 92:2 or Jub 22:23. The latter includes the encouraging but laconic admonition: "Do not be fearful."[94]

On the whole, then, Ashton seems to be correct when he claims that comfort and consolation are not overwhelmingly significant aspects of the testament form. He writes, "The truth is that the note of reassurance and the summons to faith with which Jesus prefaces his discourse in chapter 14 is not a regular element of the farewell form."[95]

Paradoxically, this claim is supported by Kurz' study – even though Kurz sees consolatory dimensions in the testament form. The difference between Kurz' study and the others noted above arises from the fact that Kurz includes classical literature in his list of testaments.[96] But

---

an die Kirche: Apg 20:17–38: Motivgeschichte und theologische Bedeutung (Munich: Kösel, 1973) 50; W. Kurz, "Luke 22:14–38"; Brown, *Gospel of John*, 2.598–99.

[94] One suggestive phrase, however, stands apart from these rare and brief comments. The *Testament of Zebulun's* patriarch utters the comforting promise, "Grieve not that I am dying . . . for I shall rise again in the midst of you . . . and I shall rejoice" (10.1–2). This bears some resemblance to Jesus' promise that the disciples will rejoice (15:11; 16:22) when he returns (14:3, 18; 16:16) Brown, *Gospel of John*, 2.599. It also differs, though, in claiming that the departed person, not the disciples, will rejoice when he returns.

[95] Ashton, *Understanding*, 453. See also the comment of Kennedy, "Deathbed speeches attributed to great figures of the Old Testament are a traditional Jewish form, but consolation is not their function," Kennedy, *New Testament Interpretation*, 77.

[96] Stauffer, Brown and Michel draw only on Jewish and Old Testament documents where they pursue consolation. Stauffer includes classical texts in his broader taxonomy, but does not see these texts as a source for consolation themes, *New Testament Theology*, 344–46.

when Kurz finds consolation in the testament form, it is not in the Jewish and Old Testament texts, but in New Testament and Greco-Roman texts.[97] This insight is critical, and requires one to look beyond the Jewish testament form for an explanation of consolatory themes in the Farewell Discourses. For, what makes Greco-Roman testaments consolatory has less to do with the fact that they are testaments than with the fact that they are Greco-Roman texts.[98] As such, they are influenced by the wave of consolation themes contained in both the broad sea of classical literature generally, as well as in the deep pools of classical consolation literature. The same insight applies to the New Testament passages mentioned by Kurz (Lk 22; Acts 20). Their consolatory quality should not be explored solely in relation to the Jewish testament, but ought to be studied in relation to the broad scope of classical consolation literature.

A further aspect of this problem requires attention as well. For, some texts that Kurz lists as Greco-Roman examples of the testament are included by classicists in the category of consolation literature. For instance, Dio's *Oration 30* is listed in Kurz' group of Greek and Latin testaments, as well as in Buresch's classic study of consolation literature.[99] The same is true of Plato's *Phaedo*. The *Phaedo* predates the flowering of consolation literature, since the form originates as an independent rhetorical style in the Hellenistic era.[100] Yet, several Platonic texts, including the *Phaedo*, are supremely important influences on consolation literature.[101]

A variety of points coincide here. Comfort and consolation are only a rare and marginal aspect of testament literature, and appear with any abundance only in the Greek and Latin examples of the farewell type scene. Whatever consolatory themes appear in these classical texts, however, are more likely due to the influence of classical

---

[97] See the helpful chart in Kurz, "Luke 22," 262–63.

[98] The texts he cites as containing consolation themes are the following: Plato's *Phaedo*; Dio's *Oration 30*; Josephus' *AJ* 4.8.45–49 (Moses' farewell); Lk 22; Acts 20. Ibid., 262–3.

[99] Ibid., 262–3, C. Buresch, "Consolationum a Graecis Romanisque scriptarum historia critica," (*Leipziger Studien zur classischen Philologie* 9, 1886) 38.

[100] See C.E. Manning, *On Seneca's "Ad Marciam."* (Mnemosyne Supplement 69; Leiden, Brill, 1981) 12.

[101] Ibid., 108. This is especially true of the *Apology*, from which arguments about the state of death are taken over by a variety of later authors. For a discussion of the consolatory dimensions of the *Apology*, see now Holloway, "Left Behind," 11f. and passim.

consolation than to the requirements of the farewell proper. If we are to understand the consolatory qualities of the New Testament texts, then, we must look beyond the evidence of Old Testament and Jewish testaments to classical consolation literature. Chapter 3 will pursue certain consolatory aspects of the Farewell Discourses in precisely this fashion.

The present study will not, however, explore the Farewell Discourses exhaustively in pursuit of consolation themes, although such an enterprise would almost certainly yield significant results.[102] After an introductory survey of general consolatory aspects of the discourses, this study will focus on one aspect of ancient consolation in order better to explain the role of the Paraclete in the consolation of the disciples. The goal is to move as quickly as possible to the larger concern of this study, the theme of presence in absence. Additionally, this effort will rely not only on consolation literature proper, but also on any and all corners of classical literature where a concern to console is present. To justify and clarify this approach, it will be helpful to outline the basic contours of consolation literature proper, as well as its relation to the larger world of classical literature.

Consolation literature in antiquity took various forms – speeches, treatises or letters[103] – and yet all of these different literary modes can be classified generally as literature designed to combat grief. Ps.-Demetrios introduces the consolatory letter as follows: "The consoling type is that written to people who are grieving because something unpleasant has happened (to them)."[104] But this definition, while simple on the surface, also indicates how diverse consolation literature can be. Any number of situations might arise that require the con-

---

[102] For an exhaustive reading of the Farewell Discourses in light of classical consolation literature, see now Paul Holloway, "Left Behind." The present study turned initially toward consolation literature after Harold Attridge indicated to me that Paul Holloway had suggested consolation literature could illumine the Farewell Discourses. See also Paul Holloway, *Consolation in Philippians: Philosophical Sources and Rhetorical Strategy* (SNTSMS 112; Cambridge: Cambridge University Press, 2001). For a briefer treatment of Holloway's ideas on John 16:1–4 embedded in a larger study, see his "*Nihil inopinati accidisse*: A Cyrenaic Consolatory *Topos* in 1 Peter 4:12," *NTS* 48 (2002) 433–48.

[103] Abraham Malherbe, "Exhortation in First Thessalonians," *NovT* 25 (1983) 65; repr. in *Paul and the Popular Philosophers* (Minneapolis: Fortress Press, 1989) lists the following as examples of each: Dio, *Orations* 27.7–9; 28; 30; Plutarch, *On Superstition* 168c.

[104] *Epist Types*, 5. Translation from Abraham Malherbe, *Ancient Epistolary Theorists* (SBLSBS 19; Atlanta: Scholars Press, 1988) 35.

solation of someone overtaken by grief. Ancient lists of specific circumstances that require consolation include poverty, loss of social status, slavery, illness, blindness,[105] legal problems,[106] loss of a slave[107] or fraud.[108] Nevertheless, the majority of surviving consolations focus on death.[109]

Consolation literature took its definitive form in the Hellenistic era.[110] Indeed, when Roman authors considered the origins of the style, they pointed to the Περὶ Πένθους πρὸς Ἱπποκλέα of Crantor, the third century BC Academician, as the original and paradigmatic consolatory treatise.[111] Crantor's work survives only in the fragments where he is quoted by other authors, but his impact on the genre is obvious in the eulogistic references to him in later authors.[112] And it is reasonable that the practitioners of consolation trace the origins of their genre to an author in the Hellenistic age, "when the prime concern of philosophy was to equip the individual to meet the changes and chances of life . . . [Consolation] was the literary counterpart to the activity of such Cynic preachers as Crates who went about with his wife Hipparchia, wearing the rough cynic cloak and approaching individuals with advice."[113]

In another sense, however, citing Crantor as the source of the consolation form can be misleading. Previous generations of scholars assumed that Crantor's work served as an archetype that all later writers aspired to copy. Mutual reliance on a single prototype was seen as an explanation for overlap between different consolation authors. Take, for instance, the supposed relationship between Plutarch's *Ad Apollonium* and Seneca's *Ad Polybium*. Because Plutarch cites Crantor repeatedly, the theory has seemed plausible that similarities stem from mutual reliance on Crantor – even though there is no secure connection between Seneca's text and the work of Crantor.[114] The truth of the matter is, Plutarch is as free in his utilization of other

---

[105] Cicero, *Tusc.* 3.34.81. Cf. Holloway, *Consolation*, 60–61.
[106] Cicero, *Ad Fam*, 5.18. Cf. Holloway, *Consolation*, 61.
[107] Seneca, Ep. 71. Cf. Holloway, *Consolation*, 61.
[108] Juv. *Sat.* 13. Cf. Holloway, *Consolation*, 61.
[109] Ibid., 61.
[110] C.E. Manning, *Seneca's 'Ad Marciam,'* 12–13.
[111] Ibid., 12.
[112] For bibliography on the fragments, see Holloway, *Consolation*, 58 n. 20.
[113] Manning, *Seneca's 'Ad Marciam,'* 12.
[114] J.E. Atkinson, "Seneca's *'Consolatio Ad Polybium,'* *ANRW* 32.2:867–871.

authors as Seneca is.[115] They both tap into deep repositories of consolatory resources. Indeed, the idea that consolatory authors follow
any model slavishly is inappropriate. For instance, Cicero's *Tusculan
Disputations* describe the different consolatory procedures of several
philosophical figures and schools (Cleanthes, the Peripatetics, the
Epicureans, the Cyrenaics and Chrysippus),[116] but consolers never
adhered solely to the tenets of their respective schools. Consolatory
texts would habitually draw on any number of arguments, from any
number of schools, to achieve their desired result.[117] Cicero himself
recognizes that the best way to ensure success in consolation is to
assemble all of the best arguments of every school. This procedure
is a way of covering all possible bases, with one school's argument
accomplishing what another might not.[118] Consolation, then, is an
eclectic enterprise, and any similarities between two consolatory texts
arise from this eclecticism.

But philosophical schools are not the only source of material for
consolation literature. Consolation texts also draw heavily on material outside the mainstream of consolation literature. Since they deal
with death and other forms of grief, they include material from any
form of literature that aids their argument. In general, venerable
authorities of the past are sought as sources for *exempla* designed
to buttress arguments against grief.[119] Seneca, for instance, draws on
Plato at great length for his arguments about the immortality of the
soul in the *Ad Polybium*.[120] Homer and the Greek tragedians are an

---

[115] Kassel's work has been instrumental in changing the view that Crantor is the
sole prototype for all subsequent consolations. R. Kassel, *Untersuchungen zur griechischen und römischen Konsolationsliteratur* (Zetemata 18; Munich, 1958). Cf. Atkinson,
"Seneca's *Consolatio*," 867–68 and passim. Kassel emphasizes instead the rhetorical
reality of the genre, wherein each author modifies his arguments to a particular
audience. This is best understood when different consolations of Seneca are compared. In his *Ad Marciam*, fate (*fatum*) reigns over fortune (*fortuna*), but in the *Ad
Polybium* the two are equated in a way that cannot be explained as Stoic, Ibid.,
871. "A common view has emerged that Seneca tempered his strict Stoic teaching
to accommodate the feelings of those to whom he addressed his consolations," Ibid.,
871. Although Seneca's arguments are basically Stoic, he allows himself to be
influenced by other thinkers and authors where it seems appropriate to him. Parallels
with Plutarch make perfect sense in light of the insight that Seneca's doctrine of
immortality is largely drawn from Platonism, Ibid., 871.
[116] Cf. Holloway, *Consolation*, 65–74.
[117] *Tusc.*, 3.22.52.
[118] *Tusc.*, 3.31.76.
[119] Ibid., 13. Cf. Manning, *Seneca's 'Ad Marciam*,' 13.
[120] Atkinson, "Seneca's '*Consolatio*,'" 871.

even more common source of material. Plutarch's *Ad Apollonium* has nineteen citations of Homer and ten from Euripides.[121] Crantor's Περὶ Πένθους often cites both Homer and Euripides as well.[122] Cicero's *Tusculan Disputations* contain three translations of Euripides, three of Homer, one from Aeschylus and one from Sophocles.[123] A particular consolation text can tap any number of philosophical and literary sources and thereby direct its arguments against any number of difficulties. Certain topoi, although they arise in one particular school, come to be fixtures in the genre, and employed by all schools.

While it is true, therefore, to claim that consolation literature, properly speaking, achieves its definitive form in the Hellenistic era, it is equally important to recognize that the constituent themes are present in the earliest stages of Greek literature. The later, fully developed form of the consolation is steeped in this earlier material.

Chapter 3 of this study will compare the Farewell Discourses to this broad spectrum of consolatory literature, meaning, both the specific genre of consolation letters, treatises and speeches, as well as the larger stock of consolation themes in classical literature generally. The chapter will not, however, attempt to isolate and explain every possible interface between ancient consolation and the Farewell Discourses. Nor will it argue that the Farewell Discourses are a sterling example of a consolation text, along the lines of Seneca's *Ad Marciam*. After exploring a few obvious connections to ancient consolation, the chapter will focus on one specific aspect of the discourses, the work of the Paraclete, in order to argue that at least one function of the Paraclete can be well explained against the backdrop of consolation themes: rendering Jesus present in his absence. This particular activity of the Paraclete is unrelated to the testament, and is better understood in light of classical consolation.

The Literary Symposium

As in the previous section on consolation, many studies have assumed that the meal in chapter 13 is yet one more link in the chain

---

[121] Manning, *Seneca's 'Ad Marciam,'* 13.
[122] Ibid., 13.
[123] Ibid., 13.

connecting the Farewell Discourses to the testament genre.[124] This
supposed link, however, snaps under the weight of closer scrutiny.
Although a few farewell texts include meals, these meals are incidental to the larger flow of the narratives in which they are embedded, and they are never as fully developed as the meal scene in John
13.[125] Meals come prior to death, for instance, in *Jubilees* (35:27;
36:17) and in the *Testament of Naphtali* (1.2), but in neither of these
cases is the meal more than a passing component of the farewell.

In *Jubilees* 35:18–27, Rebecca summons Esau and Jacob as she
approaches death. Following a series of blessings and commands
from Rebecca to her sons, the following notice appears: "And they
ate and they drank, she and her sons, that night" (35:27).

A similar event occurs one book later in *Jubilees*. When Isaac bids
farewell to Jacob and Esau, he follows the pattern of Rebecca. After
Jacob addresses to his sons commands and blessings, the text tells
us that ". . . they ate and they drank together before him" (36:17).

In the *Testament of Naphtali*, the meal is equally marginal (1.2):
"When his sons were gathered together in the seventh month, on
the fourth day of the month, and he was in good health, he gave
a feast and a drinking party." This notice is followed later with the
following information: "And while he was blessing the Lord he
confirmed that after the previous day's feast he would die" (1.4). So
incidental to the scene, the meal has come and gone within the
space of two lines. Moreover, the meal comes on the evening before
the final words of the patriarch, who speaks the day after the dinner: "After he awoke early the next morning, he told them . . ." (1.3).
Then, at the close of the *Testament of Naphtali*, we hear again, "He
ate and drank in soulful glee, covered his face and died" (9.2). Again,
the meal and the speech are disconnected. The same can be said
of the Greek and Latin texts that are often compared to the Jewish
testaments.[126]

---

[124] Brown, *Gospel of John*, 2:598; Segovia, *Farewell of the Word*, 21, 316; Moloney,
Glory, 5.

[125] E. Bammel, "The Farewell Discourse of the Evangelist John and its Jewish
Heritage," *Tyndale Bulletin* (1993) 106.

[126] See the texts in Kurz, "Luke 22," 262–3. Plutarch includes a final meal in
the deaths of Anthony (*Life of Anthony*, 75) and Cato Minor (*Life of Cato Minor*, 67).
The meal of Anthony is as cursory as that in the Jewish texts. Cato's meal is only
a little more developed. It actually follows the classical model of a meal followed
by learned conversation that will be the topic of much that will follow below. But,

The passing references to meals in the testaments, therefore, do little to explain the Johannine Last Supper. To some, the mere presence of the meal associates John's scene with the testament.[127] But John does not need to depend on farewell scenes for the inspiration to include a meal in Jesus' last night with the disciples. One can assume that the Fourth Evangelist, following the same traditions that underlie the Synoptic Gospels (whether or not he actually read the Synoptics), knew that Jesus shared a meal with his disciples before his betrayal and execution.[128] This explains the inclusion of the meal in John 13. The Evangelist was merely following traditions about the course of Jesus' last days on earth. A more important question remains, however. Regardless of where John received the idea of including a meal in Jesus' departure, he has shaped that meal in a distinct fashion, distinct at least from the similar meals in the Synoptic Gospels. This is the more pressing issue. That there is a meal is easy to explain. The particular shape of that meal is not so easy to explain. None of the basic characteristics of John's meal reflects borrowing from, or copies of, anything in the testaments. Some other source must be found for the particular shape and the elaborate development that John gives to the meal in chapters 13–17.

This pursuit leads inevitably to the literary symposium. Following in the wake of Plato and Xenophon, who both chronicled dialogues with Socrates entitled the *Symposium*, many ancient authors wrote literary symposia.[129] In addition to the writings of Plato and Xenophon, surviving meal scenes, or at least fragments of them, come from the pens of the following authors:[130] Aristotle (384–322 BC);[131] Epicurus

---

it is over in a matter of a few lines. Dio's *Oration 30* does not mention a meal, but includes in its closing paragraphs an extended metaphor that compares life to a house in which people temporarily meet to share a banquet. This is nothing like what we see in John, though.

[127] Brown, *Gospel of John*, 2.598; Segovia, *Farewell of the Word*, 21, 316.

[128] This study makes no specific claims for the relationship between the Gospel of John and the Synoptic Gospels. For the history of this question, see D. Moody Smith, *John Among the Gospels* (2nd ed.; Columbia, South Carolina: University of South Carolina, 2001).

[129] Martin, *Symposion*, 295–6, notes that there are symposiac traditions prior to Plato. That his dialogue serves as the model for so many imitators is what makes him the primary author of a new literary form. Cf. Relihan, "Rethinking," 219.

[130] List taken from K. Berger, "Hellenistischen Gattungen im Neuen Testaments," *ANRW* 25.2: 1311.

[131] Fragments of his '*Symposium*' or '*On Drunkennes*' collected in V. Rose, *Aristotelis Fragmenta* (Leipzig, 1886). Martin, *Symposion*, 169f., 204ff.

(341–270 BC);[132] Menippus of Gadara (100 BC);[133] Meleagre (140–70 BC);[134] Horace;[135] Asconius (9 BC);[136] Petronius (d. 66 AD);[137] Plutarch (d. 120 AD);[138] Lucian (d. 190 AD);[139] Athenaeus (ca. 200 AD);[140] Methodius, bishop of Olympus (d. 311 AD);[141] Julian the Apostate;[142] Macrobius.[143] Other authors are mentioned in the doxographical tradition, such as Speusippus, but their writings are completely lost.[144]

The definitive quality of the literary symposium is its dialogue form.[145] Ancient literature from Homer's epics onward is replete with meal scenes in which generous amounts of food and drink are enjoyed. Martin's classic study on the genre, however, does not label all meal scenes as symposia. The texts cited above differ from the less dramatic form of the "deipnon" in that they employ the standard meal setting as a stage for a dialogue. The meal is the critical framework for the discussion, and the literary purpose for the participants' association. But the dialogue is what makes a meal scene a symposium. The degree to which literary symposia conform to this norm will be discussed at greater length in chapter 4.

This recipe of combining a deipnon and speeches fits the Johannine Last Supper quite neatly. One qualification is necessary, however. To say that John 13–17 fits the basic symposium model is not the same as saying that it is a symposium. Aune is correct when he states that there is no Christian symposium until Methodius of Olympus in the 4th century AD.[146] But John's meal scene follows the basic pattern of a deipnon that recedes into the background and is then followed by speeches. John twice refers to the meal in chapter 13

---

[132] Fragments collected in H. Usener, *Epicurea* (Leipzig: Teubner, 1887) 115–19. Martin, *Symposion*, 208ff.

[133] Fragments in Athenaeus, 14.629e, 664e. Martin, *Symposion*, 229f, 238ff.

[134] Fragments in Athenaeus, 11.502c. Martin, *Symposion*, 111, 214.

[135] *Satire*, II 8. Martin, *Symposion*, 216ff.

[136] Cf. Pliny, *Natural History*, VII 159. Martin, *Symposion*, 243ff.

[137] *Cena Trimalchionis*. Martin, *Symposion*, 219ff.

[138] *Dinner of the Seven Wise Men, Table Talk*. Martin, *Symposion*, 247–265.

[139] '*Symposium*' or '*Lapiths*,' *Saturnalia*. Martin, *Symposion*, 222ff.

[140] *Deipnosophistae*. Martin, *Symposion*, 270ff.

[141] *Symposium of the Seven Maidens*. Martin, *Symposion*, 286ff.

[142] '*Symposium*' or '*The Caesars*'. Martin, *Symposion*, 237ff.

[143] *Saturnalia*. Martin, *Symposion*, passim.

[144] Plutarch, *Table Talk*, 612e.

[145] This distinction is established in J. Martin, *Symposion*, 149ff. and idem, "Deipnonliteratur," *RAC* 3.659, where he writes, "Das Symposion bedient sich der Dialogform." See also Berger, "Hellenistische Gattungen" 1311.

[146] David Aune, "Septem," 69.

as a "deipnon" (13:2,4), and this deipnon is followed by a conversation in chapter 14, which extends into a series of speeches in chapters 15–16 and a prayer in chapter 17. One of the key purposes of chapter 4 will be to see precisely how John's scene conforms to the typical relationship between the meal and the dialogues that follow the meal in the literary symposium.[147]

The question then arises, Why has John done this? Others have noted the similarities between the Farewell Discourses and classical dining scenarios, but they have focused on such things as the social functions of table fellowship in antiquity.[148] Chapter 4 will study, not the symposium as a social institution, but the literary symposium tradition, and especially the relationship between the meal and the conversations that follow the meal. The overall goal is to investigate contemporary claims that the symposium can be a vehicle for commemoration, as well as a time capsule that renders present that which is absent.

Summary

Before moving forward, a summary of the preceding section is in order. In response to previous scholarship that understands the Farewell Discourses solely as a testament, this study will investigate areas in which the discourses interface with classical literature, specifically the following literary styles: Greek tragedy; consolation literature; and the literary symposium tradition. The purpose of this effort is to illuminate how the Fourth Gospel bends and twists the basic expectations of the testament form. No longer designed to evoke only the themes of departure and absence, the testament of Jesus in

---

[147] Furthermore, the symposium is often combined with other literary genres in the period in which John's Gospel appears. It is not at all unusual to see him merging the symposium with the testament, as well as with other literary forms. The *Cena Trimalchionis* in Petronius' *Satyricon* is a sympotic scene that is considerably influenced by ancient comedy and embedded in a Roman novel. See above, note 69, for the blending of comic and sympotic tropes in Petronius' *Satyricon*. For Athenaeus' *Deipnosophistae*, see most recently John Wilkins, "Dialogue and Comedy: The Structure of the *Deipnosophistae*," in *Athenaeus and His World: Reading Greek Culture in the Roman Empire* (ed. David Braund and John Wilkins; Exeter: University of Exeter Press, 2000) 23–37.

[148] See Witherington, *John's Wisdom*, 236ff.; Bruce Malina and Richard Rohrbaugh, *Social-science Commentary on the Gospel of John* (Minneapolis: Fortress, 1998) 217ff.

John emphasizes instead Jesus' abiding presence. While the material from Greek tragedy will only further emphasize the theme of
departure, the material from classical consolation literature and the
symposium tradition will evoke the theme of presence. John has,
thus, twisted the testament by joining to it these three classical forms.
The result is a different kind of testament. To clarify this situation
is the purpose behind the individual arguments of the following chapters. Not every possible generic affinity is traced in each chapter,
but only those that contribute to the twin themes of presence and
absence, rendering the study admittedly somewhat selective, but more
coherent as a total monograph.

In another sense, however, this work is not only about seeing
Many instead of One. It is also about seeing One instead of Many.
To explain how this is so is the object of the remainder of the introduction. The pursuit of multiplicity can now cease, in preparation
for exploring greater unity in the discourses.

B. *Turning Many into One: Synchronic vs. Diachronic*

The question of narrative unity is a critical divide that separates literary and historical studies of the Fourth Gospel. The Farewell
Discourses are one of the key battlegrounds in this debate, particularly in the constellation of problems that circulates around the enigmatic exit of Jesus at 14:31. Chapter 2 of this study will focus on
this peculiar exit. To prepare for chapter 2, and in order to situate
its argument within contemporary discussions, the remainder of the
introductory chapter will review trends in the literary study of the
Fourth Gospel through the lens of Jesus' peculiar exit at 14:31.

The Problem: Historical Criticism

The point of controversy in 14:31 is straightforward. Jesus closes his
discourse in chapter 14 with the words, "I will no longer speak at
length with you (14:30). Arise, let us depart from here" (14:31). Yet,
chapter 15 opens in the very next line with: "I am the true vine,"
and Jesus continues to speak for three more chapters, with no indication that he has actually gone anywhere. It is only at 18:1 that
the reader is at last given the notice that Jesus has left the dinner:

"After saying these things, Jesus departed." The result is a rather substantial delay between the announcement of the departure and the actualization of the departure.

Not all interpreters see this delay as a problem. They ingeniously demonstrate that Jesus did in fact leave the supper when he said he would, and that the text contains no uncomfortable disjuncture. St. John Chrysostom provides an early example of this type. When he wonders why Jesus decides to leave the supper at this point, Chrysostom first offers the possibility that Jesus is afraid, and that he does not want Judas and the plotters to come upon him unawares and before he finishes his discourse.[149] But Chrysostom quickly dismisses this as unfitting for the all-knowing God, who himself has set the time when Judas is to come. God cannot be motivated by fear – but the disciples can. After Jesus announces to the them at the end of chapter 14, "Yet a little while and I am not with you" and "the ruler of this world is coming," the disciples are filled with dread. Jesus leads them to a safer place so that they might be more receptive to the lofty teaching he is about to present to them. Where this place is, Chrysostom never mentions.

Place is very important to B.F. Westcott, however. Like Chrysostom, he claims that Jesus leaves the supper at 14:31, but his argument is more geographical than psychological.[150] After leaving the supper, Jesus' discussion of the true vine in 15:1ff. is motivated by some external object he sees while walking, perhaps a vineyard on the Mt. of Olives. It may also be that he is in the courtyard of the Temple, especially since Josephus locates a golden vine upon the gates of the courtyard (*AJ* 15.11.3; *BJ* 5.5.4). An association with the temple is, for Westcott, strengthened by the prayer Jesus offers in chapter 17, which Westcott believes to be a high-priestly prayer.[151]

But the Gospel supports neither of these suggestions. In the first place, we are told in 14:31 that Jesus intends to leave, but not that he actually goes anywhere. Even more significant is the unshakable fact that John says only at 18:1, "After saying these things, Jesus departed." Nowhere are we told that Jesus leaves the dinner before

[149] Discussion of 14:31 is contained in his *Homiliae in Joannem*, 76.1 (PG 59:409–11).
[150] See B.F. Westcott, *The Gospel According to Saint John* (Rev. and enl. ed. James Clarke and Co. London. 1958) 211, 216.
[151] Ibid., 216.

this point. Westcott does take the announcement at 18:1 into account, but neutralizes it by referring it to Jesus' departure from wherever he is between chapters 15 and 17, i.e., the Mount of Olives or the Temple court.[152] Again, though, we cannot be sure that Jesus goes to the Temple court or the Mount of Olives, or that the setting of 15–17 is any different from 13–14. Since Jesus cannot be demonstrated to leave until 18:1, the announcement of the departure at 14:31 is a riddle.

Various reactions respond to the riddle, but the most elaborate and pervasive explanations rest on redaction or other historical theories.[153] The assumption is that the text as we have it is not the text as it originally was.[154] The original edition of the Gospel, it is argued, contained a smooth transition between what is now 14:31 and what is now 18:1. Jesus announced his departure, and then the Evangelist narrated it, which would have gone as follows:

> "Arise, let us depart from here" (14:31). Having said these things, Jesus departed (18:1).

The block of text that interrupts this smooth progression, the current chapters 15–17, was put into this position later. Either it was added by subsequent editors, or was placed here mistakenly by those ignorant of the Gospel's original order. The disjunction between 14:31 and 15:1 could not, however, have been an intentional literary move.

Such readings have carried the day among modern critics, and have branched out into elaborate sub-theories, depending on how extensive the level of editing is thought to be.[155] But regardless of

---

[152] Ibid., 211.

[153] There are a variety of other options available for reading these chapters, but they have not caught the scholarly imagination as thoroughly as those presented here. These additional views are summarized neatly in Fernando Segovia, "John 15:18–16:4a: A First Addition to the Original Farewell Discourse?," *CBQ* 45 (1983), 211–216.

[154] John Painter succinctly argues that the history of the Johannine community explains the diversity and development in the discourses. Of the disjunction between 14:31 and 15:1, he writes, "It does not seem reasonable to suggest that the evangelist wrote [Arise, let us be going in 14:31] with the intention of continuing the discourse in 15:1 as if there had been no break . . . 18:1 indicates that only then does Jesus leave with his disciples. How then can this apparent dislocation be accounted for?" See John Painter, "The Farewell Discourses and the History of Johannine Christianity," *NTS* 27 (1981) 528.

[155] See Segovia, "A First Addition," 211–216, where he recognizes that the differing approaches revolve around two issues: 1) how many separate blocks of text exist?

the degree of editorial work assumed, the belief that there was at least one editorial revision holds sway in the bulk of the scholarly literature. Or, rather, it holds sway among those people for whom this kind of interpretation would hold sway. Those scholars who believe that the history of the composition of the Gospel is a matter worth pursuing accept at least some level of editing in chapters 13–17. But not all scholars see the value of such research. In particular, a new branch of the scholarly vine has self-consciously avoided the entanglements of source and redaction theories.

The Problem: Literary Criticism

These scholars go under various theoretical monikers, and their manifold approaches create an impression that is difficult to encapsulate in a single title.[156] This study will refer to them for ease of discussion under the phrase "narrative critics." As with the redaction critics, it is not necessary to catalogue exhaustively the insights of narrative critics, or their several nuances of approach. But narrative criticism will receive more attention than redaction criticism did, since this will clarify better the ramifications of the present study. A specific

---

2) were they written by the evangelist or by someone with different theological intentions? Four options are available:

1. 15–17 are one unit of text, written by the evangelist himself, and incorporated into the text later by a redactor faithful to the evangelist's message.
2. 15–17 are one unit of text, but are the product of a mind in opposition to the evangelist.
3. 15–17 are several units of text fused together in various stages of redaction, though they were originally written by the evangelist.
4. 15–17 are several units of text fused together in various stages of redaction, though some of them are written by the evangelist and others are not.

[156] The following discussion lumps together a variety of works whose authors would call themselves either narrative critics, structural narratologists or various types of reader-response critics. Stephen Moore's eminently helpful tour guide through literary criticism of the Gospels divides literary scholarship into two categories: narrative criticism and reader-response criticism. He recognizes, however, that these general designations account neither for the tremendous variety of their subjects, nor for the overlap between the two categories. Further, reader-response criticism is an extension, really, of narrative criticism. Especially in New Testament studies, reader-response criticism is often nothing more than "reader-oriented narrative criticism." See Stephen Moore, *Literary Criticism and the Gospels* (New Haven: Yale University Press) xxii, 73, 80. Given Moore's insights, the term narrative critics will be used for the sake of ease.

concern is the manner in which narrative readings distance themselves from the questions that occupy source and redaction interpretations. Because narrative criticism operates almost entirely separately
from traditional historical criticism, there is a fruitful, but pronounced,
separation in methodological stances toward the Gospel of John, as
well as the other Gospels.[157]

The presupposition of narrative criticism that most deviates from
historical and redaction theories is its insistence on studying the
Gospel as a narrative unity. Literary critics and historians are essen-
tially studying two different texts, or at least the same text in different
time zones. As noted above, when redaction critics encounter a textual circumstance such as verse 14:31, they assume that later editors have interrupted an originally smooth narrative. The Gospel is
viewed as a document that has passed through history, and has been
changed during the journey.[158]

On the other hand, for as long as historians have noticed aporias in the Gospel, there have been others defending the need to
focus more on the text in its final, canonical form, with less concern for the historical dimensions of the text. Raymond Brown strikes
a middle ground between synchronic and diachronic concerns, when
he includes the following notice in the introduction to his Anchor
Bible commentary:

> We shall comment on the Gospel in its present order without impos-
> ing rearrangements. Some object to this procedure on the ground that
> such an approach attains only to the meaning given to passages in the

---

[157] Given this circumstance, several scholars have recently called for a rap-
prochement between historical and literary analyses of the Gospel of John. For a
critique of narrative criticism from a historical perspective, see especially John Ashton,
Studying John, particularly chapter 6 ("Narrative Criticism") and chapter 8 ("Studying
John"); M.C. de Boer, "Narrative Criticism, Historical Criticism, and the Gospel
of John." *JSNT* 47 (1992) 35–48; For attempts to span the divide between historical and narrative criticism, see M. Stibbe, *John as Storyteller*; idem, *John's Gospel*.
(New York: Routledge, 1994); M. Stibbe, ed., *The Gospel of John as Literature*; Steve
Motyer, "Method in Fourth Gospel Studies: A Way Out of the Impasse?," *JSNT*
66 (1997) 27–44.

[158] R. Bultmann's efforts to completely rearrange the canonical order of the Gospel
have not carried the day, so receive no serious comment here. But, it is important
to note the importance of 14:31 for his rearrangement of the Farewell Discourses.
Bultmann's order of the Last Supper Discourses is 13:1–30; 17:1–26; 13:31; 15:1–16:33;
13:36–14:31. Several issues are at stake in his decisions, but by placing 14:31 at
the conclusion of the scene, he has solved the problem of the delayed departure,
which is a chief preoccupation in his reconstruction. See Bultmann, *Gospel of John*,
459–461, 631.

final edition of the Gospel, and hence perhaps only to the meaning of a subordinate editor rather than to the meaning of the evangelist . . . Naturally, where there is reason to suspect that in the formative history of the Gospel a passage had another setting and meaning, we shall mention it with proper qualifications as to the certainty with which the original position can be reconstructed. But we shall give primary consideration to the passage as it now stands.[159]

It is important to note that when Brown reads the final, canonical form of the text, he does not avoid historical concerns. He attends consistently and energetically to questions of source and redaction, where the text as we have it seems to have been edited by later hands – most especially in chapters 13–17.[160]

There is, thus, nothing new about the play between the synchronic and diachronic dimensions of the Gospel.[161] What is new is the methodological presupposition of the narrative critics that they must bracket entirely the diachronic dimensions of the text, and focus exclusively on the text as a synchronic phenomenon, frozen in time. Staley writes, "[The] book has come down to us as a single entity, and thus the New Testament narrative critic may rightly seek to understand the text as a unified whole, inferring coherence and intentionality from the work."[162] His use of the terms "coherence" and "intentionality" are unsatisfying, but his intentions are clear. Even more pronounced is Culpepper, who writes,

> [Dissection] and stratification have no place in the study of the gospel and may distort and confuse one's view of the text. Every element of the gospel contributes to the production of its meaning, and the experience of reading the text is more important than understanding the process of its composition.[163]

---

[159] Brown, *Gospel of John*, xxxiv.

[160] In this, he differs from Dodd, who has the following to say about editorial questions, Dodd, *Interpretation*, 399:

> . . . I conceive it the duty of the interpreter to attempt in the first place to understand and account for the actual text which lies before him, and if possible to discover the plan on which it is arranged, whether or not any other possible plan might be discovered behind it.

[161] This is made clear in the history of research on the Fourth Gospel in J. Becker, "Das Johannesevangelium im Streit der Methoden (1980–1984)." *TRu* 51 (1986), 1–78. Cf. Ashton, *Studying John*, 143ff.

[162] Jeffrey Lloyd Staley, *The Print's First Kiss: A Rhetorical Investigation of the Implied Reader in the Fourth Gospel* (SBLDS 82; Atlanta, Georgia: Scholars Press, 1988) 23.

[163] R. Alan Culpepper, *Anatomy of the Fourth Gospel: A Study in Literary Design* (Philadelphia: Fortress, 1983) 5.

The great advantage to this approach is that it draws attention to
the manner in which the narrative communicates to the reader and
brings out elements of that communication that otherwise might go
unnoticed. The emphasis on reading a text as a linear narrative
brings to light factors in the text that are lost when the Gospel is
mined for historical information and its narrative quality is ignored.[164]

How, then, do narrative readings address the peculiar delay of
Jesus at John 14:31? It is important to say at the outset that, for all
of the ink that has been spilled on this passage by redaction critics,
the narrative critics spend disarmingly little time on it.[165] Only Tolmie
and Moloney give more than passing attention to the problem.

Tolmie investigates how the implied reader would react to 14:31
based on how the text leads up to this verse. He identifies John 13–17
as the statistically longest episode in the Gospel. Almost 20% of the
Gospel's narrative takes place in this single episode.[166] So, the pace
of the narrative slows in the Last Supper, then at 14:31 the narrative
grinds to a confusing halt. The reader should presume from John
14:30–31 that the discourse is about to conclude, and that the narrator will move on to the next episode, but this does not happen.[167]

The implied reader can react in one of three ways to this unusual
circumstance. First, "[s]/he may infer that there is an ellipsis in the
text in that the implied author failed to note a radical change in
place or time . . ." An ellipsis occurs when "an event is not narrated
in the narrative text, although it is clear that it must have happened
in the story."[168] The second option is similar to the suggestions of
Chrysostom and Westcott referred to earlier: "s/he may assume that
Jesus is moving/has moved to a new unspecified place . . ." Last of
all, "s/he may assume that Jesus has changed his mind and decided

---

[164] This, though, is a bit of a caricature of historical inquiry. Historical criticism
involves more than mere mining of the text. See de Boer, *Narrative Criticism*, 42 and
passim.

[165] Segovia recognizes the problem, but does not gauge its impact on the reader.
For him, the odd announcement of a departure that does not occur helps to mark
the conclusion of a coherent unit of text (13:31–14:31) but the issue receives no
further treatment, *Farewell of the Word*, 24–25. Culpepper, *Anatomy*, does not even
mention it as a problem. Neither does Staley in *Print's First Kiss*, which is especially
noteworthy, since his goal is to examine the way in which readers are "victimized"
by the unexpected twists of the Fourth Gospel.

[166] Tolmie, *Jesus' Farewell*, 159.

[167] Ibid., 160.

[168] Ibid., 149.

to stay longer in the same 'room' . . ." As the reader continues, he will notice that some of the material in chapters 15–16 replicates material in previous chapters, but other than that the reader will have a hard time finding his bearings. Whatever the case, Tolmie concludes with: "[The] implied reader will be unable to answer the question as to where the events that are narrated in John 15:1–17:26 occur with absolute certainty, since no clear indications are given."[169]

Moloney's interpretation of the Fourth Gospel is a model of narrative criticism, but its method runs into the same problem in addressing John 14:31.[170] Moloney defines the implied reader much as Tolmie does, so his reading of 14:31 is similar to Tolmie's as well.[171] Only now, not only is the reader confused; the reader is even "frustrated".[172] This frustration is coupled with the frustration of the disciples in the Gospel, who are caught living in the in-between time and awaiting Jesus' return. While waiting to see when the discourse will end, the implied reader shares in the tension of the disciples as they together cope with "frustrating delay". So it is with the implied reader. Not knowing what do with the text as it is, the reader experiences confusion and frustration.

This insistence of both Tolmie and Moloney that the reader will meet the passage with confusion seems to beg the question of interpretation rather than answer it. The narrative critics have recognized the same problem that the historians have: the peculiar exit of Jesus at 14:31 is confusing and perhaps even frustrating. But the narrative method is unable to provide a reading of Jesus' delay that differs markedly from those offered by historians. Very reasonably then, both Tolmie and Moloney fall back on diachronic arguments to explain the text. Moloney refers to the exit of Jesus at 14:31 as "a notorious problem [that] doubtless reflects an earlier stage in the development of the discourse before the addition of chapters 15–17, when 14:31 ran into the opening words of the Passion in 18:1."[173] But after recognizing this, he quickly moves on to his own purpose, the final form of the text, with the question, "But what does the

---

[169] Ibid., 161.

[170] Culpepper's *Anatomy* broke new ground in systematically exploring the basic narrative quality of the Fourth Gospel, but Moloney's detailed study provides a map that traces the entire narrative of the Gospel of John.

[171] See F. Moloney, *Belief in the Word* (Minneapolis, Fortress Press, 1993) 9–14.

[172] *Glory not Dishonor*, 53.

[173] Ibid., 52.

reader make of this summons to go forth, which leads nowhere?"[174]
Similar is the approach of Tolmie who writes, "From a redaction-
critical perspective this is of course a clear indication of editorial
activity."[175]

That many narrative critics recognize the validity of historical concerns, and yet quickly move past them, is what particularly rankles
historical critics. There is a sense that the advantages of narrative
criticism can only be achieved artificially, a fact that calls its value
into question for historians. More than one hundred years of research
have gone into demonstrating that the Gospel of John as we have
it, the final form of the text, is not a coherent narrative unity.
Narrative critics do not deal with this hefty bulk of scholarship at
all in their analyses, except where they are unable to explain a feature of the text.[176] It is this avoidance of the results of historical
inquiry that so disturbs historical critics. John Ashton criticizes several narrative readings of the Gospel, and then remarks specifically
about the efforts of G. Mlakuzhyil, "Mlakuzhyil, unlike the others,
recognizes that if the arguments against unity were valid they would
scupper his own project before it had got under way. But so confident

---

[174] Ibid., 52.

[175] Tolmie, *Jesus' Farewell*, 160.

[176] The first several pages of Ashton's chapter "Narrative Criticism" (*Studying John*,
143–165) are devoted to critiquing the way in which narrative critics too easily
ignore historical questions. De Boer, in general, is more positive about the potential profit of narrative readings, but shares Ashton's critiques of the manner in which
the procedure is currently practiced. As for the question of unity, De Boer, "Narrative
Criticism," 43–44, writes the following:

> Can any avowedly critical method, however, really presuppose coherence,
> whether thematic or literary, as an unquestionable principle? Many a novelist
> has thought his or her novel to be thematically coherent and narratively cohe-
> sive, but many a reviewer has thought otherwise. The critical interpreter must,
> like a discerning reviewer of a novel, go wherever the evidence – the data
> given in the extant, canonical form of the text – may lead.

Ashton, *Studying John*, 145, adds as well:

> Undaunted by the so-called aporias of the Fourth Gospel, and throwing a pair
> of enormous brackets around the historical hypotheses of their colleagues, they
> proceed *as if* the Gospel was designed from the outset in its present form ... To
> scholars who refuse to turn a blind eye to the aporias of the Gospel such a
> procedure seems foolhardy in the extreme. These, convinced that the Gospel
> was *not* originally designed as we have it now, are astonished by the pretence
> or assumption that the plan, plot, or trajectory of the Gospel should be viewed
> in its entirety as a unified whole. To rely upon this assumption is, in their
> view, to put out to sea in a very leaky vessel indeed ...

is he of their fundamental weakness that it takes him barely a page to dispose of them."[177] This is not to say that Ashton is opposed to reading the text as a unity. He simply opposes reading it as a unity when there is no regard for arguments to the contrary.[178]

There is, indeed, a sense in which narrative criticism forces a text to be seamless without actually demonstrating its seamlessness. Narrative critics endeavor to see how the text communicates, but then methodologically gag the text so that it cannot speak for itself. As Stephen Moore writes, "[Narrative criticism] may be founded unsteadily on the suppression of the older paradigm of the fragmentary, source-spliced text and may depend heavily for its success on an effective blocking out of the more disruptive data that the supplanted paradigm would bring into view . . ."[179] To Moore, this fundamental flaw in the narrative method is justification for "deconstructing" the text. The Gospel of John has aporias, and narrative criticism can only succeed if it suppresses them. Deconstruction provides a means for taking the aporias seriously.

The present study offers an alternate means of addressing the apparent aporia in 14:31. Redaction theories and narrative theories alike assume that no author would intentionally have included such an exit in the middle of the Farewell Discourses. The synchronic reading that is offered in what follows does not suppress historical arguments, but meets them head-on in an attempt to explain the peculiar pause at 14:31, not as a sloppy redactional effort, but as a legitimate, intentional literary move.

In summary, the divide that now separates historical and literary studies of the Gospel of John is an unfortunate reality. Some of the most important analyses of the Fourth Gospel have resulted from carefully attending to both the literary and the historical dimensions of the text. For example, Wayne Meeks' socio-historical investigation

---

[177] *Studying John*, 147. See George Mlakuzhyil, *The Christocentric Literary Structure of the Fourth Gospel* (Analecta Biblica 117; Rome: Pontificio Istituto Biblico, 1987).

[178] See Ashton's comments in *Studying John*, 185–7, where he also recognizes that even some historians are skeptical about the pursuit of the history of the Gospel's composition. He cites M. de Jonge as a notable example of a scholar who does not believe that the evidence is sufficient to develop elaborate theories regarding the history of the Gospel's production. Ashton accepts this criticism because de Jonge responds to historical arguments as a historian. He does not ignore the historical arguments; he simply disagrees with them. See especially M. de Jonge, *Jesus: Stranger from Heaven and Son of God* (SBLSBS 11; Missoula, Mont., 1977), viii.

[179] *Literary Criticism*, 167.

of the Johannine community is only possible because of the close attention that Meeks pays to the narrative flow of the ascent-descent scheme in the Gospel.[180]

Further, Culpepper unnecessarily equates "literary criticism" with synchronic narrative criticism, when he writes that ". . . the approach of literary criticism is clearly distinct from that of historical-critical scholarship . . ."[181] He also misrepresents historical scholarship when he sees it as nothing more than "dissection and stratification" of the text.[182] Analyzing the literary quality of a text, and its effect on a reader, can involve returning the text to its historical period, in a literary-historical fashion. When this is done, it will be possible to see that a reader could have a more specific response to the Gospel than confusion or frustration. And this is not entirely alien to narrative critical efforts, especially those of Culpepper. For, Culpepper's claim that historical and literary study are distinct is tempered by the recognition that there must be a dialogue between the two.[183] This study is an attempt at such a dialogue.

In addition, it is possible to navigate differently the divide between the synchronic and diachronic approaches to the text. The literary reading offered in chapter 2 will meet historical arguments directly by reading the Farewell Discourses through the lens of ancient drama. The goal is not so much a reconciliation of the synchronic and diachronic, as it is an attempt to offer a synchronic reading that is responsible to the diachronic arguments of historians. In this sense, the present study will not follow the very interesting work of those who interpret the Farewell Discourses in pursuit of *relecture*.[184] As the

---

[180] Wayne Meeks, "The Man from Heaven in Johannine Sectarianism," in *The Interpretation of John* (ed. John Ashton; Philadelphia: Fortress Press, 1986) 141–73; repr. from *JBL* (1972) 44–72. See on Meeks' literary concerns the comments of Stibbe, *John as Storyteller*, 61ff. The same insight is equally true for the two most thoroughly historical critics, Bultmann and Dodd, both of whom are eminently concerned with "literary" questions, with the flow of the Gospel's narrative. Cf. Ashton, *Studying John*, 208. And, of course, the same can surely be said for the universally influential work of Martyn, *History and Theology*, whose historical reconstruction of the Johannine community relies on a close reading of the literary quality of, especially, John 9.

[181] Culpepper, *Anatomy*, 5.

[182] Ibid., 5.

[183] Ibid., 5.

[184] J. Zumstein, "Le processus de relecture dans la littérature johannique," *Etud. Theol. Rel.* 73 (1998) 161–176 Dettwiler, *Gegenwart*; K. Scholtissek, "Abschied und neue Gegenwart: Exegetische und theologische Reflexionen zur johanneischen

term *relecture* (rereading) implies, these scholars mean to see redaction in a new light. Their goal is to show that editing the text is not designed merely to alter or correct the text, so that its old meaning disappears. Rather, the old and the new now stand side-by-side and each one is changed in the process. So, *relecture* simultaneously allows for editing, but does not require seeing the text as a disjointed junkyard of edited scraps. The edited material is read in light of the old material, and the old material is changed by the new additions.

Chapter 2 will also address synchronic and diachronic arguments about the Farewell Discourses, but in a very different direction. The peculiar aporia at 14:31 will receive a synchronic explanation that responds directly to diachronic theories. The argument will be based on a common dramatic device. Now, with the background of the problem clarified, that argument can commence.

Abschiedsrede 13,31–17,26," *EphTheolLov* 75 (1999) 332–358; idem, "Das hohepriesterliche Gebet Jesu. Exegetische-theologische Beobachtungen zu Joh 17, 1–26," *TrierTheolZeit* 109 (2000) 199–218.

CHAPTER TWO

"ARISE, LET US GO FORTH!"

In praising the Gospel of John, Origen writes that, if the four Gospels represent the first fruit of the New Testament, then the Gospel of John is the first fruit of the Gospels.[1] He justifies this declaration with the claim that no one else illuminated so clearly the divinity of Jesus. In modern research, however, it seems that the Fourth Gospel surpasses the others not in its illumination, nor in its clarity, but in its capacity to confound interpreters. And, to paraphrase Origen, if John's Gospel is the most enigmatic of the Gospels, then among the most enigmatic items in the Fourth Gospel is the curious narrative fissure that cuts between chapters 14 and 15. Jesus announces at 14:31 that he will leave the Last Supper, but at 15:1 he does not appear to have gone anywhere, and simply continues speaking. This elusive exit is the topic of the present chapter.

It has already been noted that a critical feature distinguishing John's Last Supper Discourses from other testaments is the dramatic action of the scene, specifically the fact that Judas and Jesus depart from the Last Supper like characters exiting the stage. Since Jesus ostensibly exits to his death, it is important to note that in ancient drama, the departure to death is a regular event with recurring characteristics. This chapter will argue that John's Last Supper Discourses can be profitably compared to the dramatic exit to death.[2]

This is but a preliminary step in the larger movement of this chapter, however. Jesus' exit to death is compared to tragic exits in general in order to argue further that Jesus' departure resembles a particular type of tragic exit, the delayed exit. Ancient dramatic figures, in all eras and in both tragedy and in comedy, commonly

---

[1] *Comm. Jo.*1, 6 (*ANF* 10:300)
[2] Jerome Neyrey, "The 'Noble Shepherd' in John 10: Cultural and Rhetorical Background," *JBL* 120 (2001) 267–91, attempts to compare the death of Jesus to noble death themes in classical literature. The present chapter is not concerned with interpreting the death of Jesus, as Neyrey does, but is an effort to understand the narrative development of interest in Jesus' death, and the way in which Jesus' impending death is cast in a dramatic form.

delay announced exits. This is particularly common among characters departing to death. Viewing Jesus' hesitation to depart at 14:31
as a dramatic delayed exit will provide new insight into critical issues
typically associated with the text. The previous chapter clarified precisely the problem posed by John 14:31, as well as previous historical and literary attempts at a solution. In this chapter, material from
ancient drama will be brought to bear on the problems involved, in
order to take seriously the various interpretive concerns, and to arrive
at a synchronic reading of the text that does not bracket and ignore
historical concerns and arguments.

The Exit to Death

When the unique and extraordinary characters of tragedy make their
way to their deaths, they do so in a very typical and ordinary fashion. No matter how dissimilar their particular circumstances, tragic
figures die in very similar ways.[3]

It is a peculiarity of tragic stagecraft that the death that so often
marks one of the climactic events in a play is not depicted before
the audience's view. Dying characters make a final, conclusive exit
to death, but the death itself happens beyond the audience's aware-
ness. Cries of pain may ring from somewhere out of sight, but only
through a messenger's report is the fate of the dead character broad-
cast, and this only after the fact.[4] Since much of the play is spent
building up to this exit, the thing most expected is not supplied; the
viewer sees only buildup and aftermath.[5] A number of theories attempt

---

[3] On the conventionality of tragic deaths, see Fiona Macintosh, "Tragic Last
Words: The Big Speech and the Lament in Ancient Greek and Modern Irish Tragic
Drama," in *Tragedy and the Tragic: Greek Theatre and Beyond* (ed. M.S. Silk; Clarendon
Press: Oxford, 1996), 414–425, as well as her *Dying Acts: Death in Ancient Greek and
Modern Irish Tragic Drama* (Cork, Ireland: Cork University Press, 1994), especially pp.
69, 94. For the conventionality of exits and entrances generally in Greek tragedy,
see Taplin, *Stagecraft*; Halleran, *Stagecraft*.

[4] There are, of course, at least two notable exceptions to this convention. Deaths
definitely occur onstage in two plays by Euripides, *Alcestis* (280ff.) and *Hippolytus*
(1438–1458). There is debate as to whether or not the *Ajax* of Sophocles should be
added to this list. Several questions of stagecraft suggest that, even though Ajax
appears to die onstage, he actually makes an exit before his death. For a recent
contribution to this debate, as well as additional bibliography, see Macintosh, *Dying
Acts*, 130–132.

[5] See Taplin, *Stagecraft*, 163–5.

to explain this treatment, or lack of treatment, of death scenes. Aesthetic, religious and practical stage concerns are all possible justifications, but no explanation enjoys universal success.[6]

For the present argument, however, it is best to set aside the search for the cause of this device, and focus instead on its effect. For, the fact that a dying character almost always dies offstage renders the last exit of that character a momentous event. The exit to death takes on a central significance, and the degree to which this potential is realized depends on the amount of preparation that an author provides for the exit.[7] It would be wrong to say that the exit to death marks every play's definitive climax.[8] Interpreters prefer to speak of a series of climactic events in the case of most plays.[9] But the exit to death is always an important moment.

For the sake of comparison with the Gospel of John, an exit worthy of close analysis is that of Eteocles in Aeschylus' *Seven Against Thebes*. Everything prior to the exit leads up to the exit, and everything after it follows from it.[10] *Seven Against Thebes* is the only surviving play of an original tetralogy on the house of Oedipus, and it would be reasonable to assume that Eteocles' exit was anticipated even in the other plays that were intended to precede *Seven*. Unfortunately, we suffer in not knowing how themes in *Seven* were prepared in the plays that did not survive.

---

[6] For a review of the options, see Macintosh, *Dying Acts*, 126–30, 133–35, 140–42.

[7] Taplin, *Stagecraft*, 163.

[8] "The final exit of a dying character may always be an important event in Greek tragedy, but the last words that precede this exit do not necessarily constitute *the* climax of the action. More often than not the action consists of a series of climaxes rather than having only one that is coincident with last words." Macintosh, *Dying Acts*, 92. See also Taplin, *Stagecraft*, 163.

[9] See, for instance, Sophocles' *Antigone*, which will be discussed below. The plot centers on the proper treatment of the corpse of Antigone's brother, Polynices. The play has three climactic confrontations: Kreon with Antigone (441–525); Kreon with Haimon (631–765); Kreon and Teiresias (988–1090). Antigone's exit to death comes immediately after her confrontation with Kreon, and yet comes relatively early in the play. It is important, however, precisely because of the way in which it works with the second confrontation, that between Kreon and Haimon, to demonstrate Kreon's intransigence. Only in his third confrontation does he reverse his stance from the previous two, thus resolving the tension created earlier. So, the death of Antigone is very important, and is preceded by a speech, which will be discussed below. But it does not mark the final climax of the play. Griffith, *Antigone*, 16–17. Indeed, in only two cases do final speeches mark the climax of their respective plays: Sophocles' *Trachiniae* and Euripides' *Hippolytus*. See Macintosh, *Dying Acts*, 92.

[10] Taplin, *Stagecraft*, 163–67, provides the basis for the following interpretation of *Seven*.

The story is clear enough in the extant *Seven,* however. The sons
of Oedipus are at war with one another. Oedipus, of course, is the
King of Thebes born under the curse that he would slay his father
and marry his mother. When the truth of his nefarious marriage is
made known, his mother/wife kills herself, and Oedipus blinds himself in order not to see the evil world he created. He leaves his kingdom to his two sons, who are to rule alternately, each for one year
at a time. This story is well known and not essential to understanding
Seven. What is important, and less well known, are the events that
follow from this point, the lives of Oedipus' sons, Eteocles and
Polynices. Legends differ regarding their fate, and *Seven* never explicitly claims to follow one specific version of the story. We know that
Oedipus has cursed his sons, but the cause and content of the curse
are not entirely clear. All we hear is one line of *Seven* (785): "And
against his sons, because of their cruelty, he launched malisons of
wrath . . ."[11] In the context of the play, the curse takes the form of
the two brothers warring against one another. Unlike certain leg-
endary accounts, however, Aeschylus blames neither brother for the
war.[12] He emphasizes their mutual destiny as the accursed sons of
Oedipus, their common fate as brothers.[13] So, we do not know the
precise nature of the curse their father has cast over them, but we
know that the brothers live under a curse. And we do not know the
precise nature of their quarrel, but we know that they are at war.

With this background in mind, it is possible now to enquire about
how the action of the play develops to a crescendo with Eteocles'
exit. Preparation for the exit is not steady, and it develops late.[14]
But as the exit becomes more likely, events unfold with increasing
momentum. Two features of Eteocles' character contribute to this
rising tempo and culminate in Eteocles' exit to death.[15]

---

[11] The translation here is slightly altered from the Loeb version, where ἀγρίας
is rendered "cruel tendance," instead of "cruelty" as here.

[12] Other versions of the myth make the blame more obvious. In the version of
the story followed by Euripides in the *Phoenician Women,* Oedipus gives his sons the
power to rule in alternate years, in an annually rotating kingship. They soon come
into conflict, however, when Eteocles refuses to relinquish the throne at the end of
the year. Thus, Eteocles is to blame for the discord. In other traditions, they divide
the kingdom in a different system, but eventually Polynices is the aggressor. William
G. Thalmann, *Dramatic Art in Aeschylus' Seven Against Thebes* (Yale Classical Monographs 1; New Haven: Yale University Press, 1978) 20–22.

[13] Ibid., 20–22.

[14] Taplin, *Stagecraft,* 163–64.

[15] Ibid., 163–64.

The curse of Oedipus is the first factor. Eteocles' eventual fate is to war against his brother, and so fulfill the curse that Oedipus set upon his sons. This theme is handled with subtlety and develops slowly. Prior to Eteocles' final exit, we are reminded of the paternal hex only in passing (line 70), when Eteocles addresses the curse personified in a prayer: "O Zeus and Earth, and you gods that guard our city, and [O] Curse, the potent spirit of the vengeance of my [father]."[16]

The additional theme that accompanies the curse is more pronounced, even early in the play. For, in addition to being the cursed son of Oedipus, Eteocles is also the defender of Thebes, another factor that results in his exit to death. As the play opens, Eteocles calms the Theban citizenry, and prepares the city for attack. He then adds the portentous notice:[17]

> Meanwhile, I will go and at the seven outlets in the walls will post six men – myself the seventh – as champions to oppose the foe in gallant style . . . (283–5).

The stage is set, then, for seven individual battles to occur as part of the larger fight. Each gate will have an attacker and a defender. Eteocles himself will defend the seventh gate, but the audience does not yet know whom he will face on the opposing side.

This information is not too long in coming. A scout enters to inform Eteocles of the enemy's movements (375). The ensuing conversation between Eteocles and the scout consists of a series of seven pairs of speeches, in which the scout identifies the attacker at a given gate, and Eteocles selects a captain appropriate to defend the respective gate. This dialogue lasts over 250 lines (375–631), during which Eteocles' own defense of the seventh gate is ignored. But it is not far below the surface. Because the arrangement of the section alternates between the announcement of an attacker by the scout and the assignment of a defender by Eteocles, an expectation lingers regarding the identity of the attacker whom Eteocles himself will face at the seventh gate. The tension gradually builds as each new gate is discussed, until the scout finally announces (631) that none other

---

[16] Zeitlin describes the tension that the curse creates as "[a] downward pull towards the final and irreversible end . . .," Froma Zeitlin, *Under the Sign of the Shield: Semiotics and Aeschylus'* Seven Against Thebes (Rome: Edizioni dell' Ateneo, 1982) 17.

[17] The translations of *Seven* are here adapted slightly from the Loeb translations.

than Polynices himself, Eteocles' brother, attacks the seventh gate. Thus, Eteocles' role as defender of the city clashes with his accursed bond with his brother. The climactic moment is marked by the collision of "the two codes, that of the city and that of the family . . ."[18] When Eteocles responds to this information, his speech unites the two elements of his character that have been developed to this point – his role as defender of Thebes and his identity as the cursed son of Oedipus. Eteocles recognizes his fate with a howl (654–6):

> O maddened of heaven and by heaven deeply loathed, O steeped in tears, our house of Oedipus! Woe is me! Now indeed our father's curses bear their fruit in deeds.

But he soon resolves to meet his fate (672–6):

> . . . I will go forth and face him – I myself. Who else has a claim more just? Chieftain against chieftain, brother against brother, foe against foe, I will take my stand. Quick, my greaves to fend off spear and stone!

The Chorus engages Eteocles in order to dissuade him from going to battle, but he concludes this conversation announcing (719), "From heaven-sent ills there's no escape!" He then exits to battle and to death.

Jesus' exit to death in the Gospel of John is similarly the culmination of thematic preparation. Like the gradual counting down of the seven defenders that culminates in the last exit of Eteocles, Jesus marches to his death in a final exit that has been prepared throughout the Gospel, slowly at first, but then with increasing intensity.

A preliminary step in presenting Jesus' exit to death is to emphasize that Jesus does *exit* to death. He urges the disciples at 14:31, "Arise, let us depart from here." This implies movement out of a scene. Although he does not actually leave at this point, he does leave at 18:1. Recognizing this is the first factor in comparing Jesus' exit to those of dramatic characters.[19]

Having emphasized that Jesus *exits* to death as a tragic character we must recognize that Jesus does not immediately exit *to death* at this point. When he finally does leave the supper, he is arrested

---

[18] Zeitlin, *Sign of the Shield*, 29.
[19] As was said in chapter 1, such a departure to go and meet death does not exist in the testaments. Death, rather, comes to meet its stationary victim. See note 35 in chapter 1.

(18:2), but does not actually die for two more chapters. Jesus' exit, then, is an exit to his arrest and trial, and only subsequently, to his death. But this is not at all unlike the exit of Cassandra in Euripides' *Trojan Women* (294–461). When Cassandra is escorted off the stage, she goes not to die, but to become Agamemnon's concubine. The exit, however, initiates her journey with Agamemnon to Argos where she finally will die. For this reason, the exit of Cassandra has been analyzed in conjunction with exits to death.[20] Just like Cassandra, Jesus does not exit at 18:1 to immediate death. But, also like Cassandra, he does exit to certain death.

And this certainty arises from the careful preparation that culminates in the exit at 18:1. Jesus marches off to a death that has been thematically prepared and gradually foreshadowed, just like the exit of Eteocles, and just like the characters in all other well-prepared exits to death. The Gospel anticipates this exit by gradually entwining and extending several themes: the Jews' pursuit of Jesus; the increasing imminence of Jesus' "hour" (ὥρα/καιρός); and the cycle of Jewish festivals.[21]

The bloody plans of Jesus' opponents are brought into clearer focus as the Gospel of John develops. A key gauge of the escalation is the dramatic progression of the theme of Jesus' hour. When Jesus says at John 2:4 "my hour has not yet come," the phrase means something more than "it [is] too early for me to begin my work."[22] The phrase "my hour" is a coded statement that refers to a special point in the development of the divine plan for Jesus.[23] Jesus' hour will soon be understood more clearly.[24] The term appears several times again in the following chapters, each one building a sense of urgency as the reader understands that the hour is coming closer.

The conflict with the Jews also gains momentum in chapter 2, immediately following the Cana miracle and the reference to Jesus'

---

[20] Macintosh, *Dying Acts*, 95 note 12: "Cassandra's exit here is analogous to other exits for death, because, although Talthybius is taking her away to become Agamemnon's concubine, this exit marks the beginning of her passage to Argos where she is to die."

[21] Moloney, *Glory not Dishonor*, 12.

[22] E.K. Lee, "The Drama of the Fourth Gospel," *Expository Times*, 65 (1953), 174.

[23] Ibid., 174. For a recent discussion of the peculiar narrative quality of Jesus' conversation with his mother, see Sjef Van Tilborg, *Imaginative Love*, 6ff. See Staley, *Print's First Kiss*, 83–90, 95–118, for more on "victimization" of the reader in the Fourth Gospel, and its particular effect in this passage.

[24] Lee, "Drama," 174.

hour. In the cleansing of the Temple, Jesus first comes into conflict with the Jews and in this context also refers to the destruction of his body: "Destroy this temple and in three days I will raise it up" (2:19). The narrator then adds, "He was speaking of the temple of his body" (2:21).

Further, the conflict with the Jews that opens in chapter 2 takes place in the context of the Passover (2:13,23). The themes of Jesus' hour and his treatment at the hands of the Jews are thus linked from the start with the cycle of Jewish festivals. The conflict that was engaged at the Temple in chapter 2 already becomes critical by chapter 5, where Jesus justifies healing on the Sabbath by referring to God as "my Father" (5:17).[25] By chapter 7, the quarrel has become so acute that Jesus will not travel in Judea, because the Jews seek to kill him (7:1). He will not, at first, even attend the Feast of Tabernacles, since his time has not yet arrived.[26]

The growing tension grows further in chapters 11–12, where the Sanhedrin condemns Jesus to death (11:53), so that Jesus confines himself to the town of Ephraim in the desert (11:54). His seclusion and the pursuit of the chief priests and Pharisees (11:57) cause many to wonder, "What do you think? Will he come to the feast?" (11:56). Jesus' fate and the coming feast of Passover are thereby linked.[27]

The decisive "now" arrives at 13:1, where, just before the feast of Passover, the narrator informs the reader that Jesus knew clearly "that his hour had come to be taken from this world to the Father . . ." The slow escalation of interest in Jesus' death follows the trajectory of the gradual increase in the hostility of Jesus' opponents. Two chronological devices orient this struggles: the awaited arrival of Jesus' hour and the continued interest in Jewish feasts, often as places of

---

[25] The evangelist then informs the reader, "This is why the Jews sought all the more to kill him, because he not only broke the Sabbath but also called God his Father, making himself equal with God" (5:18).

[26] Nevertheless, Jesus does go up to the feast privately (7:10). While there, he asks the Jews directly, "Why do you seek to kill me?" (7:19), and they do not own up to their plots. The crowd, though, knows that this is the man whom the leaders seek to kill (7:25). And their restraint is clear at 7:30: "So they sought to arrest him, but no one laid hands on him, because his hour had not yet come." A similar scene takes place in chapter 8. We are told once again that the Jews stay their hand when Jesus debates with them in the temple "because his hour had not yet come" (8:20). Later, two times more Jesus mentions their desire to kill him (8:37, 40), and then narrowly escapes at the end of the chapter when they pick up rocks to stone him (8:59).

[27] Meeks, "Man from Heaven," 174.

conflict, culminating in the final Passover.[28] The gradual association of his death with his hour has reached a high point in the Last Supper.[29] The two time patterns have run parallel to one another up until chapter 13. "Now they coalesce: There is a feast of 'the Jews' that is also the hour of Jesus."[30]

The exit of Jesus, then, marks the culmination of carefully wrought themes, signaling the point at which related strands are finally united to mark a definitive narrative moment that leads to his death.

A considerable theological point is also scored in Jesus' exit from the Last Supper. Parallel to the increasing attention to Jesus' eventual exit to death is the growing emphasis on Jesus' identity as the descending and ascending redeemer. This omnipresent theme focuses the reader's attention further on Jesus' departure to death, and therefore from the world.[31] Like the motif of Jesus' hour, the motif of descent/ascent (καταβαίνειν/ἀναβαίνειν) enters the Gospel in an enigmatic fashion at 1:51, but gradually becomes clearer. Its introduction at the inception of the Gospel story suggests that it will have some later role in the narrative, and that it is critical to understanding the story of Jesus.[32] Indeed, the descent/ascent scheme emphasizes that Jesus is beyond the understanding of people of "this world."[33] "The pattern, descent and ascent, becomes the cipher for

---

[28] Cf. 2:13, 23; 4:45; 5:1,9; 6:4; 7:2; 10:22; 11:55–57; 12:1.

[29] Moloney writes of the interplay between "the hour" and the festal cycle, "There have been two 'times' running through the story . . .," *Glory Not Dishonor*, 12.

[30] Ibid., 12.

[31] The motif has been analyzed variously, from both a history of religions perspective, as well as from a social perspective. On the standard history of religions perspective, see Ashton, *Understanding*, 337ff.; C.H. Talbert, "The Myth of a Descending-Ascending Redeemer in Mediterranean Antiquity," *NTS* 22 (1975/76) 418–43. Meeks, "Man from Heaven," is a classic expression of the sociological insights that can be culled from this motif. Culpepper refers to the Gospel's focus on this theme of descent/ascent as an example of the stereoscopic vision of the Gospel's narrator. He defines a stereoscopic image as one in which two slightly different perspectives are combined to give a richer, fuller image of the same picture. The Fourth Gospel's stereoscopic perspective combines the twin themes of Jesus' "whence" and "whither," *Anatomy* 33.

[32] Meeks, "Man from Heaven," 146.

[33] In his conversation with Nicodemus in chapter 3, Jesus proclaims, "No one has ascended into heaven except the one who descended from heaven, the Son of Man" (3:13). Followed as it is by this ascent/descent language in 3:13, it is clear that being born ἄνωθεν, "anew/from above" refers to the descent and ascent of Jesus. In vv. 31–33, Jesus is the one who comes from above (ἄνωθεν):

The one who comes from above (ἄνωθεν) is above all; the one who is of the earth belongs to the earth and speaks about earthly things. The one who comes

Jesus' self-knowledge as well as for his foreignness to the men of this world."[34]

The alternation between descent and ascent reaches a critical moment at precisely the same point as Jesus' hour, in the early verses of chapter 13. In the first half of the Gospel, the Book of Signs,[35] the descent theme predominates.[36] There is much more attention to the "whence" of Jesus than to his "whither," often to underscore the inability of people to understand his true identity and origin.[37] Only

---

from heaven is above all. He testifies to what he has seen and heard, yet no one accepts his testimony. Whoever has accepted his testimony has certified this, that God is true.

In chapter 6, this motif appears again. Jesus tells the crowds (6:27): "Do not work for the food that perishes, but for the food that endures for eternal life, which the Son of Man will give you." And the food that the Son of Man gives is from heaven: "For the bread of God is that which comes down from heaven and gives life to the world" (6:33). And Jesus is himself the bread that comes down from heaven (6:35, 38, 48–51).

[34] Meeks, "Man from Heaven," 154.

[35] I accept the generally posited division of the Gospel of John into two parts, and use Brown's language of Book of Signs and Book of Glory for the two portions of the text. I understand the difference between them as Brown does. The Book of Signs is defined as follows: "The public ministry of Jesus where in sign and word he shows himself to his own people as the revelation of his Father, only to be rejected" (*Gospel of John*, cxxxviii). The Book of Glory is defined as follows: "To those who accept him Jesus shows his glory by returning to the Father in 'the hour' of his crucifixion, resurrection, and ascension. Fully glorified, he communicates the Spirit of life" (Ibid., cxxxviii).

[36] It was noted above that the conversation with Nicodemus in John 3 also shows considerable concern for the ascent of Jesus, so it would be overstating the case to say that the ascent motif is absent from the first 12 chapters of the Gospel. Also, in chapter 7, at the same time that people are debating Jesus' origin, they puzzle over one of his statements about his destination as well. In 7:33–34, Jesus says the following to the representatives sent from the Pharisees and chief priests: "I will be with you a little while longer, and then I am going to him who sent me. You will search for me, but you will not find me; and where I am, you cannot come." Their response is confusion:

Where does this man intend to go that we will not find him? Does he intend to go to the Dispersion among the Greeks and teach the Greeks? What does he mean by saying, 'You will search for me and you will not find me' and 'Where I am, you cannot come?'

[37] In chapter 7, when Jesus attends the feast of Tabernacles, his doubters think they know his origin. On the last day of the festival, Jesus' words amaze the crowd (7:37–40), and they wonder about his identity: ". . . some in the crowd said, 'This is really the prophet.' Others said, 'This is the Messiah'" (7:40b–41a). But all of the concern for Jesus' identity soon leads to questions about his origin: "Surely the Messiah does not come from Galilee, does he?" A similar failure to understand Jesus' origin occurs later in 9:29: "We know that God spoke to Moses, but this man – we do not know where he is from." This ignorance of Jesus' origin marks a definitive condemnation against those who do not know him.

with the opening of chapter 13 does Jesus' ascent displace his descent in importance.[38] Now, it is no longer important to know whence Jesus has come. Attention is centered on his departure, his return to the place of his origin and his exit from the world. 13:1 reads: "Now before the festival of the Passover, Jesus knew that his hour had come to depart from this world and go to the Father." This is repeated in 13:3: "Jesus, knowing that the Father had given all things into his hands, and that he had come from God and was going to God . . ." The emphasis on Jesus' departure continues throughout the discourses.[39]

The arrival of the Last Supper, therefore, marks the climactic union of several themes and threads that push the narrative forward, clarifying for certain that when Jesus exits from the supper, he is exiting to his death/exaltation. Jesus takes this exit to death in the same way that Eteocles and Cassandra exit to death. When Jesus moves to leave the supper, and announces, "[T]he ruler of this world is coming . . . Arise, let us go forth from here" (14:30–31), he announces his exit to death. One verse after he departs from the supper (18:1), he is arrested (18:2). He is crucified a chapter later. The careful preparation of Jesus' exit certainly raises nagging questions about the delay between the announcement of the exit at 14:31 and its actualization at 18:1, and this matter will be addressed in the latter portion of this chapter. For now, it is enough to show that Jesus' exit is strikingly similar to a dramatic exit. Like tragic characters whose exits mark critical developments in a dramatic plot, Jesus' exit from the Last Supper marks a critical narrative shift. Having avoided and evaded capture in previous chapters, he now marches headlong

---

[38] Meeks, "Man from Heaven," 155.

[39] In the Last Supper, Jesus announces his departure to the circle of the disciples by referring back to his comments to the Jews in chapter 7: "Little children, I am with you only a little longer. You will look for me; and as I said to the Jews so now I say to you, 'Where I am going, you cannot come'" (13:33). This statement inspires Peter to ask the question that will lead to the prediction of his betrayal, "Lord, where are you going?" (13:36). Chapter 14 opens with a similar discussion about whither Jesus will go when he departs (14:1–5), and the expected fear of the believers who will be like orphans in the wake of his departure. And verse 16:5 of the Farewell Discourses returns to this theme, when Jesus rebukes the disciples by saying, "But now I am going to him who sent me; yet none of you asks me, 'Where are you going?',". Ibid., 157f. Finally, chapter 17, Jesus' final prayer "is only intelligible within the descent/ascent framework, for it is the 'summary debriefing' of the messenger who . . . has accomplished his work in the lower regions and is returning . . ." Jesus prays to the Father, "I am no longer in the world, . . . but I am coming to you" (17:11), Ibid., 159.

into his arrest and trial. Everything prior to this exit culminates in
it, and everything posterior to this exit follows from it. So, Jesus'
exit to death is a fundamental narrative device, around which much
of the narrative flow of the Gospel is set into place. This is precisely
how the exit to death can work in ancient tragedy.

Even further association between Jesus' exit and the dramatic exit
to death is clear in the conversation that Jesus shares with his disciples before his death. Many tragic characters deliver what one
interpreter has dubbed the "Big Speech" prior to their exit to death.[40]
When Eteocles leaves for battle, the Theban citizens question why
he feels compelled to go, and they beg him to save himself. While
his exit is imminent, Eteocles debates with the Chorus about whether
or not he should depart and, so fulfill the curse (lines 677–719). And
during the entire debate, his exit hangs in the background.[41] To thus
engage a dying character in conversation on the brink of the exit
to death is standard in ancient tragedy. One scholar defines the
device as follows:[42]

> When an exit from the stage will lead to certain consequences, then
> a dispute over whether the exit should be made at all serves to explore
> the dramatic situation and at the same time puts it in concrete terms
> on the stage. . . . This simple and strong dramatic technique recurs
> throughout Greek tragedy.

Eteocles defends his decision to depart through lines 679–719. The
conversation is as follows in 714–719:

> Chorus: Do not go forth on this mission to defend the seventh gate!
> Eteocles: Your words shall not blunt my sharpened purpose.
> Chorus: Indeed, but victory, though inglorious, is held in honour by
>   the gods.
> Eteocles: No soldier may brook an utterance like that.
> Chorus: What! Will you make a harvest of your own brother's blood.
> Eteocles: From heaven-sent ills there's no escape.

With this last line, he exits to his death. The exit has been debated
and discussed from several angles, sometimes emotional, sometimes
logical – "then, in the end, Eteocles breaks the suspense . . . He goes;

---

[40] See Macintosh, *Dying Acts*, passim for the phrase "Big Speech."
[41] Taplin, *Stagecraft*, 165.
[42] Ibid., 165.

and in his going he fulfills the curse. For the audience, he is dead."[43]

Jesus' departure takes very much the same form. As soon as Jesus has announced, "Where I am going, you are not able to come . . ." (13:33), he begins to receive questions about the nature of his departure. The first question comes from Peter (13:36) and leads into the famous prediction of Peter's betrayal, contained in Mk (14:29–31) and Lk (22:31–34) as well. What distinguishes John's treatment of the prediction from the Synoptic versions is that Peter's question is not isolated. It is followed by several other questions around which the nature of Jesus' departure is explained more fully at 14:5, 14:8 and 14:22. As with the dramatic example above, there is concern about the imminent departure, and Jesus justifies and explains the departure in light of these questions. Questioning why and whether or not Jesus should make his exit is cast in the form of the dramatic debate that precedes his exit to death.

Thus, the first half of this chapter argues that Jesus' exit from the Last Supper is reasonably read as an "exit to death" in ancient tragedy. Several important themes related to Jesus' death and glorification gradually develop to a crescendo in the Farewell Discourses in much the same way that exits to death in ancient drama are the culmination of gradual preparation. For John, furthermore, this narrative device underscores the fundamental Christological characterization of Jesus as the descending and ascending redeemer.

But to notice this is only a start. Drawing parallels to the exit to death still leaves unresolved the most troubling narrative feature of the discourses, the peculiar exit of Jesus at 14:31. In fact, to see the scene as an exit to death only heightens the confusion that this verse creates. For, the dialogical sections in chapters 13–14 may push the narrative forward in those chapters, but this dialogical style abruptly stops in chapter 15. Jesus' dialogue with the disciples turns into a monologue.[44] This shift suggests that something has changed, and changed abruptly, at 14:31.

---

[43] Ibid., 165.

[44] In chapter 16, the dialogue makes two brief returns: "Therefore, they said, "We do not know what he means by saying 'a little while'" (16:18); "Therefore, his disciples said to him, "Behold, now you speak plainly, and no longer speak in a parable" (16:29).

The Delayed Exit

Enter the delayed exit. In almost every era, in both tragedy and
comedy, in both Greece and Rome, ancient dramatists employed a
device that modern scholars call the "delayed exit."[45] As Frost defines
it, "A delayed exit takes place when an announced or actual exit
movement is halted either by outside intervention or by second
thoughts on the part of the character himself."[46] In order to investigate how closely the delay of Jesus' exit from the Last Supper functions like a delayed exit from ancient drama, it is necessary first to
explain the function of the dramatic device.

The delayed exit works in various ways, depending on the author
deploying it. In Menander, the delay can add to characterization,
or serve to introduce an important scene.[47] Examples of the first type
follow a standard pattern: "one speaker instructs another to follow
him off the stage, but his companion fails to comply and raises some
momentary objection whose purpose is, apparently, to cast light on
his own character."[48] Notice, for example, how the delay at *Dyskolos*
871 provides an opportunity for displaying the bashfulness of Gorgias.
When they realize their friend Knemon is not around to join them
with their mothers and a stepsister, Sostratos and Gorgias prepare
to join the women. But Gorgias pauses to reveal his shy character:

> Sostratos: Goodbye to him, then! Let us go inside.
> Gorgias: But, Sostratos, I'm shy of being in
>   The company of women –
> Sostratos: Nonsense, man! Come, in you go![49]

Cases where the delay is used to introduce some significant activity
also follow a rough pattern. But in such cases, the delay is generally not the result of a companion losing his nerve. It arises from
some external intervention. Menander's *Epitrepontes* 858–9 exemplifies

---

[45] For Athenian tragedy, see Taplin, *Stagecraft*, 162–3, 184, 212, 300, 307, 319–21,
419, 459n. For Menander, see Frost, *Exits and Entrances*, 15f. For New Comedy in
general, see K. Bennet, *Motivation*, passim. Also, useful for Roman comedy is John
Hough, "Plautine Technique in Delayed Exits," *CP* 35 (1940) 39–48.
[46] Frost, *Exits*, 15. See also Taplin, *Stagecraft*, 162: "the delayed exit is "an exit
movement which is begun and then stopped."
[47] Frost, *Exits*, 15.
[48] Ibid., 15.
[49] The translation here of Menander is taken from *Menander: The Plays and Fragments*
(Transl. Maurice Balme. Intro. Peter Brown; Oxford: Oxford University Press, 2001).

this type.[50] Pamphile is about to enter her house with the announcement, "I'll go," but is stopped short by Habrotonon with "Wait, lady, for a bit." The delay sets off a chain of events that leads to the identification of Pamphile as the previously unknown mother of an abandoned child, which is a critical point in the comedy. This use of the delay for the purpose of introducing an important scene is adopted from its use in tragedy.[51] And it is the tragic use that needs now to be explored further, as a close analog to the Gospel of John.

An extensive use of the device in Greek tragedy occurs in Sophocles' *Philoctetes*, where characters repeatedly move to leave a scene, but are halted by their own initiative or by some other character.[52] Of the many examples in the *Philoctetes*, the most interesting one for the present study is the final departure of Neoptolemus and Philoctetes at the end of the play. This, the play's final exit, appears to resolve the complicated struggle between Neoptolemus and Philoctetes that has been the center of the drama's conflict.

As the Greeks sail to Troy, Philoctetes suffers a severe wound. Useless for the coming war, he is left against his wishes on the island of Lemnos. He has with him, however, the bow and arrows of Heracles and a seer has informed the Greeks that they will only win the war if they fight with these weapons. Odysseus, therefore, sails to Lemnos with Neoptolemus in order to trick Philoctetes into coming to Troy after all. This is no small task, given the grudge Philoctetes bears for being abandoned by his compatriots. The deceit requires Odysseus and Neoptolemus to convince Philoctetes that they will sail him home to Greece, so that they can secretly transport him, and his precious weapons, to Troy. Neoptolemus, though, soon refuses to trick Philoctetes. Instead, he reveals the plot to Philoctetes and promises to take Philoctetes home, and not to Troy. Philoctetes and Neoptolemus prepare to sail home to Greece, but at the very point where they resolve to depart, a major delayed exit intervenes, and a message from Zeus changes their plans. In the excerpt here provided (lines 1402–15), Neoptolemus is nervous that the Greeks will punish him for his treason, while Philoctetes assures him, and they head off together:

---

[50] Frost, *Exits*, 15.
[51] Ibid., 15; Taplin, *Stagecraft*, 162–3.
[52] See ibid., 163 as well as idem, "Significant Action in Sophocles' *Philoctetes*," *GRBS* 12 (1971), 26–7, 29–31, 33–9.

Neoptolemus: If you wish, let us depart!
Philoctetes: O speaker of a noble word!
Neopt.: Plant your steps firmly after mine.
Phil.: To the best of my strength!
Neopt.: But how shall I escape blame from the Achaeans?
Phil.: Do not think about it!
Neopt.: What if they ravage my country?
Phil.: I will be there.
Neopt.: What will you do to help?
Phil.: And with the arrows of Heracles.
Neopt.: What do you mean?
Phil.: I will prevent them from coming near.
Neopt.: . . . Come when you have kissed the ground!
Heracles: Not yet, before you have listened to my words, son of
Poeas . . . For your sake I have come, leaving my home in heaven, to
tell you the plans of Zeus . . .

The stage production of the scene is not entirely clear. The command "Let us depart" from Neoptolemus at 1402 might indicate
that Philoctetes leans on him for support, and that they are head-
ing off together.[53] When Neoptolemus, afraid that the Greeks will
seek revenge for his allegiance with Philoctetes, wonders, "But how
shall I escape blame from the Achaeans?" this could mark a hesitation, but then they start off again with: "Come when you have
kissed the ground." Or, perhaps they have been slowly making their
way as they speak the lines. At any rate, Heracles stops short the
departure they undertook at 1402. For a moment, the tension building throughout the play appears to resolve, with the two departing
for Greece. Then Heracles arrives to deliver Zeus' will, and they turn
instead for Troy. The *deus ex machina* delays the exit until the proper
destination is chosen and the play can have a fitting conclusion.

Thus, delayed exits often introduce moments of dramatic significance,
sometimes great, sometimes small. But none of the above examples
much resembles the delay of Jesus at 14:31. To see delays that resemble Jesus', we must look to delays that stop an exit to death. A striking example of such a delay occurs in Aeschylus' *Agamemnon*, when
Cassandra makes her final departure from the stage to her death at
the hands of Clytemnestra. Like Philoctetes and Neoptolemus,
Cassandra is once stopped short by outside intervention but, unlike
those others, she also stops herself.

---

[53] Ibid., 33–9.

The scene makes complete sense only in light of Cassandra's peculiar role throughout the play.[54] Agamemnon returns home from Troy not knowing that his wife intends to kill him. Her murderous anger increases when Agamemnon arrives at his door with Cassandra in tow. But Cassandra is a silent participant for much of the drama. In the herald scene that opens the play, no mention is even made of her. When she enters at line 783, no attention is paid to her until 950. Even when she is directly addressed by Clytemnestra (1035) and told to go inside the house, she remains silent. It is not even certain she can speak Greek (1062–3). She is a silent presence. But her very silence makes her the center of dramatic attention.

At line 1035 when Clytemnestra addresses Cassandra, Agamemnon has already entered the house, where his death awaits. Clytemnestra returns from the house to order Cassandra inside, to share Agamemnon's death. When Clytemnestra retreats alone back into the house at 1068, Cassandra's refusal to move reveals much about herself. Clytemnestra has been in control of the action throughout the play. But this is a critical moment where action takes place beyond her control. Cassandra gains stature as a character by acting independently from, and in spite of, Clytemnestra's will. And it is then that Cassandra speaks.

At first, there is no coherence to her words. Her stage movements are also unclear. She may or may not move toward the house at 1072 when she begins her lament.[55] At any rate, she definitely turns to enter the house at 1290 with the statement: "I must be brave. It is my turn to die."[56] She then turns to the doors of the house: "I address you as the gates of death . . ." (1291) and makes her way. Then follows a delay (1296–9), apparently, when the Chorus questions, "But if you see it coming, clearly – how can you go to your own death, like a beast to the altar driven on by god, and hold your

---

[54] This discussion of the exit of Cassandra is dependent on Taplin, *Stagecraft*, 306–322.

[55] The matter depends on the significance of her addressing Apollo in line 1087. It was common for Greek houses to have some cult stone for Apollo before the door, and it is certain that this stone was depicted on both the tragic and comic stages. So, when she pauses to reflect on her bloody fate by addressing Apollo, this may indicate that she has begun moving toward the house, where the cultic votive of Apollo sits. See ibid., 318–19.

[56] The translations here from *Agamemnon* are those of Robert Fagles in *Aeschylus: The Oresteia* (Transl. Robert Fagles; New York: Penguin, 1984).

head so high?" She pauses (1299) to respond that she has no escape, and then resolves to move forward again (1305).

But as soon as she heads toward the house, she stops short again. Her pause is indicated by the chorus' question, "What now? What terror flings you back?" (1306).

After this second (or third) delay, she gathers her wits yet again and at 1313 she resolves to enter with: "Well, I must go in now, mourning Agamemnon's death and mine. Enough of life!" But even this is not the final departure. She stops again: "I'd like a few more words, a kind of dirge . . ." (1322). At the conclusion of this brief speech, she moves finally to go into the house.

Cassandra starts toward the door and stops three (or four) times before entering on the fourth (or fifth) movement. Her final entry is met with a brief choral ode (1331ff.), and then immediately Agamemnon cries out from within, "Aagh! Struck deep – the death blow, deep –." Cassandra soon follows him in death. The action of the play, therefore, just as it is to reach its climax and Agamemnon and Cassandra are to die, is halted with the delay of her exit. And her exit hangs by a thread as she moves toward the house and then stops, again and again and again.

A similar use of the delayed exit is present in the final form of the Gospel of John at verse 14:31. Jesus announces that he is going to depart but does not leave. The comparison with the delayed exit must include just as much contrast as comparison, for the delayed exit in John does, and does not, look like the delayed exit in ancient drama. But the similarities are compelling.

The similarities operate on a grand level, encompassing the whole narrative. The delayed exit in *Agamemnon* and *Philoctetes* comes imme- diately prior to the point where the great conflict of each play is brought to a conclusion. Jesus' exit to death in the Gospel of John is also the culmination of thematic preparation. Jesus marches to his death in a final exit that has been prepared throughout the Gospel, slowly at first, but then with increasing intensity. In the *Agamemnon*, the audience knows Cassandra and Agamemnon are to die when they enter the house. By drawing out so painfully long Cassandra's departure into the house, the significance and expectation of the event is heightened. Moreover, as Taplin indicated, the effect of this delay is to wrest, even for a moment, control from Clytemnestra. Cassandra ignores Clytemnestra's order to enter the house and delays her exit until she has finished her speech. Cassandra takes charge of her fate. Jesus' delay functions in the same way. As his critical hour arrives, Jesus demonstrates control over his hour by determining when it will proceed, when it will pause.[57]

One feature of Jesus' departure, however, cannot be immediately explained by comparison with the exit of Cassandra. When Cassandra halts her departure, the text clearly indicates her hesitation. There is no question that she has stopped. In the same way, Heracles interrupts Philoctetes and Neoptolemus with his message from Zeus. Precisely the lack of any such notice is the source of confusion in the case of Jesus. We are told that he wants to leave, but then we do not know whether he stays or goes. He merely keeps talking and enters a state of dramatic limbo when he begins 15:1 with "I am the true vine . . ."

This apparent confusion, however, is not a cause for distancing the exit of Jesus from tragic exits, but actually a reason for closer association. A typical feature of the delayed exit to death is a separation between the speaker and the action around him or her. In the "Big Speech" that accompanies exits to death, the speaker is commonly transported into a state above the action occurring around him or her. "The 'Big Speech' gains its prominence in Greek tragedy very often from a suspension or displacement of the action, which makes the dramatic time in these interludes qualitatively different . . ."[58] "The action is very often frozen in the background whilst the preoccupations of the dying character dominate the scene."[59]

In Sophocles' *Antigone*, for instance, Antigone delivers a speech of farewell before her death. In the midst of her speech, Creon enters and orders her to be arrested. Without pausing in her speech, and without acknowledging Creon at all, Antigone continues her lament. The scene plays out as follows:

> Antigone: (876ff.) Unwept, friendless, unwedded, I am conducted, unhappy one, along the way that lies before me! No longer may I, poor creature, look upon the sacred eye of the shining sun; and my fate, unwept for, is lamented by no friend.

---

[57] See, for Jesus and the Father's control over the time of his hour, Gail R. O'Day, "'I Have Overcome the World' (John 16:33): Narrative Time in John 13–17," *Semeia* 53 (1991), passim. On the common christological point that Jesus controls his destiny, see, for instance, Moloney, *Glory not Dishonor*, 52.

[58] Macintosh, *Dying Acts*, 94.

[59] Macintosh, "Tragic Last Words," 415.

Creon (enters): (883ff.) Do you not know that no one would cease to
pour forth songs and lamentations before death, if need be? Will you
not lead her off as soon as possible, and when you have enclosed her
in the encompassing tomb, as I have ordered, leave her alone, isolated, whether she wishes to die or to be entombed living in such a
dwelling. For we are guiltless where this girl is concerned; but she shall
be deprived of residence with us here above the ground.

Thus, the command to remove Antigone has been given: ". . . lead
her off as soon as possible!" But this is not what happens. As soon
as Creon ends his order, Antigone begins to speak: "Tomb, bridal
chamber, eternal prison in the caverned rock whither I go . . . " (891).
And Antigone continues speaking for over forty more lines, when
she is finally led away (943). Creon recognizes that she is ignoring
him when he shouts to his attendants, "Therefore there shall be
trouble for those conducting her on account of their slowness!"
(931–2). Thus, although the order to depart has been given, Antigone,
obvlivious to the command, launches into a speech that lasts over
30 lines.[60] In this and similar instances like it, the speech of the
dying character is given prominence through the suspension or displacement of the action surrounding the speech. There is no reality
outside the words of the character approaching death. The action
is in limbo and the plot is frozen until the speech concludes.

A similar circumstance occurs in another speech of Cassandra,
this time not the Cassandra of Aeschylus' *Agamemnon*, but the Cassandra
of Euripides' *Trojan Women* (294–461).[61] With the Greek victory in
the Trojan War, a messenger informs Cassandra that she must accompany Agamemnon to his home. The messenger demands that he is
in a great hurry to remove her (294–296), but she delivers two
lengthy speeches that cover almost 200 lines of text. Even when he
repeats his order (419–420), Cassandra continues, oblivious to his
concerns.

---

[60] The suspension of action here is an especially nice parallel to John 14:31
because the delay in Sophocles, stretching from 891–928, has also been attributed
to later editorial meddling. The displacement of the action is so extreme that some
have assumed that much of these verses are later additions. Lines 904–920 are
especially problematic, Macintosh, *Dying Acts*, 94–5. Today, however, the tendency
is to accept 904–920 as genuine, David Bain, *Masters, Servants and Orders*, 25. But
even if these lines (904–920) are later interpolations, there are still twenty undis-
puted lines (891–903, 921–928) of Antigone's speech separating Creon's order from
Antigone's departure, Macintosh, *Dying Acts*, 94–5.
[61] Ibid., 95–6.

An even more extreme detachment of a character from contextual surroundings appears in Sophocles' *Ajax*. Here, there is no exit command, but the last speech of Ajax involves a drastic separation between Ajax and the activity of the other *dramatis personae*. ". . . Ajax' death speech is delivered in an indeterminate place at an indefinite time."[62] The chorus, which is typically the means of fixing the place of an event in Sophocles, is absent.[63] And Ajax' speech gives no indication of his surroundings. In the speech prior to this one, Ajax claims that he will take himself to the "meadows' streams by the shore" (654–655), but he only refers to his environment casually and sparingly in his final speech.[64] This makes the place of the speech rather abstract. By distancing Ajax from the action, the focus of the audience is "unerringly on the speaker."[65]

In all of the above, there is a separation between the last speech of the dying character and the activity surrounding that character. The final words "break through the confines of the dramatic present in significant ways . . . to stress their intrinsic separateness from the action proper."[66] This parallels the manner in which Jesus' discourses begin as a conversation with his disciples at a dinner, but lose their moorings to their surroundings as he announces an order to depart that he does not follow. The parallels are, of course, not perfect. Antigone and Cassandra ignore the orders of others, while Jesus, by contrast, disregards his own order. Nevertheless, there is a breakdown between the dramatic action and the delivery of the "Big Speech." Jesus announces his departure, but then delays, and his speech takes place removed from the action occurring – or not occurring – around him. He is not totally separated from the disciples; he addresses them in the second person throughout the remainder of his farewell. But his exit movement has stopped, and the setting is unclear. O'Day helpfully writes:

> In many ways, chaps. 13–17 can be understood as the fourth evangelist's attempt to freeze the time of the hour in order to explain what the hour will mean before the events of the hour play themselves out in full.[67]

---

[62] Ibid., 96.
[63] See Taplin, *Stagecraft*, 103–4, and Macintosh, *Dying Acts*, 96.
[64] Ibid., 96.
[65] Ibid., 96.
[66] Ibid., 92.
[67] O'Day, "I Have Overcome," 159.

Thus, the shape of Jesus' exit from the Last Supper roughly parallels the delay of the exit to death of dramatic characters. If this claim is correct, then at least one useful exegetical insight naturally follows. The aborted exit of Jesus at 14:31 need not be considered the result of sloppy editing. It has every chance of being an intentional literary device. This calls more broadly for a re-evaluation of the literary unity of the Last Supper Discourses. The remainder of this chapter will briefly address the overall narrative unity of the discourses, in light of the preceding argument.

The Delayed Exit and Narrative Unity

The feature of the Farewell Discourses that most raises suspicions about their composite character is the very verse in view in this chapter, 14:31.[68] Dodd refers to the problems circulating around 14:31 as "one of the most difficult problems in the structure of these discourses."[69] If this obstacle is removed, then the nature of the debate shifts considerably and the discourses can more easily be read in a more unitary light. This is certainly true in Bultmann's interpretation. Bultmann, after all, thought that the only obstacle to seeing the discourses as a unity was their displacement. He did not recognize any major disjunctions in the thought of the discourses. He rejects the notion that 15–17 have been inserted between 14 and 18 by a later editor by recognizing that chapters 15–17 ". . . are fully Johannine in both content and form."[70] He then argues: "And it would not be reasonable to suppose that an independent editor, writing in the form and spirit of the Gospel – and he would have to be such and not just an opportunist interpolator – would put [15–17] in this impossible position, rather than insert it e.g. between 14:24 and 25."[71]

---

[68] Ashton, *Understanding*, 28–31.
[69] Dodd, *Interpretation*, 406.
[70] Bultmann, *Gospel of John*, 459.
[71] Ibid., 459. Bultmann, of course, sees more problems in these chapters than that presented by 14:31. 14:31 is his primary concern, however: "The question whether the present order of the text of chapters 13–17 is the correct one is prompted by the observation that 14:25–31 is obviously the conclusion of the farewell discourses," *Gospel of John*, 459. Other matters are raised by him in ibid., 459–461.

But the delay of Jesus at 14:31 is not as difficult and impossible as Dodd and Bultmann suggest. The delay that has been difficult and impossible to explain by other than historical theories does not require such theories. A great obstacle to narrative unity, therefore, is no longer insurmountable. Indeed, the painfully long pause at 14:31 is perhaps the only feature of the discourses not able to sustain a synchronic interpretation in previous work. Other apparent obstacles are not so overwhelming.

For instance, self-professed historical and narrative critics can both explain the peculiar comment of Jesus at John 16:5 without recourse to redaction theories. Jesus reprimands the disciples because none of them asks him where he is going, but he thereby seemingly contradicts verses 13:36 and 14:5, in which Simon Peter and Thomas both wonder where Jesus is going. Jesus has, therefore, been twice asked about the whither of his departure, and yet still claims that no one asks him where he is going. Many interpreters assume that the incongruence between the disciples' questions and Jesus' ignorance of those questions is a sign of editing, and very sloppy editing.[72] But not all interpreters see so great a problem here, and this is true for more than just narrative critics. Although Schnackenburg sees editorial seams in John 16, he does not believe that 16:5 contradicts 13:36 and 14:5.[73] Jesus' reproach about the disciples' lack of curiosity is actually not about their lack of curiosity as such. Jesus' larger concern is the disciples' sorrow at his departure, their incomprehension and speechlessness. Immediately after his reprimand about no one wondering where he is going, Jesus adds, "But because I have said these things to you, sorrow has filled your hearts" (16:6). He then goes on to explain that it is better for him to leave. In noting that no one now asks where he is going, he admonishes the disciples for the terror that renders them speechless. They asked him earlier, but now their fear prevents them. It is the fear that Jesus rebukes.

Dodd similarly interprets 16:5 in relation to the earlier questions in 13:36 and 14:5. He writes, ". . . [T]he apparent contradiction does not perhaps go so deep as is sometimes supposed."[74] His reading relies on two steps. First, in 13:36 and 14:5 the disciples are

---

[72] Brown, *Gospel of John*, 2.583.
[73] Schnackenburg, *Gospel of John*, 3.126.
[74] Dodd, *Interpretation*, 412–13 n. 1.

concerned about where Jesus is going. Jesus tells them that they cannot know where he is going (13:36b) but they can know the path
that will lead there (14:5). Jesus is himself the Way. Dodd writes,
"What Jesus is saying is, 'You know the way, you do not need to
know where it leads.'"[75] Second, in 14:28, Jesus finally informs the
disciples that he is going to the Father. Now, the disciples know
both the way (14:5) and the destination (14:28). Therefore, in 16:5,
when Jesus mentions their lack of curiosity, he is not concerned
about the fact that no one asks where he is going. He is more concerned about the fact that, even though they know where he is going
(to the Father), they are still distressed. 16:5 then is not a reproach
about a question not asked, but a recognition of the disciples' misplaced distress. As with Schnackenburg, the real concern is 16:6,
where Jesus recognizes the disciples' sorrow "But because I have said
these things to you, sorrow has filled your hearts."[76]

The point of the above argument is that the conflict between16:5
and 13:36/14:5 is not as insurmountable as 14:31 has seemed to be.
It can be explained by other than redactional arguments. Other factors further suggest the unity of 13–17. A certain logic, for instance,
binds chapters 15–17.[77] The chapters have a flow and coherence

---

[75] Ibid., 412 n. 1.

[76] To put these arguments forward is not to suggest, however, that there is no
connection between the questions in 13:36 and 14:5 and Jesus' reproach in 16:5.
While they do not necessarily contradict one another, they are nevertheless very
much connected, Segovia, *Farewell of the Word*, 226–7. The return to the earlier concerns of Peter and Thomas indicates that the same themes discussed earlier will be
taken up again. The discourse material in 13:31–14:31 had as one of its primary
foci the announcement of Jesus' departure. 16:5 marks a return to this concern,
and signals this by a repetition of the disciples' previous questions. From 15:1 to
16:4, Jesus' discourse had shifted to discussing the future that the disciples would
have in community with one another after his departure. 16:5 marks a return to
the concerns of chapter 14, treated in a new light. This return is signaled by a reference to the disciples' earlier questions, Schnackenburg, *Gospel of John*, 3.90.

[77] To support notions about the coherence of the discourses, it is important to
recognize how sure some commentators are that chapters 15–16 constitute one unit
of discourse. While Brown distinguishes in 15–16 three discrete blocks of text
(15:1–17; 15:18–16:4a and 16:4b to 16:33), and further assumes that these blocks
all have separate origins, he also recognizes that these originally distinct units have
been carefully and effectively edited together into a unified discourse. For instance,
the theme about Jesus' selection of the disciples in the first unit of discourse (15:16)
is carried over into the second block (15:19). The dominant theme of love in 15:1–17
is balanced by the theme of hatred in 15:18–16:4a. And the theme of the world's
opposition to Jesus and to the disciples prepares for the Paraclete to be introduced
as the prosecutor of the world in 16:7–11. Brown, *Gospel of John*, 2.586ff. Furthermore,
chapter 17 is not an unconnected concluding prayer to the preceding discourses.

obvious even to historical critics like Brown and Schnackenburg. And Segovia has presented a thorough reading of the discourses that reconciles all of the competing tensions.[78]

It is beyond the scope of the present study, however, to cover every position now. All that is needed is to note that the one insurmountable obstacle that separates 14 from 15–17 is the assumption that 14:31 indicates sloppy editing of the discourses. No matter how many ways one can overcome the theories that see disunity elsewhere in the discourses, 14:31 remains a problem. But, if 14:31 is seen as a dramatic delayed exit, then one less obstacle separates 14 from 15–17.

To argue this is not to deny that the Gospel was unaffected by the historical circumstances that surrounded its production. But redaction theories insist that a previously pristine text was later interrupted, even if by the later work of the original composer(s).[79] However one understands the composer(s) of the Gospel, the final editing of the discourses need not be seen as the work of a later hand, but as part of the initial production of the Gospel. This is in keeping with the claims of De Jonge, who writes in regard to John's editing of his sources that[80]

> ... the author may have introduced subtle changes in what he had before him, or he may be quoting from memory or just re-telling a story. Everything which does not obviously bear the stamp of the author's mind may, nevertheless, go back to the author, including certain tensions or (seeming) inconsistencies.

The mere presence of inconsistencies or seams in the Gospel does not suggest that the Gospel has been, after its production, set upon by several editors. It is just as likely that the Evangelist himself left these tensions in the work. And, as this chapter has argued, not all of the seeming tensions are actually seams and tensions. The delayed

---

"[The] redactor showed a touch of genius in putting it at the end of the Discourse. Its soaring, lyrical quality provides a perfect climax . . .," Ibid., 2.587. Schnackenburg sees additional connections between chapter 17 and what precedes it. Because the prayer is so fundamentally concerned with the situation of the disciples in the world, it is a very effective conclusion to chapters 15–16, for which this is a very important concern. Schnackenburg, *Gospel of John*, 3.167–69.

[78] Segovia, *Farewell of the Word*, especially 283–319.

[79] Dodd rightly insists that we cannot be sure the Evangelist was not the editor of his own work, *Interpretation*, 407.

[80] Marinus de Jonge, *Jesus: Stranger from Heaven*, vii, 197–199. See also Godfrey Nicholson, *Death as Departure* (SBLDS 63; Chico: Scholars Press) 13ff.

exit to death is a legitimate literary move. So, if editing there must be, perhaps we should think of the editing as a step in the creation of the text by its original author(s). The editing was not a later intrusion on the text, but part of its original production. For, regardless of whatever repetitions and inconsistencies one might find in the discourses, care went into bringing the final discourses into a coherent shape. The editing took place in light of some larger literary plan. The delayed exit is a critical part of this larger plan.[81]

To summarize the preceding argument, this chapter attempts to reconcile the competing methodological voices in the study of the Farewell Discourses. Contemporary Gospel studies are marked by far too sharp a divide between historical and literary analysis. The present study is simultaneously historical and literary in that it explains the literary flow of the narrative by reference to a device from ancient

---

[81] For the sake of completeness, an interesting theory requires attention here. The present study uses the delayed exit to argue against employing source theories to explain the Farewell Discourses. But it was argued variously in the first half of the last century that the Roman comic Plautus (c. 254–c. 184) used the delayed exit precisely to splice together different Greek sources, or to edit Greek sources. See the following representative essays by John Hough: "The Structure of the *Asinaria*," *AJP* 58 (1937) 19–37; "Plautine Technique in Delayed Exits," *CP* 35 (1940) 39–48; "The Structure of the *Captivi*," *AJP* 63 (1942) 26–37. But Hough's arguments rest on several faulty premises. First, Hough assumes that every delayed exit in a play of Plautus is an innovation of Plautus, on the assumption that Plautus' models like Menander never used the delayed exit, "Plautine Techniques," 40. The several comedies of Menander now in our possession demonstrate that this is no longer the case, Frost, *Exits and Entrances in Menander*, 15f. Plautus, then, is not necessarily importing into his plays delays that did not previously exist. Further, Hough relies on the now generally discredited assumption that Plautus is merging multiple Greek originals into his Roman plays, an assumption which is entirely hypothetical. Critiquing this line of approach, and specifically the work of Hough, Duckworth insists, "[The] intricate combining and interweaving of two Greek plays cannot be definitively proved for any Plautine comedy," G. Duckworth, *The Nature of Roman Comedy*. (Princeton: Princeton University Press, 1952; repr., London: Bristol Classical Press, 1994) 208. See also W.G. Arnott, *Menander, Plautus and Terence* (Clarendon Press: Oxford, 1975) 37–8. For a more positive assessment, however, of at least the heuristic value of pursuing Plautus' hypothetical Greek originals, see the review of research in David M. Christenson, *Plautus, Amphitruo* (Cambridge: Cambridge University Press, 2000) 50–55, where serious attention is given to the idea that even Greek tragedies like Euripides' *Bacchae* lie behind Plautus' *Amphitruo*. Plautus certainly reworked his Greek sources, but Hough's assumption that the delayed exit is one of the primary sites of such reworking is open to too much suspicion to alter the present argument. For the history of the relevant problems, with reference to the fact that Hough's theories have not achieved wide acceptance, see J.C.B. Lowe, "Aspects of Plautus' Originality in the *Asinaria*," *Classical Quarterly*, 42 (1992) 152–75, especially 159, where he writes of Hough's arguments, "[T]hese theories have gained little support . . ."

analogs. Modern literary theories employed by narrative critics help mightily in explaining the structure of the Gospel of John. But, to ignore other ancient texts in exclusive favor of modern theories is to define too narrowly what can be classified as "literary."

Furthermore, literary unity cannot merely be assumed. It must be demonstrated. Narrative criticism helps us to pay more attention to the final form of the Gospel, but sometimes by ignoring arguments about its possible history of composition. The present chapter has proceeded differently. In claiming that 14:31 does not indicate editorial revision, the chapter meets directly the arguments of redaction critics, and offers an alternative, synchronic way to explain the evidence.

To summarize the preceding argument, then, the puzzling delay of Jesus at 14:31 appears to mimic tragic models. The delay of the exits of Antigone, Cassandra and others, as well as the contextual confusion surrounding their delays, serves to focus attention on the speakers, lifting them beyond their immediate surroundings. Their exits are thus made more significant, and the speeches that accompany the exits receive greater attention and total focus. Jesus' exit, and the discourses that accompany it, share the same quality. Jesus' exit is a critical point in the Gospel for a host of reasons, and so the progress of the narrative pauses immediately prior to the exit, in order to reflect on and underscore the exit's significance. The delay of the exit need not be seen as a sloppy set of footprints left by people who did not know how to cover their tracks. It is a legitimate literary move.

Now, as a way to transition to the next chapter, one final matter deserves attention regarding the "Big Speech" that precedes the tragic exit to death. In Jesus' "Big Speech," he responds to his disciples' confusion and grief as they contemplate his absence. The delay of Jesus' exit halts the progress toward death, permitting Jesus to reflect on his triumph over death and to comfort his disciples. The pause is an opportunity for consolation. But, the "Big Speech" that precedes death in Greek tragedy is not regularly focused on consolation,[82] while Jesus' "Big Speech" has as one of its primary goals to console the disciples. For John, the delay of the tragic exit to death provides an opportunity for the decidedly un-tragic character of Jesus'

---

[82] Macintosh, *Dying Acts*, 93.

approach to death. So, just as the Fourth Gospel has bent the testament genre by binding it to the dramatic exit to death, the Gospel also bends the conventions of the dramatic exit by infusing it with elaborately consolatory elements. Precisely how Jesus consoles is the topic of the next chapter.

CHAPTER THREE

THE THEMATICS OF TOKENNESS

The *Wisdom of Solomon* explains the rise of idolatry as a father's attempt to deal with the grief of losing his son. The relevant account reads as follows:

> For a father, consumed with an untimely bereavement, made an image of his child, who had been suddenly taken from him; he now honored as a god what was once a dead human being, and handed on to his dependents secret rites and initiations. Then the ungodly custom, grown strong with time, was kept as law ... (14:15–16a).

The previous chapter focused on Jesus' departure from the disciples and from the world. The next two chapters of this study will come to grips with Jesus' ensuing absence. Or rather, they will explore the ways in which the Gospel asserts that Jesus is present even in his absence. This chapter will argue that Jesus' presence is underscored by the use of common tropes from classical consolation literature, reflected in writers like Plutarch, Seneca, Cicero and others, as well as from Greco-Roman literature generally. In particular, the chapter will explore the consolatory function of the Paraclete. The quotation about the origins of idolatry from the *Wisdom of Solomon* expresses a common means in antiquity for dealing with the loss of a loved one, wherein a trace of presence assuages the pain of the beloved's absence. The Paraclete is just such a token of Jesus' presence.[1] Since previous work has connected the Paraclete's "tokenness" to the testament form, it is necessary first to clarify previous scholars' insights regarding the relationship of Jesus and the Paraclete in the Fourth Gospel.

---

[1] For the language of presence-in-absence in regard to the Paraclete, see Ashton, *Understanding*, 443–59 and Brown, *Gospel of John*, 644ff., 1137ff., and passim.

The Paraclete and Jesus

No less than the Johannine Jesus, the Johannine Paraclete is an enigmatic figure.[2] In five passages in the Farewell Discourses (14:15–17,
25–26; 15:26–27; 16:5–11, 12–15), Jesus promises that his departure
from the kosmos will be followed by the appearance of a figure to
which he gives the title "Paraclete" (παράκλητος). Much of the confusion surrounding the Paraclete arises from efforts to define this
term precisely. A particular problem presents itself in applying to
the Greek word παράκλητος an appropriate meaning that coincides
with the activities assigned to the Johannine Paraclete. Additional
problems arise in placing the Paraclete into a history of religion context. These two areas of controversy – the title and the background
of the figure that carries the title – have still not been completely
resolved.[3]

---

[2] Against Bultmann, who argues that Jesus reveals only that he is the revealer
(see, for example, *Gospel of John*, 145 and passim), Meeks writes: "He reveals rather
that he is an enigma," in "Man From Heaven," 151.

[3] The title παράκλητος is a peculiarly Johannine noun in the New Testament.
Among the books of the New Testament, the term appears in the Gospel of John
in the passages listed above from the Farewell Discourses, as well as one time in
the First Epistle of John (2:1). In 1 John, however, not the Holy Spirit, but Jesus
is called the Paraclete. This fact underlines the Paraclete's role as Jesus' successor.
If Jesus is the Paraclete, and the Spirit is his successor, the Spirit is naturally, then,
"another Paraclete" (14:16), Brown, *Gospel of John*, 2.639. Schnackenburg, *Gospel of
John*, 3.74–5, sees the Spirit as succeeding Jesus as the Paraclete on earth, while
Jesus is the Paraclete with the Father, in heaven (1 John 2:1). But there is no need
for such a distinction in roles, Windisch, *Spirit-Paraclete*, 4–5. While no exact Hebrew
equivalent has been discovered for the term, the Greek verb παρακαλῶ and its cog-
nates παράκλησις and παράλκητος have a history in Septuagint and New Testament
usage, as well as in the broader current of Greek literature. For surveys of the
meaning of the term, see Brown, *Gospel of John*, 2.1136; Schnackenburg, *Gospel of
John*, 3.139–41; K. Grayston, "The Meaning of PARAKLĒTOS," *JSNT* 13 (1981)
67–82. Attempts to clarify the Johannine use of the term based on non-Johannine
literature, however, have been inconclusive. Each different appearance of the word
resembles one or another aspect of the Paraclete, but no single usage explains the
entire range of functions that John assigns to the Paraclete in the Fourth Gospel.
The various functions of the term in classical literature seem to ricochet off of John's
figure, but do not connect precisely with what John presents. The term can, for
instance, carry a passive meaning, in the sense of "one called alongside to help,"
as a defense attorney. But, the Johannine Paraclete is more a prosecuting attorney
against the world than he is a defense attorney of the disciples (16:8–11), Brown,
Gospel of John, 2.1136–37. Other uses of the term are equally able to explain individual aspects of the Paraclete's functions, but are not relevant for all of them,
Ibid., 2.1136–37. Not only is the name of the Paraclete a puzzle; it is equally
difficult to find in the history of religion a figure that serves as an obvious model
for the Paraclete. Several personalities help individually to clarify one or another

The Paraclete is obviously the Holy Spirit and is so identified in 14:26. And, in 14:17, 15:26 and 16:12, the Paraclete is the "Spirit of Truth."[4] Brown has also demonstrated that what is said of the Paraclete is not inconsistent with what is said of the Holy Spirit throughout the New Testament.[5] Even so the relation of the Paraclete in the Farewell Discourses to the Holy Spirit in the remainder of the Gospel has been a matter of debate.[6]

Nevertheless, for all of the difficulty in trying to understand the background of the Paraclete, the figure's actual functions in the Gospel are relatively straightforward.[7] Further, and even more to the present argument, the Johannine Paraclete is best understood, not in relation to other biblical figures outside the Gospel of John, but in relation to the Johannine Jesus. The close connection between Jesus and the Paraclete is a primary concern of this chapter.

---

aspect of the Paraclete, but no single figure serves as an obvious model for the range of functions attributed to the Johannine Paraclete. Brown, *Gospel of John*, 2.1137–38, sees, for the teaching aspects, the inspiration of the Old Testament prophets, since they speak the words of God to human beings. For the forensic character of the Spirit, he looks to Late Jewish angelology. George Johnston, *The Spirit-Paraclete in the Gospel of John* (SNTSMS 12; Cambridge: Cambridge University Press, 1970), 80–118, provides a useful summary of possibly analogous figures, with special attention to relations to Gnostic figures and figures from Qumran. In the end, the Paraclete is partly all of these figures, and yet none of them completely.

[4] See, for instance, Windisch, *Spirit-Paraclete*, 20–21.

[5] Regardless of the Paraclete's similarity to the Spirit in other New Testament books, however, the portrayal of the Paraclete in the Farewell Discourses and the portrayal of the Spirit in the rest of the Gospel of John have been debated in the history of scholarship, Brown, *Gospel of John*, 2.1139–40. See also Windisch, *Spirit-Paraclete*, 9.

[6] In the Farewell Discourses, the Paraclete will not arrive until after Jesus has departed (14:16–17; 16:7). But, it is unclear whether or not the Spirit operates according to this same time scheme throughout the rest of the Gospel. While 7:39 operates from the same perspective of the Farewell Discourses ("for as yet there was no Spirit, because Jesus was not yet glorified"), the Spirit is also spoken of as being already present in Jesus' ministry (1:32–33). For this reason, a long line of scholars has claimed that the Paraclete was originally a salvific figure who had nothing to do with the Holy Spirit, but who was later connected, albeit loosely, to the Holy Spirit in the Gospel of John. See, for instance, Windisch, *Spirit-Paraclete*, 22–24, passim; Brown, *Gospel of John*, 2.1135. Several recent interpreters have seen greater association between the Holy Spirit and the Paraclete, however. See Brown, *Gospel of John*, 2.1139–43, and more recently, Gary Burge, *The Anointed Community: The Holy Spirit in the Johannine Tradition* (Grand Rapids: Eerdmans, 1987); and F. Porsch, *Pneuma und Wort. Ein exegetischer Beitrag zur Pneumatologie des Johannesevangeliums* (Frankfurter Theologische Studien 16; Frankfurt: Knecht, 1974). Cf. Ashton, Understanding, 420.

[7] One common and convenient way for explaining the Paraclete's various duties is to separate them into two broad categories: 1) how the Paraclete will interact with the disciples; 2) how the Paraclete will interact with the world. See, for instance,

To begin, the Paraclete continues Jesus' work.[8] The Paraclete will teach and remind the disciples of all that Jesus said to them (14:26), testifying on behalf of Jesus (15:26), and proclaiming only what is heard from Jesus (16:13). More to the point, as Jesus says, ". . . he will take what is mine and declare it to you" (16:14).

But, there is a deeper aspect to the association of Jesus and the Paraclete. The Paraclete does not merely succeed Jesus and complete his earthly work; the Paraclete somehow "re-presents" Jesus. That the Paraclete makes Jesus present is implicit in Jesus' promise that he will send to the disciples "another Paraclete" (14:16). The phrase demands that Jesus himself is the first Paraclete. This implicit association is made explicit in a number of statements about the Paraclete.[9] The similarities start somewhat humbly. Where the Paraclete is termed "the Spirit of Truth," (14:17; 15:26; 16:13), Jesus is himself the Truth (14:6). Jesus is said to be the Holy One of God (6:69), while the Paraclete is the Holy Spirit (14:26). Likewise, the Paraclete will "come" (15:26; 16:7, 8, 13), just as Jesus has "come into the world" (5:43; 16:28, 18:37). Both the Paraclete (ἐκπορεύεσθαι) and Jesus (ἐξέρχεσθαι) come forth from the Father. The Father "gave" the Son (3:16), and will likewise "give" the Paraclete when the Son requests it be done (14:16). In the same way, just as the Father sent the Son (3:17, passim), he will send the Paraclete (14:26).[10]

When it comes to interaction with the disciples, the connections become even more explicit. For instance, while the world cannot recognize or know the Paraclete, the disciples can know him (14:17), just as they know and recognize Jesus (14:7, 9). Both the Paraclete

---

Ignace De la Potterie, "The Paraclete," in *The Christian Lives by the Spirit* (transl. John Morris; New York: Alba House, 1971) 77; Brown, *Gospel of John*, 2.1136. Each separate saying functions in one of these two ways. The second (14:26) and the fifth (16:12–15) sayings present the Paraclete as the teacher of the disciples. The first emphasizes the Paraclete's abiding presence. The third (15:26–27) and the fourth (16:7–11) sayings refer to the opposition between Jesus and the world, and the Paraclete's role in this struggle. More generally, the Paraclete teaches the disciples and reminds them of Jesus' words (14:26). He also bears witness to Jesus in the world (15:26) and prosecutes the world (16:8–11). See De La Potterie, "Paraclete," 72–77; Schnackenburg, *Gospel of John*, 3.75.

[8] Ashton, *Understanding*, 422.

[9] The following list is a modified version of Brown's list, *Gospel of John*, 2.1140–41 and his essay "The Paraclete in the Fourth Gospel," *NTS* 13 (1996–67) 113–132.

[10] This further suggests that the Paraclete is to Jesus, as Jesus is to the Father, and that the Paraclete will be sent in Jesus' name, just as Jesus was sent in the Father's name (5:43), Brown, *Gospel of John*, 2.1140.

(14:17) and Jesus (14:20, 23; 15:4, 5; 17:23, 26) are to remain with –
and within – the disciples. Where the Paraclete will guide (ὁδηγήσει)
the disciples "into all the truth" (16:13), Jesus is the Way (ἡ ὁδός)
and the Truth (14:6). The Paraclete teaches the disciples (15:26–27),
just as Jesus teaches (6:59; 7:14, 18). The Paraclete testifies as a witness (15:29), just as Jesus testifies as a witness (8:14). Furthermore,
the teaching and the testimony of the Paraclete are exclusively about
Jesus (14:26; 16:12–13). This is functionally equivalent to the way in
which all of Jesus' teaching and testimony are about the Father (8:28;
7:27–28; 14:13; 17:4).

These similar patterns of interaction in regard to the disciples are
mirrored by similar patterns of interaction with the "world". The
world cannot accept (14:17), or see (14:17), or know the Paraclete
(14:17), just as it cannot accept (5:43) or see (16:16) or know (16:3)
Jesus.

In a variety of contexts and fashions, therefore, the work of Jesus
and the work of the Paraclete overlap. Brown expresses the consequences of this association as follows:[11]

> Thus, the one whom John calls "another Paraclete" is another Jesus.
> Since the Paraclete can come only when Jesus departs, the Paraclete
> is the presence of Jesus when Jesus is absent.

Windisch is correct, then, in identifying the Paraclete as Jesus' "doppelgänger" or double.[12]

This notion of the Paraclete as Jesus' double comes through most
clearly in the first Paraclete passage (14:16–17). In this passage, none
of the other tasks of the Paraclete (teaching, reminding, prosecuting)
appear.[13] All we are told, in the words of Schnackenburg, is that
"he is given to the disciples," and "his significance for the disciples
in the world is emphasized."[14] Jesus promises that "another Paraclete"
will come to the disciples after Jesus himself has departed. Up to
this time, Jesus has fulfilled the role of "Paraclete" but now another

---

[11] *Gospel of John*, 2.1141.
[12] The term doppelgänger comes from Hans Windisch, "Die fünf johanneische
Parakletsprüche," in *Festgabe für Adolf Jülicher* (Tübingen: J.C.B. Mohr, 1927) 129.
The English translation "double" is found in the English translation of this article
contained in idem, *The Spirit-Paraclete in the Fourth Gospel* (trans. J.W. Cox; Philadelphia:
Fortress, 1968) 20 and passim.
[13] Schnackenburg, *Gospel of John*, 3.75.
[14] Ibid., 3.75.

will be sent in his place. This means more than that the Paraclete
will do what Jesus did in Jesus' absence. It is not merely a matter
of activity. When 14:16 claims that the Paraclete will "be with you
forever," the phrase calls to mind the saying from Matthew, where
Christ promises to his disciples, "And remember, I am with you
always, to the end of the age" (28:20). What Matthew depicts Christ
saying about himself, John applies to the Paraclete. The Paraclete is
Christ's agent of eternal presence with his disciples.[15] As Johnston
notes, "After Jesus' departure the spirit of truth will come to help
the faithful and to represent their Lord. For the presence of the
spirit-Paraclete makes up for the absence of Christ."[16] In a different
form and manner, the Paraclete makes Jesus present to the disciples. Without actually being Jesus, he fills the place of Jesus and
makes Jesus present.

There is a close association between the Paraclete saying in 14:15–17,
and the ensuing statements about Jesus' return in 14:18–21. This
connection extends the present discussion. The descriptions of the
Paraclete's "coming and indwelling" and the "coming back and
indwelling of Jesus" are placed in a parallel relationship.[17] The following chart best demonstrates the connections:[18]

	Paraclete 14:15–17	Jesus 14:18–21
Necessary to love Jesus, keep his commands	15	21
Giving of Paraclete; coming back of Jesus	16	18
World will not see Paraclete or Jesus	17	19
Disciples will recognize Paraclete and Jesus	17	19
Paraclete and Jesus will dwell in the disciples	17	20

"Such parallelism is John's way of telling the reader that the presence of Jesus after his return to the Father is accomplished in and
through the Paraclete. Not two presences but the same presence is
involved."[19]

With the last phrase of Brown's quotation, a corrective, or at least
a caution, can be included in the harmony of presence that very

---

[15] Windisch, *Spirit-Paraclete*, 5.
[16] Johnston, *Spirit-Paraclete*, 86.
[17] Brown, *Gospel of John*, 2.644.
[18] Modified from ibid., 2.644–645.
[19] Ibid., 2.644ff.

clearly exists between Jesus and the Paraclete. Following the promise in the first Paraclete passage (14:16–17), Jesus promises to come to the disciples (14:18). What is the significance of this? Much modern commentary connects these promises to the post-Resurrection appearances of Jesus.[20] As the resurrected one, Jesus will not leave the disciples orphans, but will come to them "in a little while" (14:18–19). But, the idea that this will keep the disciples from being orphans is not satisfying. For, if this is the right reading, then Jesus will once again leave them orphans after his final departure. A more permanent presence is needed, and, for this reason, many people, in ancient and modern commentary, have argued for some other form of Jesus' coming to the disciples.[21] It seems best to follow Aune, Brown, La Potterie and Moloney in arguing that this permanent presence is reflected in the sending of the Paraclete.[22] Justification for this lies above in the various sets of parallels between the consonant activity of Jesus and the Paraclete, especially in the close connection between what is promised about the Paraclete in 14:16–17 and what is promised of Jesus in 14:18–21. The sending of the Paraclete seems to fulfill the promise that Jesus will return. Brown, however, may go too far in referring to the Paraclete as "another Jesus."[23] The Paraclete and Jesus can be closely associated only if one recognizes that they are also distinct.[24] Even though the disciples can experience Jesus' life-giving presence through the Paraclete, Jesus is, in fact, departing from the kosmos (14:19). "The distinction between the physical Jesus, who is departing, and the "other Paraclete," who will be given (see v. 16), must be maintained."[25] The Paraclete is "another Jesus"

---

[20] For example, see Schnackenburg, *Gospel of John*, 3.77; Edwyn Hoskyns, *The Fourth Gospel* (2nd ed.; ed. Francis Noel Davey; London: Faber and Faber), 359, passim.

[21] See David Aune, *The Cultic Setting of Realized Eschatology in Early Christianity* (NovTSup 28; Leiden: E.J. Brill, 1972) 128–29, for a list of options. See Moloney, *Glory not Dishonor*, 43–4 for more recent bibliography on the problem.

[22] Aune, *Cultic Setting*, 126–135; Brown, *Gospel of John*, 2.638–657; La Potterie, "Paraclete," passim; Moloney, *Glory not Dishonor*, 43–44.

[23] Brown, *Gospel of John*, 2.1141.

[24] Moloney, *Glory not Dishonor*, 44.

[25] Ibid., 43. See also Moloney's critique of Dettwiler, *Gegenwart* where Moloney writes, "[Dettwiler] rightly interprets 13:31–16:33 as the fruit of a 'Relecture' within the Johannine community, by means of which the absent Jesus is rendered present. However, he collapses the presence of the Paraclete in the post-Easter period into the presence of the glorified Christ and underestimates the importance of the physical absence of Jesus," ibid., 100.

only in the sense that he is Jesus' representative.[26] Yet, he does make Jesus present, inasmuch as he *re-presents* Jesus.[27] This is akin to what is said in 1 John 3:24: "We know that he abides in us by the Spirit which he has given us."[28] This distinction will become important below.[29]

Before moving on, it will be useful to summarize the preceding comments. Although the place of the Paraclete in the history of ancient religious thought is hard to pinpoint precisely, the role of the Paraclete within the Gospel is relatively clear. He represents Jesus, after Jesus has departed. What is said of the Paraclete is modeled on what is said about Jesus, especially in the first Paraclete passage (14:15–17). Here, none of the specific tasks of the Paraclete are spelled out, except that one of his primary, underlying purposes is to represent Jesus after Jesus' departure.

This is certainly not his only function. The most difficult thing about John's Paraclete is that the Paraclete is resembles loosely a variety of other figures (prophets, angels, Moses/Joshua typology)[30] but corresponds precisely to no single one of them. Although the character of the Paraclete combines traditional elements, it combines them in a unique way. John borrows from existing materials, but does not replicate anything exactly.[31] A variety of models are uniquely combined in order to present the Paraclete as a substitute for Jesus in light of Jesus' departure from the world.

---

[26] Johnston, *Spirit-Paraclete*, 87.

[27] Ibid., 86.

[28] Such a saying is very close to John 14:16ff.; 16:13, 15. Cf. Johnston, *Spirit-Paraclete*, 78.

[29] One more qualification is necessary. Overemphasis on Jesus' post-Resurrection presence suggests an utterly realized eschatology for the Gospel. While the Paraclete certainly presents a period of eschatological blessings for the community in the wake of the Resurrection, this Spirit-filled time does not exhaust Johannine eschatological thinking. There is still future expectation in the Gospel's eschatology. To paraphrase John 4:23 and 5:25: the time "now is," but it is also "coming." For the idea that John's eschatology is realized, but still contains futuristic elements, see Jörg Frey, *Die johanneische Eschatologie. Band II: Das johanneische Zeitverstandnis* (WUNT 110: Tübingen, Mohr Siebeck, 1998) 283 and passim.

[30] See Windisch, *Spirit-Paraclete*, 18ff.; Brown, *Gospel of John*, 2.1137–39; Schnackenburg, *Gospel of John*, 3.144–49.

[31] Attridge, "Genre Bending," passim.

Testament and Commission

The understanding that various figures contribute to John's Paraclete does not always carry over into formal considerations of the Farewell Discourses. Variety yields to unity when the testament genre enters the discussion. The Paraclete follows Jesus, it is assumed, as other successor figures appointed in testaments. But, in the first place, not all of the supposed examples of this phenomenon are relevant to the study of John's Gospel.[32] The one case that bears resemblance to the Jesus-Paraclete relationship is the connection between Moses and Joshua, as expressed in both the *Testament of Moses*, a rewriting of Deuteronomy's portrayal of Moses, as well as in Deuteronomy 31:14ff.; 34:9 and Joshua 1:1–9.[33] The fact that John's Farewell Discourses contain so many allusions and parallels to Deuteronomy supports the idea that Jesus' farewell follows that of Moses.[34] For instance, in

[32] Brown follows Bornkamm, for instance, in arguing that there exists a series of "tandem relationships" that serve as a model for the relationship between Jesus and the Paraclete. Günther Bornkamm, "Der Paraklet im Johannesevangelium," in Geschichte und Glaube (Gesammelte Aufsätze; 3 vols.; München: Kaiser, 1968) 3: 68–69 (revised form of "Der Paraklet im Johannes-Evangelium," in *Festschrift für Rudolf Bultmann* [Stuttgart: Kohlhammer, 1949] 12–35); Brown, *Gospel of John*, 2.1137–38. Moses is followed by Joshua, Elijah is followed by Elisha, just as John the Baptist is followed by Jesus. In all of these paired associations, the latter figure is charged with the task of continuing the work of the predecessor, and carries out this work under the guidance of the spirit of God. In Deut 34:9, the spirit of wisdom fills Joshua after Moses commissions him, just as in 2 Kgs 2:9, 15, the spirit of Elijah is bestowed upon Elisha. John the Baptist, likewise, is instrumental in the descent of the Spirit onto Jesus at his baptism (1:32–34; cf. Mt 3:13–16; Mk 1:10; Lk 3:21–22). There are problems with this neat picture, however. These tandem relationships are only loosely parallel to the relationship between Jesus and the Paraclete. The easiest to remove from consideration is the pairing of John the Baptist and Jesus, since Jesus is not John's successor and follower, at least as the Gospels present the pair, but John's superior. Jesus does not complete John's work, he accomplishes the work that John heralds and for which he prepares the way (John 1:6–9). As for the case with Elijah and Elisha, Elisha receives twice the amount of Elijah's spirit, but is not commissioned to complete tasks that Elijah left unfinished, Ashton, *Understanding*, 471. Johnston also provides a necessary caution to the possible view that the Paraclete, as a successor of Jesus, is somehow seen as a second mediator of salvation. One of the Paraclete's critical functions is to demonstrate that Jesus is the only savior of the world. Such a belief in Jesus does not seem to leave room for a successor who needs to complete the work of salvation, *Spirit-Paraclete*, 95.

[33] In regard to the *Testament of Moses*, see especially books 1.6–2.1 and books 10–12. Cf. the translation in Ashton, *Understanding*, 470–84.

[34] See for a wide range of associations between John 13–17 and Deuteronomy A. Lacomara, "Deuteronomy and the Farewell Discourse (Jn 13:31–16:33)" *CBQ* 36 (1974) 65–84.

the same way that Moses chooses Joshua as his successor in his testament in Deuteronomy, Jesus chooses a successor who will complete his work, the Paraclete. This neat parallel works very well – to a point. For instance, Joshua is filled with the spirit of wisdom when Moses lays hands upon him (34:9), while the Paraclete actually *is* the Spirit.[35] Likewise Joshua, in the *Testament of Moses* is called his people's "guide on the way" (11:10), and the Paraclete will guide the Johannine Christians to the truth (16:13).[36] Finally, and most important, Joshua will succeed Moses, and complete his work by taking the Israelites into the Promised Land (Deut 31:23; Joshua 1:1–9). "Joshua . . . is specifically enjoined by God – or by Moses speaking on God's behalf – to carry out tasks that were originally to have been performed by Moses."[37] In the same way, the Paraclete is sent in order to lead the Johannine community into the fullness of what was promised to them in the work of Jesus.[38] He is Jesus' successor, whose job is to complete Jesus' work. The testament of Moses includes the appointment of a successor, Joshua, so the testament of Jesus appoints a successor as well, the Paraclete.

This interpretation explains much about the Paraclete, but not everything. The Paraclete is a successor, true, but the Paraclete is more than a successor. The Paraclete is also Jesus' double, what Windisch calls Jesus' doppelgänger.[39] Ashton clearly recognizes these twin qualities of the Paraclete, as well as the inability of the testament to cover both of them. He approaches the problem by connecting the two characters of the Paraclete to the form of the Farewell Discourses.[40] The two roles of the Paraclete correspond to the two genres that Ashton sees behind the Farewell Discourses, the testament and the commission. The successor themes derive from the testament genre, while the doppelgänger themes come from the closely related commission form. Thus, in the first Paraclete passage (14:15–17),

---

[35] Cf. Brown, *Gospel of John*, 2.1138. The Spirit also plays a role in the other "tandem relationships" that Brown recognizes. Elisha receives a double share of Elijah's spirit (2 Kings 2:9, 15), while John the Baptist is central to the descent of the Spirit upon Jesus.

[36] Translation taken from Ashton, *Understanding*, 476. Ibid., 476.

[37] Ibid., 471.

[38] Ibid., 476.

[39] Ibid., 470.

[40] For more on the commission form, see N. Lohfink, "Deuteronomistische Darstellung." Cf. Ashton, *Understanding*, 468.

in which it was argued above that the notion of presence-in-absence is most pronounced, the Evangelist has employed motifs from the commission form. In those places where the successor theme is most pronounced, such as in the second Paraclete passage (14:25–26), the testament form is more to the fore.[41]

The present study will follow both of Ashton's claims, agreeing that the testament is inadequate to explain the Paraclete's role as double, and that the Paraclete is a composite figure whose presentation draws from various generic backgrounds. But, examining Ashton's arguments more closely now will clarify how the present study also deviates from Ashton.

The idea that the Farewell Discourses combine two genres – testament and commission – arises from Ashton's belief that the Farewell Discourses are not modeled after the fully developed testament form as it is presented in later testaments like the *Testaments of the Twelve Patriarchs*.[42] Rather, the discourses follow more closely the testament, as it is understood in the Old Testament passages where the testament is actually united with the closely allied commission form. Examples of such texts are 1 Kgs 2:1–9, Deut 31 and Josh 1:1–9.[43] The definitive components of the commission will receive further attention below, but at a basic level the testament and commission can be distinguished by one general quality: the nature of the commands they give.[44] Testament commands are often general exhortations that can be applied to a broad range of experiences and circumstances. The commission form includes a command to a specific act, such as Joshua completing Moses' work (Deut 31; Josh 1:1–9).

Our immediate concern, however, is to determine whether or not the commission form adequately explains the Paraclete's role as Jesus' doppelgänger. The details of Ashton's argument, therefore, require greater attention.

Ashton cites as an example of the commission a text from Haggai, which reads as follows (2:4–5):

---

[41] Ashton supports this argument by recognizing that Windisch calls the Paraclete "doppelgänger" in one article ("Die fünf Parakletsprüche," 129), but "caliph" or "successor" in another article ("Jesus und der Geist," 311), *Understanding*, 470. Both articles are translated in Windisch, *The Spirit-Paraclete*.

[42] Ibid., 470ff.

[43] Ibid., 471.

[44] Ibid., 457.

> Yet now take courage, O Zerubbabel, says the Lord; take courage, O
> Joshua, son of Jehozadak, the high priest; take courage, all you peo-
> ple of the land, says the Lord; work, for I am with you, says the Lord
> of hosts, according to the promise that I made you when you came
> out of Egypt. My spirit abides among you; do not fear.

Three definitive elements of the commission are prominent here:[45]

> 1. Encouragement, which appears in Haggai with the a phrase like
> "take courage."
> 2. The actual commission, which here is the injunction to work. In
> the case of Joshua, the commission is to bring the Israelites into the
> promised land (Deut. 31:23).
> 3. "The promise of divine assistance," which is not actually a com-
> mon element of the form. Here it takes the form of "I am with you,"
> as it does in Deuteronomy 31:23 (Cf. 1 Chron 22:16; Joshua 1:9).

For Ashton, it is significant that the Haggai text unites the promise
of divine assistance ("I am with you") with the additional promise
that "my spirit abides among you." God bestows his divine assistance and presence, therefore, through the presence of the Spirit.
Indeed, the presence of God is often connected to the spirit of God,
as in Psalm 51:11: "Do not cast me away from your presence, and
do not take your holy spirit from me."[46] Consequently, the Paraclete
renders God present just as the Spirit has always done. In this way,
the Paraclete is a doppelgänger of Jesus. He is a successor, according to the conventions of the testament, because he completes Jesus'
work. But he is also Jesus' presence among God's people, following
the convention that Ashton attributes to the commission form. John
has thus bent and twisted the testament form by uniting to it this
aspect of the lesser-known commission form.

A critical problem, however, prevents one from seeing the commission form as the influence on John's portrayal of the Paraclete
as Jesus' double. A substantial point of difference separates how God
bestows his presence through the abiding nearness of his spirit in
Haggai, and the way in which Jesus sends the Spirit into the world
as a token of his presence in the Gospel of John. What might be
called a mechanical distinction divides the two types of presence-in-
absence. God, in the Old Testament, does not assume human flesh.
But, in Jesus, the Son of God has become flesh (1:14). When he

---

[45] Ibid., 468–69.
[46] Ibid., 468–69.

departs from the world, he leaves the Paraclete as a token of his former physical presence. The Paraclete represents Jesus on earth, since Jesus was once present, and has now departed. In the commission, by contrast, God certainly indicates that he will be present in his Spirit, but this is not as a substitute for a former bodily presence. This mechanical distinction is the first shortcoming of the commission form. There is another problem as well.

To Ashton, the commission form is helpful not only as a way of explaining Jesus' presence-in-absence, but also as a means for explaining the various consolatory statements in the Farewell Discourses in John. Although such consolatory gestures are almost completely absent in the later testament literature and are not really an integral element even in the early texts that combine the testament and the commission, in those commissions where God himself lays a commission on someone, his presence is offered as a consolatory gesture (LXX Ps. 26:1, 14).[47] God's promised presence reassures and, in some sense, consoles. In three different ways, Jesus promises that he will continue to be present with the disciples: first, in his own coming (14:18); second, through the indwelling of Father and Son with the disciples – whatever form this will actually take (14:2, 23); and, third, by the sending of the Spirit as Jesus' double.[48]

But the promise of divine assistance is, as Ashton even recognizes, not a regular feature of the commission form.[49] Even if it were, these three gestures do not exhaust the consolatory character of the Farewell Discourses. Various statements in the Farewell Discourses represent Jesus calming his disciples, as in 16:6–7 where he says, "But because I have said these things to you, sorrow has filled your hearts. Nevertheless I tell you the truth: it is to your advantage that I go away, for if I do not go away, the Advocate [Paraclete] will not come to you." Such statements may have something to do with the coming divine presence, but they also seem to represent attempts to argue the disciples out of their grief. They are not just promises but arguments, attempts to persuade the disciples not to bemoan Jesus' departure. Furthermore, the Johannine arguments are much more

---

[47] Ibid., 453, 455.

[48] Ibid., 462ff.

[49] The notion of divine assistance and presence does not appear in all examples of the commission (cf. 2 Sam 13:28; 1 Kings 2:1–9), but does appear in some examples, sometimes in the form of a prayer: "The Lord be with you" (1 Chron 22:16), Ibid., 468.

developed than the very bare statements in the commissions such as "be strong" or "do not fear."

The consolatory dimension of the Farewell Discourses, then, is only partly like what is seen in either the testament or the commission. By contrast, Greek and Latin consolation literature bears several striking resemblances to the discourse material in John 13–17.

Consolation Literature

Chapter 1 emphasized that consolation is a form of moral formation, a manifestation of the moral improvement that Greek and Roman moral philosophers enjoined on their followers. Consolation is not mere sympathy, a distinction that consolers are quick to make.[50] Plutarch, in his *On Exile*, writes as follows:

> ... [It] is not partners in tears and lamentation, like tragic choruses, that we need in unwished-for circumstances, but people who speak frankly and instruct us that grief and self-abasement are everywhere futile.[51]

The role of consolation in character formation is obvious to Pauline scholars, who recognize the crisis faced by converts in Paul's churches.[52] Consolation softens these converts' suffering and teaches them how to handle hardship as they continue in their new life. What woes, then, does the Gospel of John seek to assuage? Seneca is instructive here. Exiled by the Emperor Nero, Seneca sets out to alleviate his mother Helvia's pain by writing to her a lengthy consolatory treatise. Early on, he notes:

> Now there are two possibilities. For what moves you is either the thought that you have lost some protection, or the mere longing for me is more than you can endure.[53]

---

[50] Already as early as Thucydides, Pericles says in his funeral oration, "I do not lament; rather, I shall console" (οὐκ ὀλοφύρομαι μᾶλλον ἢ παραμυθήσομαι) 2.44. Cf. Holloway, *Consolation*, 62.

[51] 599b. Even so, some consolation texts contain brief signs of sympathy, such as, "I could not help sharing in your feeling," Plutarch, *Ad Apollonium*, 102a. Cf. Holloway, *Consolation*, 63.

[52] For Philippians, see Holloway, *Consolation*, and for First Thessalonians, see Abraham Malherbe, *Paul and the Thessalonians* (Philadelphia: Fortress Press, 1987), esp. 46–60.

[53] *Ad Helviam*, 14.1.

Chrysostom sees precisely these two factors in Jesus' consolation of the disciples: fear about losing the Lord's protection, and grief at losing his companionship. In regard to the sadness of loss, Chrysostom writes that

> ... they would miss that companionship with which they had grown so familiar: His conversation, His presence in the flesh, and would receive no consolation if he were absent.[54]

And, commenting on Jesus' prediction of future persecution (John 15:18–16:4a), Chrysostom attributes the disciples' distress to the following fact: "they are so few in number, [and] are in consternation at the prospect of being the target of ... hostility."[55] Elsewhere he insists that Jesus must "store up for [the disciples] ahead of time great courage for the frightful things that were to come upon them."[56] By isolating these two themes – the desire for Jesus' continuing presence and the fear of persecution by the synagogue – Chrysostom is in accord with contemporary scholarship. Common opinion agrees that the Gospel of John was produced by and for a group of people locked in combat with the synagogue.[57] And the Gospel is clearly concerned for those "who do not see and yet believe" (20:29).[58] In other words, the Gospel is written for people who lack the presence of Jesus and who need his protection. As both Seneca and Chrysostom illustrate, consolation literature is appropriate for both matters. The

---

[54] *Hom. Jo.*, 75.1 (PG 59:403/Goggin, 300).

[55] Ibid., 77.2 (PG 59:416/Goggin, 328–9).

[56] Ibid., 70.1 (PG 59:382/Goggin, 252).

[57] The classic expressions of this struggle are in the works of Meeks, "Man from Heaven;" J.L. Martyn, *History and Theology*; R. Brown, *The Community of the Beloved Disciple* (New York: Paulist Press, 1979). See also recently, Jaime Clark-Soles, *Scripture Cannot Be Broken: The Social Function of the Use of Scripture in the Fourth Gospel* (Leiden: Brill, 2003).

[58] The entire set of discourses from 13:31 to 16:33 explores either the meaning of Jesus' departure, or its consequences for the disciples, who must remain faithful to Jesus even after he has gone. Segovia believes that explanations about the meaning of the departure are connected to the consequences of the departure in a chiastic structure that appears in an ABBA pattern. The outer portions of the structure, labeled A, (13:31–14:31; 16:4b–33) deal with the meaning of the departure, together with the positive consequences – both in the immediate and distant future – for the disciples. The inner elements of the chiasm, labeled B, (15:1–17; 15:18–16:4a) are, for the most part, concerned with the negative consequences of the departure of Jesus, and focus only on the distant, not the immediate, future. *Farewell of the Word*, 284ff., especially 288–89. See also Schnackenburg, *Gospel of John*, 3.48, 90, who insists that the Farewell Discourses, whatever their diachronic twists and turns, remain focused on the meaning and the consequences of the departure of Jesus.

following discussion will treat the two themes separately for the sake of organization.

The argument will first focus on the matter of persecution. When Seneca writes to his mother, he passes quickly over the possibility that she fears any danger following his absence. Quite the contrary, she has always protected him, so will not miss a protector when he is gone (*Ad Helviam*, 14.2–3). The Johannine community is not so fortunate. The Farewell Discourses address their problems directly.

The warnings of persecution in chapters 15 and 16 about impending persecution conform to consolatory convention in two ways. First, Jesus establishes the world as inherently a place of pain for the disciples, stating flatly, "In the world you face persecution" (16:33b). Jesus more fully explains the nature of the trouble with the world in an earlier comment:

> If the world hates you, be aware that it hated me before it hated you. If you belonged to the world, the world would love you as its own. Because you do not belong to the world, but I have chosen you out of the world – therefore the world hates you (15:18–19).

The "world" clearly functions here within the larger frame of Johannine dualism as a place in opposition to God.[59]

But the insistence that the world is inevitably a place of pain, whatever the theological or philosophical ground of such a claim, is a common feature of consolation literature. Ancient consolers often remind their grief-stricken audiences that suffering is a normal, expected part of life, especially since life inevitably and always will end in death.[60] The *Ad Apollonium*, ascribed to Plutarch, insists that

---

[59] Ὁ κόσμος can, of course, have the (literally) mundane meaning of earth, as opposed to heaven, as well. For a recent study of the term in John, see Stanley B. Marrow, "Κόσμος in John," CBQ 64 (2002) 90–102. See also Ashton, Understanding, 205–237; James Charlesworth, "A Critical Comparison of the Dualism in 1QS 3:13–4:26 and the Dualism Contained in the Gospel of John," in *John and Qumran* (ed. James Charlesworth; London, Geoffrey Chapman, 1972) 76–106; Dodd, *Interpretation*, passim.

[60] Take, for instance, the notion that death is inescapable for all in Seneca, *Ad Polybium*, 11.1: "Every man is deceived by his own credulity, and in the case of those whom he loves he willfully forgets mortality. Yet Nature has made it clear that she will exempt no man from her stern law." Several Egyptian papyrus letters, all dated to after the second century AD, express the same sentiment about the inevitability of death. One stock phrase is "οὐδὲν δύναταί τις πρὸς τὰ τοιαῦτα," which indicates that death is the lot of all, and unable to be avoided. See Juan Chapa, *Letters of Condolence in Greek Papyri* (Papyrologia Florentina 29; Florence: Edizioni Gonnelli, 1998) 34f.

a youth who died too early is not thereby more to be mourned, but in fact, ". . . for this very reason his lot is happier, and he is spared many evils; for Euripides says, 'Life bears the name of life, being but toil.'"[61]

Precisely because the world is an arena of endless discomfort, consolers insist that suffering is less if pain is anticipated. The *Ad Apollonium* elsewhere adds:

> For one ought to realize, not merely that he himself is mortal by nature, but also that he is allotted to a life that is mortal and to conditions which readily reverse themselves. For men's bodies are indeed mortal, lasting but a day, and mortal is all that they experience and suffer, and, in a word, everything in life . . . (103f–104a).

Many people suffer more than necessary because they are oblivious to life's painful reality. Because unexpected pain is far harder to bear than that which is expected, consolers consistently warn their audiences not to be caught unawares, or else chide them for having already been caught unexpectedly by grief. Cicero ascribes the idea to the Cyrenaics, writing:

> The Cyrenaics, for their part, claim that distress is not produced by every misfortune, but only by a misfortune which was not foreseen and anticipated. And it is true that unexpectedness makes our distress considerably worse, for everything seems more serious when it happens suddenly.[62]

Seneca similarly writes to Marcia, consoling her on the death of her son, in the following way (9.2):

> So many rich men are stricken before our eyes with sudden poverty, yet it never occurs to us that our own wealth also rests on just as slippery a footing! Of necessity, therefore we are more prone to collapse; we are struck, as it were, off guard; blows that are long foreseen fall less violently.

---

[61] *Ad Apollonium*, 119f–120a, quoting an unknown play of Euripides, fragment 966 of Euripides documented in A. Nauck, *De Tragicorum Graecorum Fragmentis Observationes Criticae* (Berlin, 1855). For a review of the issues involved in attributing the text to Plutarch, see Jean Hani, *Plutarque: Consolation a Apollonios* Etudes et Commentaires 78 (Paris: Klincksieck, 1972) 27ff.

[62] *Tusculan Disputations*, 3.13.28. Translation from Margaret Graver, *Cicero on the Emotions: Tusculan Disputations 3 and 4* (Chicago: University of Chicago Press, 2002) 15. Cf. Grollios, *Seneca's 'Ad Marciam.'* (Athens: G.S. Christou and Son, 1956) 44.

Along these same lines, Seneca often compares the toil of life to the circumstances of an embattled soldier, who expects to be killed at any moment.[63]

These quotations provide a new realm of possibilities for understanding Jesus' warning to the disciples that they must expect future suffering in 16:1–2b, 4:

> I have said these things to you to keep you from stumbling. They will put you out of synagogues . . . But I have said these things to you so that when their hour comes you may remember that I told you about them.

Jesus' prediction of the future is certainly an expression of his divinity.[64] But on another level, Jesus has warned the disciples of their persecution, in order to keep them from stumbling. They will not stumble, because they will anticipate suffering, and not be caught by it unawares.[65]

There is also a particularly Christian dimension to the suffering that Jesus offers his followers in the face of persecution: they do not suffer alone. In the first place, the world that hates them hated Jesus before them (15:18ff.). Additionally, by hating Jesus, the world hates the Father (15:24). But God has a response to the activity of the world, the sending of the Paraclete: "And when he comes, he will prove the world wrong . . ." (16:8).[66] In suffering, Christians are on the side of God against God's opponents. Thus, in condemning Jesus and his followers, the world condemns itself. This eschatological perspective is no small consolation to the suffering Johannine community.[67] This

---

[63] See *Ep.* 95.5: "To live, Lucilius, is to battle." He elsewhere adds that life is like being besieged (*Ep.* 113.27), or akin to taking a soldier's oath (*Ep.* 65.18). Cf. Grollios, *Seneca's Ad Marciam*, 46ff.

[64] Chrysostom insists that 16:4 will prove that Jesus has divine foresight, which is no small comfort in sorrow. *Hom. Jo.* 75.4 (PG 59:408).

[65] It is of course, important to recognize that predictions of the future are also a common feature of the testaments. 1 Enoch (91.1) is able to see all that will befall his descendants forever. Brown, *Gospel of John*, 2.600. The point of the present argument is, Jesus insists that the reason he tells them of the future is to prevent them from stumbling. This very much fits the consolatory device discussed here. More generally, such prophetic predictions on the eve of death are common in Jewish literature, and are especially apt for Jesus, since he is a prophet (4:44; 7:40). Greek and Latin literature also ascribes prophetic vision to people on their deathbeds. See Fitzgerald, *Jesus' Last Will and Testament*, 74–77.

[66] Precisely what is intended here in the judgment of the Paraclete is difficult to assess, but such questions are beyond the scope of the present argument. See Brown, *Gospel of John*, 2.711–14.

[67] Malherbe notes the consolatory quality of the same eschatological tone in 1 Thessalonians, *Paul and the Thessalonians*, 59.

hope is supported even further by Jesus' reassurance to his disciples as they struggle in the world: "But take courage; I have conquered the world" (16:33).

The disciples' fear of persecution, however, is only half of the matter. For the disciples not only require consolation for the trials that will befall them in the world. They also lack Jesus, and need comfort and consolation on that account as well. Here, several consolatory themes are at play. The next few pages will turn, then, to a brief discussion of Jesus' efforts to comfort the disciples' sadness at his departure.

In the first place, joy is a critical component in the Farewell Discourses. In response to his disciples' sorrow and confusion, Jesus in several places speaks of joy and rejoicing. In 14:28, for instance, he urges, "If you loved me, you would rejoice (ἐχάρητε) that I am going to the Father, because the Father is greater than I."[68] In other words, the disciples' sorrow at his departure is misplaced. If only they could see rightly, the disciples would recognize that Jesus' going away is a cause of delight rather than of dismay. His return to the Father should lead them to joy, not sadness, since the departure fulfills his work, and marks the successful completion of his mission.[69] Furthermore, when Jesus has been glorified, he will bestow eternal life upon the disciples (17:2).[70] Once this is understood, their sorrow should turn to joy. Their joy, then, is dependent on seeing the situation correctly. Such a pattern of argument fits the standard scheme for discussing joy in consolation literature.

Stoic ethics are the source of joy-related tropes in Hellenistic and Roman moral philosophy, and, therefore, also in consolation literature.[71] Stoic ethics urge the eradication of the passions (πάθη), and

---

[68] Moloney writes, "Untroubled hearts, without fear in face of his departure, are the guarantee that they have heard his words and are holding fast to them." *Glory not Dishonor*, 50.

[69] Chrysostom paraphrases 14:28 in the following way: "Therefore He said: 'Even if you are afraid for Me because you think that I am not powerful enough to protect Myself, and if you have no confidence that I shall see you again after the crucifixion, still, on hearing that I am going to the Father, you ought to rejoice at length, because I am going to One who is greater and who can therefore solve all difficulties'." *Hom. Jo.* 75.4 (PG 59:408/Goggin, 309–10).

[70] Brown, *Gospel of John*, 2.655. See also chapter 2 of this study, where the descent/ascent scheme of Jesus' coming from and returning to the Father is discussed as a critical aspect of the Gospel's theology.

[71] In this survey of joy in consolation literature, I am dependent on Holloway, *Consolation*, 78–83.

their replacement with the "rational emotions" (εὐπάθειαι) of the
Stoic sage. In this scheme, joy (χαρά) is the opposite of grief (λύπη),
and, therefore, very relevant for consolation. But, the appropriate-
ness of joy depends on whether or not the objects of joy are actually items of moral indifference (τὰ ἀδιάφορα) or things that truly
matter (τὰ διαφέροντα). A Stoic sage navigates his joy between things
that matter and things that do not in two ways. In the first way,
the sage refrains from placing too much value on an item that is
actually ἀδιάφορον. The sage might attach joy to this thing, but with
appropriate sobriety, recognizing the true status of the thing. A posture like this keeps the passions in check. Or the sage can, rather
than restrain joy, express it totally, but only towards things that are
really of importance, τὰ διαφέροντα. To the Stoic, the joyful life is
the life of true virtue, a rejoicing in the virtues of the sage. By reserv-
ing one's joy for the things that truly matter, one is able to transcend the vicissitudes of life. Death, pain, and poverty do not harm
a person who recognizes that life, comfort, and wealth do not bring
the true joy that the virtues sustain.

In the grammar of Christian consolation, the object of joy differs
in detail, but not in structure. Recognizing that what truly matters
is still intact softens grief.[72] For the Johannine Christian, then, the
departure of Jesus should not cause suffering, since his departure
expresses the essence of his work. Jesus' place is above with the
Father, whence he came, and only if he returns to the Father can
he bestow eternal life upon the disciples (17:2). In Stoic terminology, this departure is something that "really matters" and should
therefore be a source, not of pain, but of joy. The Farewell Discourses,
especially in chapter 16, consistently alternate between the two poles
of the disciples' sorrow, λύπη (16:6, 20, 21), and the joy, χαρά, that
Jesus urges (14:28; 15:11; 16:20, 22, 24).[73] The disciples should rejoice
that the Father's plan is coming to a successful completion.

---

[72] Holloway argues that, in Philippians, Paul consoles the Church at Philippi by
directing their joy toward the progress of the Gospel (1:12); Paul's preaching (1:20)
and the Lord (3:1). *Consolation*, 81. For discussions of later Christian uses of classical consolation themes and forms, see Robert C. Gregg. *Consolation Philosophy: Greek
and Christian Paideia in Basil and the Two Gregories*. Patristic Monograph Series 3
(Cambridge, MA: Philadelphia Patristic Foundation, 1975); J.H.D. Scourfield, *Consoling
Heliodorus: A Commentary on Jerome "Letter 60"* (Oxford: Clarendon Press, 1993). See
also Holloway, *Consolation*, 60 note 29, for a list of primary sources.

[73] See also Schnackenburg, *Gospel of John*, 3.124.

Consolers also emphasize the joy of the one supposedly suffering. This is especially helpful in consolations for exile. When Seneca writes to his mother during his exile, he assures her in a variety of ways that he is happy in his exiled state, in order to console her.[74] His expression of joy intends to elicit joy from her. In the same way, the Johannine Jesus hopes that the disciples will take up his joy in the following quotations:

> I have said these things so that my joy may be in you, and your joy may be complete (15:11).
>   But now I am coming to you, and I speak these things in the world so that they may have my joy made complete in themselves (17:13).

Thus, by recognizing the deeper realities that are at stake in Jesus' departure, the disciples are enjoined to see this departure with joy. By training their minds to rejoice in the proper objects, they will rejoice, not sorrow, in Jesus' departure. They should share his joyful understanding of the Father's will.

This discussion of joy returns the present argument to the concern for the Paraclete that opened the chapter. For, the disciples are told that the path to joy is to recognize the purpose of Jesus' departure. When he speaks of the Paraclete, Jesus continues this line of argumentation: "Nevertheless I tell you the truth: it is to your advantage that I go away, for if I do not go away, the Advocate will not come to you; but if I go, I will send him to you" (16:7). Only if he departs will "another Paraclete" bring to them a host of benefits.

This, too, resembles a standard argument in consolation literature. Related to the need to rejoice where appropriate, consolers also argue, "[C]onventional misfortunes often actually advance the cause of things that really matter."[75] Musonius Rufus insists that exile is not the evil (κακόν) that some people believe it to be, and that exile is actually a good thing, "since it furnishes men leisure and a greater opportunity for learning the good and practicing it than they formerly enjoyed."[76] Seneca also writes (*De tran. an.* 9.3):[77]

---

[74] *Ad Helviam*, 4.2–5.1. Cf. Holloway, *Consolation*, 82.

[75] Ibid., 105.

[76] Cf. ibid., 105. Frag. 9.43.8–15 in *C. Musonius Rufus. Reliquiae.* (Ed. Otto Hense; Leipzig: Teubner, 1905).

[77] Plutarch writes of the benefits of exile in a similar vein (*On Exile* 603e–f).

> When the mind is disobedient to precepts and cannot be restored by
> gentler means, why should it not be for its own good to have poverty,
> disgrace, and a violent overthrow of fortune applied to it . . .

The sending of the Spirit-Paraclete is portrayed in a similar fashion.
Jesus' absence is not to be lamented, because it serves a higher good.
"If I do not go away, the Advocate will not come to you" (16:7).
The disciples should not suffer at Jesus' departure, but recognize that
his going away serves to advance the plan of the Father. An apparently grievous development actually advances the beneficial plan of
salvation, by resulting in the gift of the Paraclete.

Indeed, the very sending of the Paraclete is a consolatory act. This
chapter opened with a survey of the scholarly consensus which holds
that the Johannine Paraclete is designed, at least in part, to be Jesus'
double. The preceding discussion has added to this scholarly consensus the insight that the farewell discourses in various ways include
aspects of ancient consolation. These two realities can be combined
now, by claming that the very identity of the Paraclete as Jesus' double conforms to ancient practices of consolation. In consolation literature, and in the larger spectrum of classical literature where
consolation themes enter a story, a void that remains after a person
dies or departs is often filled by some token or substitute of that
person's presence.

Most superficially, surviving friends help one another in a time of
trial by sharing pain, so that each individual's pain is easier to shoul-
der. Seneca writes to Polybius (*Ad Polybium* 12.1–2):

> Do you turn, rather, from the thoughts that torture you to the many
> and great sources of consolation you have, and look upon your admirable
> brothers, look upon your wife, look upon your son; it is for all their
> lives that Fortune has settled with you for this partial payment. You
> have many on whose affection to rest . . . Moreover, to share one's
> grief with many is in itself a kind of consolation; because, if it is dis-
> tributed among many, the part that is left behind with you must be
> small.

This sentiment is at least a rough parallel to Jesus' new commandment in John 13:34. When the disciples lose Jesus, they turn toward
one another to fill the void.[78] In the Farewell Discourses, Jesus' rela-

---

[78] It also accords well with the ancient practice of wills for Jesus to disclose his
testamentary wishes to his friends. In an interesting twist on ancient practice, how-

tionship with his disciples is characterized by love and friendship. He loves them "to the end," "εἰς τέλος" (13:1); and they are no longer his slaves, but his friends (15:15). His relationship of loving them, however, is announced at his departure and is, therefore, intimately connected to that departure (13:34; 15:12). In some sense, the disciples' love and friendship for one another is intended to help them in their deprivation of the one whom they together love.[79] For Jesus only urges them to love one another at the point that he says that he is leaving them. In 13:33 he says to his disciples:

> Little children, I am with you only a little longer. You will look for me; and as I said to the Jews so now I say to you, 'Where I am going, you cannot come.'

Then, he adds in 13:34:

> I give you a new commandment, that you love one another. Just as I have loved you, you also should love one another.

This is how John Chrysostom reads the giving of the love command:[80]

> Now, since on hearing these things they were likely to become greatly perturbed, because they were about to be left alone, He comforted (παραμυθεῖται) them by placing about them the protection of the root and guarantee of all blessings: charity (τὴν ἀγάπην). It was as if He said: 'Are you grieving because I am going away? But if you love one another, you will be stronger.'

---

ever, Jesus calls his disciples his friends after he has already disclosed his message to them. In ancient practice, the process is reversed. Because one is a friend, one is worthy to hear a dying person's will. For a copious treatment of the interaction of friendship and wills, see Fitzgerald, *Jesus' Last Will and Testament*, 70ff. and passim. Sharon Ringe, *Wisdom's Friends: Community and Christology in the Fourth Gospel* (Louisville: Westminster/John Knox, 1999) 64–82, has recently compared ancient ideas about responsibilities that friends have for one another in times of trouble with the Gospel of John. But, she mainly focuses on the manner in which friends assist one another in times of difficulty, as they do in all of life's daily circumstances. This is not specifically tied to the way in which friends soften the loss of another friend by filling the void themselves, as we see in consolation literature.

[79] To be sure, however, the command to love is also a common feature of testament literature. I do not mean to suggest that this must be read exclusively as an aspect of classical consolation literature. But it is very much like consolation literature inasmuch as the survivors do not miss the missing person so deeply, because they have new objects of love and friendship. For love commands in the testament, see Brown, *Gospel of John*, 599, 611.

[80] *Hom. Jo.* 72.4 (PG 59:393/Goggin 277).

Thus, the love they share with one another provides a means of comfort in their communal loss of the one they love.[81]

Friends and family members compensate for the loss of a loved one in even more direct ways. In Seneca's *Ep. 63* to Lucilius, relatives and companions serve as agents that fill the void of a departed loved one.[82] The lost friend is to be replaced by new friends. Seneca writes as follows:[83]

> If we have other friends, we surely deserve ill at their hands and think ill of them, if they are of so little account that they fail to console us for the loss of one . . . (*Ep.* 63.10)
> If a man who has lost his one and only tunic through robbery chooses to bewail his plight rather than look about him for some way to escape the cold, or for something with which to cover his shoulders, would you not think him an utter fool (63.11)?
> You have buried one whom you loved; look about for someone to love. It is better to replace your friend than to weep for him (63.12).

Something like this may be involved in the gesture of Jesus from the cross, when he unites his mother to the Beloved Disciple (19:26–27). Jesus does not tell the Beloved Disciple to be "like" a son to his mother, nor his mother to be "like" a mother to the Beloved Disciple. The mother has lost a son, and now the Beloved Disciple becomes her new son.[84]

At times, this device is expressed even more strongly. The replacement is not only a replacement for the lost loved one, but also a reminder of the departed, and a token of the lost friend's continuing presence. Because Marcia is distraught over the loss of her son, Seneca tells her to look for comfort in her still surviving daughters, as well as in her lost son's children, her granddaughters. The purpose of this is not to forget her son or to "move on." It is to help her remember her son all the more. Seneca writes (16.6–7):

---

[81] Brown writes, "Since the disciples cannot follow Jesus as he leaves this life, they receive a command that, if obeyed, will keep the spirit of Jesus alive among them as they continue their life in this world," *Gospel of John*, 2.612.

[82] Manning, *Seneca's 'Ad Marciam,'* 39, 94.

[83] For more on this trope throughout classical literature see ibid., 94; Constantine C. Grollios, *Seneca's 'Ad Marciam'*, 67–68.

[84] Fitzgerald, *Jesus' Last Will and Testament*, 53–60, copiously documents the common practice of using a will to assign friends to care for one's loved ones after death. He then connects this practice to Jesus' act on the cross as an extension of this practice in the care of his mother. See also ibid., 88ff.

And even the son whom you . . . mourn so deeply has not been utterly taken from you: you still have the two daughters he left – great burdens if you are weak, great comforts if you are brave. Do bring yourself to this – whenever you see them, let them remind you of your son and not of your grief! . . . Do you now put these daughters of your son Metelius in his stead, and fill the vacant place, and lighten your sorrow for one by drawing comfort from two![85]

This passage from *Ad Marciam* helps the present argument flow into the second, and even more important, way in which a token of presence replaces a lost loved one. The first passages cited above demonstrate the manner in which other friends or family members fill the hole left by death or departure. They are replacements, or they help to share the burden of a lost loved one. This device is certainly present in the passage quoted from *Ad Marciam*. But there is also something else in this passage. Marcia's family members are to serve not only as replacements for her son but as reminders of him. He is absent, but they are tokens of his presence, "in his stead."[86] Now, to be sure, the mechanism of presence-in-absence is muted in this passage, but it is implicit: "whenever you see them, let them remind you of your son and not of your grief."

And, this is precisely how the Paraclete functions in ch. 14. John Chrysostom sees the consolatory quality of this first Paraclete passage (14:16) as follows:

It was probable that, because they did not yet rightly know Him, they would miss that companionship with which they had grown so familiar: His conversation, His presence in the flesh, and would receive no consolation if He were absent. Therefore, what did he say? 'I will ask the Father and he will give you another Paraclete,' that is, 'another like me.'[87]

---

[85] *Ad Marciam* 5.6. Seneca likewise exhorts his mother to compensate for his loss by noticing her still surviving sons. He promises her, "They will vie in their services to you, and the blank that one has caused will be filled by the devotion of two" (*Ad Helviam*, 18.4).

[86] See also the *Ad Polybium* 7.4: "And besides, since you always declare that Caesar is dearer to you than your own life, it is not right for you to make complaint of Fortune while Caesar is alive. So long as he is alive, your dear ones are alive – you have lost nothing. Your eyes ought to be not only dry, but even happy; in him you have all things, he takes the place of all."

[87] *Hom. Jo.*, 75.1 (PG 59:403/Goggin, 300–01).

The Paraclete, then, is different from Jesus, but is a consolation because it fills the absence of Jesus with the presence of "another Paraclete."

Furthermore, the act of replacing a lost loved one is not only attested in letters and treatises on consolation. Classical literature abounds with similar circumstances. The selection from the *Wisdom of Solomon* that opened this chapter is instructive. A father was grieved at the loss of his son, so constructed a statue in order to keep a token of his son's presence.

Recently, Maurizio Bettini has exhaustively explored this mechanism.[88] Bettini isolates what he refers to as a "Fundamental Story" in which "the characters consist of two lovers and a portrait."[89] Ancient literature and lore abound with stories in which a lost loved one is made present to a bereaved survivor by some token of presence, what Bettini calls a "portrait." The portrait can assume various forms and perform any number of functions, but the basic mechanism is invariable: the pain of losing a loved one is softened by rendering the departed beloved present-in-absence by means of a token. The loved one is gone, but a token of presence somehow makes the loved one present as well. A survey of this "thematic of tokenness" in ancient literature will clarify precisely how it operates.

The basic story, reflected in the passage from the *Wisdom of Solomon* about the rise of idolatry is paralleled in a relatively similar tale from the writings of Pliny the Elder. Here, however, there is no worship of the image. The sole concern is with the origin of artistic sculpture. The story centers on Butades, a potter from Sicyon who later creates pottery in Corinth. Pliny writes as follows (*Natural History* 35.151):

> It may be suitable to append to these remarks something about the plastic art. It was through the service of that same earth that modeling portraits from clay was first invented by Butades, a potter of Sicyon, at Corinth. He did this owing to his daughter, who was in love with a young man; and she, when he was going abroad, drew in outline on the wall the shadow of his face thrown by a lamp. Her father pressed clay on this and made a relief, which he hardened by exposure to fire with the rest of his pottery . . .

---

[88] Maurizio Bettini, *The Portrait of the Lover* (transl. Laura Gibbs; Berkeley and Los Angeles: University of California, 1999).
[89] Ibid., 4.

Thus, whether in the *Wisdom of Solomon* or in Pliny the Elder, whether used in idolatry or not, whether by a father or by a young girl, the ancient etiologies for the origin of sculpture represent a desire to render the absent one present.[90] The token image is not exactly the same as the model on which it is based and which it replaces, but it resembles and evokes the model.

A similar token, also based on the real presence of the departed, appears in Aeschylus' *Agamemnon*. The chorus speaks of the pain felt by Menelaos when his wife, Helen, left him for Troy. His loss is not exactly like that of the figures above. Unlike the daughter of Butades, or the father in the *Wisdom of Solomon*, Menelaos does not miss and long for one with whom he shared a happy love. Rather, he longs for a wife who has left him to be with another man.[91] But the same basic structure prevails. The passage reads as follows (*Agamemnon* 409–426):[92]

> The soothsayers of the palace greatly lamented, saying, "Alas, alas for the palace, the palace and the princes; alas for the bed and the hus-band-loving traces [στίβοι] she left there . . . Because of his longing [πόθος] for the woman who has crossed the sea, a phantom seems to reign in the palace! The charm of the lovely statues [εὔμορφοι κολοσσοί] is hateful to the husband; in the eyes' emptiness all the charm of Aphrodite has vanished. Appearing in dreams, sorrowful apparitions bring empty pleasure – because it is surely vanity when a man thinks that he sees joyful things, but the vision suddenly slips from his embrace, and wings its way along the paths of sleep.

It is not entirely clear whether the εὔμορφοι κολοσσοί are statues of Helen herself, or merely female statues.[93] If they are statues of Helen, then they serve in precisely the same way as those statues mentioned above in the etiologies of idolatry. If they are not specifically stat-ues of Helen, though, there are other deposits of her presence that

---

[90] Ibid., 7
[91] Ibid., 15.
[92] Translation from ibid., 14.
[93] Arguments in favor the statues being replicas of Helen are supported by the standard Greek procedure of using statues to replace the dead. See, for instance J.P. Vernant, "Figuration de l'invisible et catégorie psychologique du double: Le colossus," in Mythe et pensée chez les grecs (Paris, 1966) 325–338 (English translation: "The Representation of the Invisible and the Psychological Category of the Double: The Colossus," in Myth and Thought among the Greeks (London, 1983) 305–320. In response, Fraenkel insists that these *kolossoi* are merely the standard statues adorn-ing palaces, *Agamemnon* 2.218f. Cf. Bettini, *Portrait*, 241 note 32 and 242 note 38.

trouble Menelaos: her appearance in his dreams, and the στίβοι she has left behind in the palace, either footprints that she made on her way to their bed, or else the impressions of her body preserved in the bed.[94]

Euripides' *Alcestis* also relies on the plastic arts. The *Alcestis* is very much a treatise on how to deal with death, loss and mortality.[95] The shape of the plot is complex, but the basic thrust of the story is straightforward. Apollo, wishing to repay the kindness of Admetus coaxes the Fates into postponing the day of Admetus' death, as long as Admetus is able to find a substitute to take his place. The only substitute he can find is his wife Alcestis. As soon as she descends into death, however, and he extols the virtues of so great a wife, he recognizes that to lose her is worse than his own death. In the end, Heracles brings Alcestic back to Admetus and to life.[96]

Even though Alcestis eventually returns to Admetus, however, Admetus is inconsolable during his wife's absence. He struggles to preserve some token of Alcestis' presence. The following speech expresses his sorrow (328–330, 343–356):

> While you lived you were my wife, and in death you alone will bear that title . . . I shall put an end to revels and the company of banqueters and to the garlands and music which once filled my halls. I shall never touch the lyre, or lift my heart in song to the Libyan pipe. For your death takes all the joy from my life. An image of you shaped by the hand of skilled craftsmen shall be laid out in my bed. I shall fall into its arms, and as I embrace it and call your name I shall imagine, though I have her not, that I hold my dear wife in my arms, a

---

[94] Ibid., 16. Whatever the *stiboi* represent, it is interesting to recognize the power attributed to such bodily impressions. A saying of Pythagoras preserved by Iamblichus (*Protrepticus*, 29) "required that the body's impression be erased in the morning upon getting up from bed, apparently because the impression of the limbs preserved something of the actual person, something it would be dangerous to expose to others," Ibid., 16, 243 note 43.

[95] For various interpretations of the *Alcestis'* view and treatment of death, see the following: Charles Segal, "Euripides' *Alcestis*: How to Die a Normal Death in Greek Tragedy," in *Death and Representation* (ed. Sarah Webster Goodwin and Elisabeth Bronfen; Baltimore: Johns Hopkins University Press, 1993) 213–241; J.W. Gregory, "Euripides' *Alcestis*," *Hermes* 107 (1979) 259–70; Wesley D. Smith, "The Ironic Structure in *Alcestis*," *Phoenix* 14 (1960) 127–45; Anne Pippin Burnett, "The Virtues of Admetus," *CP* 60 (1965) 240–55.

[96] The play, however, does not represent a triumph over death. Rather, Alcestis' return to life is, on a larger scale, a return to the status quo that existed prior to Admetus' escape from death. It was his escape from death that set his world into complete disarray and confusion. Alcestis' return signals a recovery of normal mortal existence, wherein death is an inescapable fact of life, Gregory, "Euripides' *Alcestis*," 259–70.

cold pleasure, to be sure, but thus I shall lighten my soul's heaviness. And perhaps you will cheer me by visiting me in dreams. For even in sleep it is a pleasure to see loved ones for however long we are permitted.

This passage is a synopsis of many of the themes that Bettini traces. Like so many other figures, Admetus relies on dreams to make his wife present to him (see Menelaos' dreams of Helen above), as well as calling on her name. But, also, like so many other cases in ancient literature, a simulacrum of his wife is constructed in order to render his wife present.[97]

These examples do not nearly exhaust this widespread mechanism in classical literature. Bettini covers many more, but all examples share the same basic storyline. "The absent lover is replaced by an image: the portrait is a substitute, a consolation."[98] And, whether one looks to Aeschylus, Euripides, Seneca, Pliny, or the *Wisdom of Solomon*, the basic mechanism is the same. Some token of the lost one's presence – whether another person, a vision in a dream, a statue – will soften the pain of absence. People who are intimately connected by bonds of love and friendship will miss their loved ones less if they have some token of their lost one's presence. The Paraclete is just such a simulacrum that makes Jesus present to the community. Without actually being Jesus, he makes Jesus present.

Finally, having argued that classical literary themes lie behind the presentation of the Paraclete, it is necessary to recall that consolation is an aspect of moral formation. Philosophical consolation encourages people to deal with loss in a philosophically acceptable fashion. It is one more area in which a teacher guides a pupil. In the present case of Jesus, of course, the person who is lost is the teacher himself. This is an unusual circumstance for a consoler. Seneca faces a similar situation in consoling his mother on his exile, and writes as follows:

> Moreover, although I unrolled all the works that the most famous writers had composed for the purpose of repressing and controlling sorrow, not one instance did I find of a man who had offered consolation to his dear ones when he himself was bewailed by them; thus, in a novel situation I faltered . . .[99]

---

[97] Bettini, *Portrait*, 24.
[98] Ibid., 10.
[99] *Ad Helviam*, 1.3.

However unique Seneca's situation is in this particular case of consolation and exile, ancient teachers often deal with being absent from their pupils. In discussing the condition of the Thessalonian church, Malherbe emphasizes the difficulty that Paul's converts undergo during Paul's absence. Comparing Paul's relationship to his disciples with the relations of Greco-Roman moral philosophers and their teachers, Malherbe writes, "When one was separated from one's teacher, one yearned for him and remembered in detail what he taught and the example he set."[100] A lengthy passage from Lucian's *Nigrinus* demonstrates the sentiments of a pupil who is apart from his teacher. The *Nigrinus* is a dialogue between two unidentified characters, one of whom describes to the other his association with the philosopher Nigrinus. The comments of the philosophical pupil are as follows (*Nigrinus*, 6–7):[101]

> Then, too, I take pleasure in calling his words to mind frequently, and have already made it a regular exercise: even if nobody happens to be at hand, I repeat them to myself two or three times a day just the same. I am in the same case with lovers. In the absence of the objects of their fancy they think over their actions and their words, and by dallying with these beguile their lovesickness into the belief that they have their sweethearts near; in fact sometimes they even imagine they are chatting with them and are as pleased with what they formerly heard as if it were just being said, and by applying their minds to memory of the past give themselves no time to be annoyed by the present. So I too in the absence of my mistress Philosophy, get no little comfort out of gathering together the words that I then heard and turning them over to myself. In short, I fix my gaze on that man as if he were a lighthouse and I were adrift at sea in the dead of night, fancying him by me whenever I do anything and always hearing him repeat his former words. Sometimes, especially when I put pressure on my soul, his face appears to me and the sound of his voice abides in my ears. Truly, as the comedian says, "he left a sting implanted in his hearers!"

Recalling the teacher's words, then, accomplishes what other survivors, like Admetus, accomplish through a clay figure: the absent one is present. Only here, the recollected words of the teacher are the token of presence. And this presence is so real that the teacher's visage appears to the eyes and his words echo in the ears. The pupil

---

[100] Malherbe, *Paul and the Thessalonians*, 67.
[101] Cf. ibid., 67.

here beguiles himself into believing that he is in the presence of his teacher.

For the Johannine Christians, there is no need to rely on imagination. The same Paraclete that makes Jesus present to them is also charged with facilitating the recollection of Jesus' words.[102] There is another sense, then, in which the Paraclete renders the absent Jesus present. He will remind the disciples of all that the Lord taught them: "But the Advocate, the Holy Spirit, whom the Father will send in my name, will teach you everything, and remind (ὑπομνήσει) you of all that I have said to you" (14:26). Here, however, the consolatory work of the Paraclete begins to overlap with the role of the successor figures in the testament. The Paraclete continues Jesus' teaching ministry even after Jesus has returned to the Father, just as Joshua completes and continues the ministry of Moses. We are again, then, in bilingual territory. Whatever the overlap with successor figures, however, being reminded of Jesus' words is yet another way of putting the disciples in the presence of their Lord.[103]

This reality anticipates the argument of the next chapter. For the Johannine community will continue to need instruction from its Lord. Since ancient pupils required instruction even when separated from their teachers by many miles, moral philosophers relied on letters to bridge the distance between themselves and their charges.[104] The

---

[102] Paul also sends Timothy to both the Thessalonians and the Philippians, to reflect his ongoing concern for their moral development, and to guide them when he cannot be present. Holloway sees this in Philippians 2:19–24, where Timothy serves not only as Paul's messenger, but as his "surrogate." *Consolation*, 126–27.

[103] Here, Holloway's recent study should be consulted. The present argument stresses that the Paraclete is a token of Jesus' presence simply by, in some form, being present. Holloway now nuances this further by recognizing that such a simulacrum of the departed can be either a mediator of presence, along the lines argued here, or a surrogate teacher, along the lines of Paul's sending Timothy to the Thessalonians and Philippians (see previous note). Thus, the Paraclete renders Jesus present as a mediator and a surrogate. Holloway creatively and convincingly distinguishes both functions in the classical examples of the simulacrum, "Left Behind," 7–8, 22–24, passim.

[104] See Malherbe, *Paul and the Thessalonians*, 68–78; For the use of the letter in moral formation, see Stanley Stowers, *Letter Writing in Greco-Roman Antiquity* (Philadelphia: Westminster, 1989). A fourth century letter of Basil of Caesarea demonstrates well the convention (*Epistle* 297):

Judging it to be quite proper for me, both because of my elderly age and because of the sincerity of my spiritual affection, to visit your incomparable Nobility not only in bodily presence, but also when you are absent not to fail you, but by letter to supply the want, now that I have found this fitting messenger for my letter . . .

Johannine Christians have no such letter from their Lord and teacher.
This is not to say, however, that they do not have a record of their
Lord's words. They have his discourses on the night before his death,
preserved in a time capsule for the benefit of future disciples who
are also separated from the Lord, not by many miles, but by the
boundary between above and below. The next chapter will connect
the Johannine effort to preserve Jesus' discourses for later believers
to the literary symposium tradition in a way reminiscent of the moral
philosopher's pedagogical use of letters.

Before discussing the literary symposium in the coming chapter,
however, a summary of the preceding chapter is in order. There is
nothing new in claiming that the Paraclete is a consolatory figure.
Ashton, Brown, Schnackenburg and Segovia, to name only a few
prominent interpreters, all view the Paraclete's work in the Johannine
community as consolatory in some form or another.[105] What this
chapter has tried to provide, however, is a more appropriate framework for understanding the Paraclete's role as a consoler. The Paraclete
is not only a successor, as Joshua is to Moses, but the presence of
Jesus himself, now present in a token until Jesus himself returns in
the Parousia. To explain how the Paraclete makes Jesus present, the
notion of succession in the testament is not completely helpful.
The successor model does illumine how the Paraclete will carry on
the teaching and witnessing roles of Jesus. But this activity only partly
defines the Paraclete, and has little to do with the first Paraclete passage (14:16–17). Joshua may be "like" another Moses in the way
that each new President of the United States is "like" the previous
one, inasmuch as he or she discharges the duties of the President.
But each new President is not a token of the specific presence of
George Washington. The Paraclete makes Jesus present. At the most
basic level, then, the Spirit is "another Paraclete" inasmuch as the
Spirit represents Jesus at a time when Jesus himself is no longer
physically present. The Paraclete is not, as Brown says, "another
Jesus," but the Paraclete does somehow render Jesus present, without being Jesus.[106] And this presence consoles the disciples.

---

[105] See Segovia, *Farewell of the Word*, 119; Cf. Brown, *Gospel of John*, 2. 1137, passim; Schnackenburg, *Gospel of John*, 3.147–48. J.G. Davies, "The Primary Meaning
of PARAKLHTOS," *JTS* n.s. 4 (1953) 35–38, argues that, following Septuagint
usage of the verb παρακαλῶ, the noun παράκλητος should best be read in the
active sense of "the consoler."

[106] Brown, *Gospel of John*, 1141.

That the Paraclete is Jesus' doppelgänger has long been recognized. That the Paraclete is a consolatory figure has long been recognized. But these two insights are more richly integrated when fused with the insights of classical consolation. Only then is it obvious precisely how the doppelgänger is consolatory.

The next chapter will extend the discussion of Jesus' continuing presence introduced in this chapter. But in what follows, Jesus will not be present in and through the Paraclete. He will be present in the very words of the Farewell Discourses.

CHAPTER FOUR

AND THE *FLESH* BECAME *WORDS...*[1]

Athenaeus' *Deipnosophistae* purports to narrate the events and conversations surrounding a party at the house of a Roman host named
Larensis. Near the close of the book, the most prominent guest at
the gathering, Ulpian, concludes his final speech, and the narrator
informs the reader that Ulpian's death will soon follow. The relevant passage reads as follows (15.686 b–c):

> [Ulpian said], 'As for myself, I shall at this point stop speaking for
> today, yielding the discussion of perfumes to those who want to carry
> it on... Thus, indeed, will I make my exit, as in a play, after my
> speech.' Not many days after that, as if he himself had had a pre-
> monition of the silence that was to be his, he died happily, allowing
> no time for illness, but causing grief to us his companions.

This passage resonates with both of the preceding chapters of this
study. As with Jesus' dramatic exit, Ulpian departs "as in a play"
after his "Big Speech," and death awaits him soon after he departs.
Further, in his going, he causes "grief to his companions" just as
Jesus grieves his companions by leaving them behind. That Jesus
departs from a supper further likens him to Ulpian. Unlike Ulpian,
however, Jesus comforts his companions when he exits. Precisely how
Jesus comforts his table companions, the topic of the previous chapter, will continue to occupy the present analysis.

In this chapter, however, center stage goes not to the exit of Jesus,
but to the exit of Judas. The first half of the argument will culminate in the exit of Judas, and the latter half will develop out of
Judas' exit. As in the previous chapters, the purpose here is not to
explore every possible connection between the Farewell Discourses
and the literary symposium tradition. The emphasis will be on the
form and function of Jesus' discourses, and, more specifically, on
how the particular style of symposium that John presents preserves

---

[1] The phrase is a modified borrowing from Patrick Chatelion Counet, *John, A
Postmodern Gospel: Introduction to Deconstructive Exegesis Applied to the Fourth Gospel* (Biblical
Interpretation Series 44; Leiden: E.J. Brill, 2000) 301.

the discourses of Jesus for later generations.[2] The broad thesis of the chapter is that the form of the supper, which is not a feast of food but a feast of words, is designed to render the absent Jesus present to the readers of the Gospel. The Word who became flesh is now present in his words.

The Symposium: Friendship and Enmity

Although a peculiar way to begin, the first step in this argument is to insist that John's Last Supper is not a symposium *per se*.[3] Aune correctly notes that no Christian example of the literary symposium exists prior to the work of Methodius, the 4th century bishop of Olympus.[4] Just as the second chapter compared Jesus' farewell to the dramatic exit to death, without thereby claiming that the Fourth Gospel is in fact a tragic poem, the present chapter will stop short of declaring John's Last Supper scene to be a paradigmatic example of a symposium. Josef Martin's *Symposion: Die Geschichte einer literarischen Form* represents what amounts to a grammar of the literary symposium. Of the several key figures and circumstances that typify the literary symposium, John's Farewell Discourses include perhaps only one major figure.[5] Even so, Martin concludes his study

---

[2] Each of the canonical Gospels, in some sense, renders Jesus present to later generations through the commemoration of his words and deeds. Moreover, the Gospels depict Jesus' past words and deeds through the filter of the Resurrection. But the Gospel of John is most obvious in this type of *anamnesis*, articulating explicitly what the Synoptic Gospels imply. Cf. Nils Dahl, "Anamnesis: Memory and Commemoration in Early Christianity," in *Jesus in the Memory of the Early Church* (Minneapolis: Augsburg, 1976) especially 28–29.

[3] See, for instance, Martin, *Symposion*, 314ff.; Aune, *The New Testament in its Literary Environment*, 122, who mentions that both Luke and John employ sympotic tropes, though he then only analyzes Luke along these lines. See also idem, "Septem," passim; Witherington, *John's Wisdom*, 236ff.; Malina and Rohrbaugh, *Social-Science Commentary on John*, 217ff.; Van Tilborg, *Imaginative Love*, 133ff.; Relihan, "Rethinking," 216, 241–2.

[4] Aune, "Septem," 69.

[5] The primary topoi of the genre are surveyed under two headings: *Stehende Figuren* (*Symposion*, 33–115) and *Situationstopoi* (ibid., 116–148). The stock figures are characters such as "the Host" (*Der Wirt*); "the Jester" (*Der Spaßmacher*); "the uninvited Guest" (*Der ungebetene Gast*); "the Physician" (*Der Arzt*); "the late Guest" (*Der späte Gast*); "the Drunkard" (*Der Weinende*); "the Offended Guest departs" (*Der Gekränkte geht*); "the long-lasting Drinker" (*Der große Zecher*); "the pair of lovers" (*Das Liebespaar*). The *Situationstopoi* investigate either the typical events that inspire a symposium (*Szenische Motiv*), such as a victory celebration; or common occurrences at the table,

with a brief review of sympotic tropes in the Gospel of John, and makes some basic connections with less significant aspects of the genre.[6] His insights will become obvious in the following pages, and indicate the need to push a little further in the pursuit of sympotic undertones in John's Last Supper. At this point, a basic survey will clarify loose but discernible connections between the Farewell Discourses and the literary symposium tradition.

When heard accurately, the meal and discourses in John 13–16 sound very much like the conversation of the symposium, particularly in regard to the continuing concern for the themes of love and friendship. The vocabulary of love takes a central place in the Farewell Discourses. The concepts of life and light that dominated the first twelve chapters of the Gospel do not entirely disappear, but take a secondary place behind the emphasis on love (ἀγάπη) and friendship (φιλία).[7] The purpose of this shift in emphasis is certainly not to undermine the claim that Christ is both light and life, but rather to clarify the manner in which Christ manifests himself as light and life. The Father and Son are united by divine love (14:31; 15:9), which Christ demonstrates toward human beings through his self-sacrifice (15:9–10), and which humans return by obedience to Christ and by their relationships of love with one another (15:12–13).[8]

That John so emphasizes love in Jesus' last meal with his disciples is striking because love and friendship are among the most popular topics associated with table-talk scenes in ancient literature.[9] The relation between friendship and the symposium can operate on two levels. In the first place, for Plutarch, a central purpose of table

---

such as a conflict among the guests (*Der Streit*); or the various ways in which a symposium can adjourn or conclude (*Unterbrechungen und Schluß des Symposions*).

[6] Ibid., 314–17.

[7] Cf. Dodd, *Interpretation*, 398–99, where a small chart appears, indicating that in chapters 1–12, terms related to light, life and darkness appear 82 times, as opposed to 6 instances of the terms ἀγάπη and ἀγαπᾶν. By contrast, in chapters 13–17, terms related to light, life and darkness appear only 6 times, while forms of ἀγάπη and ἀγαπᾶν appear 31 times. Φιλεῖν and φίλος are used with roughly the same frequency, six times in chs. 1–12, seven times in chs. 13–17.

[8] Ibid., 398. See also Fernando Segovia, *Love Relationships in the Johannine Tradition: Agape/Agapan in I John and the Fourth Gospel* (SBLDS 58; Missoula: Scholars Press, 1982).

[9] See Martin, *Symposion*, 316. Smith cites several comments of Plutarch, among which is the notice, "A guest comes to share not only meat, wine and dessert, but conversation, fun and the amiability that leads to friendship (*philophrosyne*)," Plutarch, *Table Talk*, 660b. Cf. Smith, *From Symposium to Eucharist*, 55.

fellowship is to foster stronger feelings of friendship among the participants. He writes of the "friend-making character of the dining-table" in *Table Talk* (1.612d) and his *Life of Cato* includes a quotation of Cato in which the dining table is mentioned as being "highly friend-making" (25.351f). Indeed, Plutarch also insists that the advice for a visit to the market applies equally well to the symposium: "[W]e should not let a party break up before we have made a new friend and well-wisher among the other guests and fellow-diners" (4.660a). Second, love and friendship are common conversation topics in literary symposia. Plato's *Symposium*, for example, is nothing more than a series of speeches on the nature of love.[10]

Judas, of course, offends this friendly association. He represents the enmity that cannot tolerate, or be tolerated by, the love and friendship expressed between Jesus and his disciples in the Farewell Discourses.[11] Enmity and friendship are common companions in

---

[10] Secondary literature on the *Symposium* and on Plato's theory of love more generally is massive, but see especially the introduction in Kenneth Dover, *Plato, Symposium* (Cambridge: Cambridge University Press, 1980). For an interesting study of the interaction between the form and content of the dialogue, see David Halperin, "Plato and the the Erotics of Narrativity," in *Methods of Interpreting Plato and His Dialogues*; (eds., J.C. Klagge and N.D. Smith; Oxford: Oxford University Press, 1992) 93–129. For the sake of clarity, however, it is important to note that there is nothing necessarily sympotic about the statements on love and friendship that John employs. One might be tempted to think otherwise. Plato's *Symposium*, for instance, includes a phrase strikingly similar to Jesus' praise for dying on behalf of one's friends (15:13). Phaedrus claims in his speech on love: ... "only lovers are prepared to sacrifice themselves" (Καὶ μὴν ὑπεραποθνήσκειν γὲ μόνοι ἐθέλουσιν οἱ ἐρῶντες, 179b). But the idea of dying for one's friends has no exclusively sympotic associations, and is a commonplace in Greek and Latin discussions of friendship. See the texts cited in Ronald F. Hock, "An Extraordinary Friend in Chariton's *Callirhoe*: The Importance of Friendship in the Greek Romances," in *Greco-Roman Perspectives on Friendship* (ed. John T. Fitzgerald; Atlanta: Scholars Press, 1997), 156–57 and in Van Tilborg, *Imaginative Love*, 151–154. However, this fact presents no problem to the present argument. There need not be a direct link between John and a specifically sympotic friendship topos. The discussion of the themes alone is sufficient.

[11] The struggle between love and enmity is not confined to the character of Judas, of course. For, after Jesus dubs the disciples his friends in 15:14, he then gives the following notice in 15:18–19: "If the world hates you, be aware that it hated me before it hated you. If you belonged to the world, the world would love (ἐφίλει) you as its own. Because you do not belong to the world, but I have chosen you out of the world – therefore the world hates you." As Brown writes, "Jesus loves his disciples because they remain or abide in him; the world hates them for the same reason," *Gospel of John*, 2.692. The "world" hates the disciples because it hates Jesus, who has called the disciples his friends. This notion of being on one side or another, of being a friend of Jesus or a friend of the world, is obviously an extension of the various dualisms that are the bedrock of John's Gospel. Associated with Jesus are light and life, while the world is associated with darkness and death.

ancient presentations of friendship.[12] One way of expressing the connection is to say that a friend of a friend is a friend; a friend of an enemy is an enemy. Sophocles' *Philoctetes* neatly expresses the convention when Neoptolemus says in regard to Philoctetes,

> I am the enemy of the Atreids, and this man is my closest friend precisely because he hates them. Since, then, you have come kindly disposed towards me, you must not hide from us any part of their plans that you have heard (585–6).[13]

Literary symposia often dramatize this tandem relationship of love and hatred. Because the table is the locus of friendly interaction, characters intent on causing discord and confusion (or worse) often invade the supper setting. In the Johannine supper, Judas personifies the enmity that opposes the loving association of Jesus and his disciples.[14] Examining the activity of Judas in light of other literary

---

Being or not being a friend of Jesus is yet another way of standing on one side or another of this dualism. But this particular image is consistent with classical notions of friendship, where discussions of friendship often go hand in hand with discussions of enmity. This is significant for the Farewell Discourses because the interplay between friendship with Jesus and enmity with the world is not confined to verses 18–19 of chapter 15. It is also part of the larger plan of the discourses. In the first order, commentators are unanimous in dividing chapter 15 according to these notions. 15:1–17 discuss the disciples' relationship with Jesus, while 15:18–16:4a discusses the hatred from the world that can be expected in light of the disciples' relationship with Jesus, Moloney, *Glory*, 56–59.

[12] Cf. David Konstan, *Friendship in the Classical World* (Cambridge, Cambridge University Press, 1996) 58. For the pairing of friendship and enmity in a variety of circumstances, see the essays in Fitzgerald, *Greco-Roman Perspectives on Friendship*, especially Johan C. Thom, "'Harmonious Equality': The *Topos* of Friendship in Neopythagorean Writings," 84–5, 87–90, 92–3, 95–6, 100; David L. Balch, "Political Friendship in the Historian Dionysius of Halicarnassus, *Roman Antiquities*," 123–44.

[13] A helpful introduction to the relationship between enmity and friendship, as well as an exhaustive study of the phenomenon in Sophocles, is contained in Mary Blundell, *Helping Friends and Harming Enemies: A Study in Sophocles and Greek Ethics* (Cambridge: Cambridge University Press, 1989).

[14] Moloney joins Witherington in noting that the introduction of Judas' enmity interrupts "the intimacy of a supper" Moloney, *Glory*, 13; Witherington, *John's Wisdom*, 236ff. Because the deipnon is a locus of friendly, loving association, Judas' betrayal is all the more egregious for taking place in such a setting. This is certainly the aspect of Judas' activity that most appalls John Chrysostom. When he comments on 13:2, he indicates that Judas' betrayal is all the more nefarious because Judas was a companion of Jesus' table, *Hom. Jo.* 70.1 (PG 59:381). Later, in regard to 13:26 ("It is the one to whom I give this piece of bread when I have dipped it in the dish"), Chrysostom states: "Even the method He used was calculated to shame the traitor, for, after sharing the same bread, he was dishonoring the table. Granted that his partaking of Christ's hospitality did not shame him, whom would it not win over to receive the morsel from Him? Yet it did not win Judas," ibid., 72.2 (PG 59:391/Goggin 271).

symposia will fruitfully demonstrate some of the more obvious sympotic undertones in the Farewell Discourses, and so the next several pages will compare Judas to similar figures in sympotic scenes.

John's portrayal of Judas in the Last Supper differs from the presentation in the Synoptic Gospels. In Matthew, Mark and Luke the following rough sequence of events transpires: Judas meets the priests before the meal, Jesus predicts the betrayal within the meal, and then Judas betrays Jesus after the meal.[15] The act of betrayal is oriented around the Last Supper, but spills out both before and after the meal. John, by contrast, focuses the act of betrayal more clearly within the meal scene. Judas does not meet with the chief priests prior to the meal. His intention to betray Jesus is established squarely within the dinner.[16] Indeed, the very next words after the sentence "there was a dinner" are the words that connect Judas to the devil

---

[15] None of the Synoptic accounts presents such a concentrated, clear connection between the betrayal and the meal. In Mark (14:10–11) and Matthew (26:14–15), Judas betrays Jesus prior to the Last Supper. Only after Judas speaks to the priests does the Last Supper commence. Luke follows the same basic outline of events (22:14ff.). Judas' meeting with the chief priests (and the temple officers) is thus the prelude to the supper. Because the Synoptics position the betrayal before the meal, they expend little energy on the betrayal within the course of the meal. In Mark 14:17–21 Jesus announces at the table that he will be betrayed, but the identity of the betrayer is not mentioned. Matthew (26:20–25) follows Mark closely, but includes an exchange between Jesus and Judas. When Judas denies any wrongdoing with the phrase "Surely not I, Rabbi," Jesus responds, "You have said so" (26:25). But there is nothing beyond this. Both Mark (14:20) and Matthew (26:23) include the notice that the betrayer is the one who dips his bread into the bowl at the same time as Jesus, but do not identify the figure. Luke (22:21–23) follows a slightly different sequence of events within the supper, but concludes the meal with a notice that one of the disciples will betray Jesus, and that the betrayer's "hand is on the table" (22:21). All of the Gospels, then, place a statement about the betrayal within the context of the Last Supper. But in the Synoptics, the acts of betrayal are clustered around the supper. In John, the betrayal is focused more closely within the supper. The Synoptics also contain narrative confusion in the act of betrayal. None of the Synoptics explains how Judas could have shared the Last Supper with Jesus and then also arrived with the chief priests when Jesus was arrested. Luke informs the reader that Jesus went to the Mount of Olives with the disciples (22:39). Presumably, Judas was among the disciples, so it is a narrative mystery how Judas could be in the company of the chief priests when they arrive to arrest Jesus. In Mark (14:32) and Matthew (26:36), when Jesus goes to Gethsemane, the disciples are with him. But then Judas appears with the priests when it is time to arrest Jesus. John has no such narrative confusion. As the introductory chapter of this study demonstrated, Judas elaborately exits the Last Supper to meet Jesus' betrayers (13:30). For discussion of the relationship between John and the Synoptic Gospels, see especially D. Moody Smith, *John Among the Gospels*.

[16] Relihan sees the same significance in this fact, "Rethinking," 241.

(13:2). The themes of love (of Jesus) and enmity (of Judas) are combined in the first two verses of the scene.[17] The close connection between (1) Jesus' love, (2) the enmity of Judas and (3) the meal setting is obvious even in the grammatical structure of 13:2.[18] Starting as it does with two genitive absolutes, verse 13:2 is cumbersome and top-heavy. This syntactical construction allows the meal to be the link between Jesus' love and Satan's control of Judas. The text reads as follows:

> . . . ἠγάπησεν αὐτούς. Καὶ δείπνου γινομένου τοῦ διαβόλου ἤδη βεβληκότος εἰς τὴν καρδίαν ἵνα παραδοῖ αὐτὸν Ἰούδας Σίμωνος Ἰσκαριώτου . . .

> . . . He loved them. And during the supper, the devil having already put it into the heart of Judas son of Simon Iscariot to betray him . . .

The words follow one another closely, and are jumbled together to underscore their association. Jesus' love and the devil's hostility interconnect in the context of a meal. Furthermore, the overall structure of the Johannine deipnon in chapter 13 emphasizes these two themes. By focusing first on the footwashing (vv. 3–17), which is an expression

---

[17] 13:1 has been seen in recent commentary as a summary statement of all that is said in 13–18:1. To some commentators, it introduces the entire second half of the Gospel. When analyzing the discourses rhetorically as an epideictic speech, Kennedy, *Rhetorical Criticism*, 73–75 labels 13:1 as the proem of the speech, but ignores 13:2. 13:1 introduces what he considers to be the relevant topics that will be developed for the next several chapters. He also gives scant attention to 13:2–30. After noting that these verses correspond to the 'narrative' section of an epideictic speech, he adds that they introduce a new theme: the devil. Segovia's *Farewell of the Word* 43–47 follows Kennedy completely in this assessment of 13:1, and continues to follow Kennedy in that the work gives no meaningful attention to 13:2–30. The body of Segovia's analysis (59ff.) begins with the speech that opens at 13:31, after the departure of Judas. For more on this topic, see below.

[18] This joining of themes so early in the Last Supper scene has not escaped the notice of commentators. Moloney elaborates fully on the connection between the verses. In v. 1 Jesus prepares to depart "from the sphere of everyday human events." As he departs, his love for the disciples is underscored because his death is for them. The Gospel expresses this with the phrase (13:1), ". . . he loved them until the end (εἰς τέλος)." Whether "until the end" here means that he loved them to the end of his life, or that he loved them to the fullest possible extent, is immaterial. Either way, verse 1 communicates that Jesus is about to pass over to the Father as a symbol of his boundless love for the disciples. But this is not all, because the Gospel indicates how Jesus is to "pass over" when verse 2 introduces Judas and informs the reader that he has been compelled by Satan to betray Jesus. Moloney sees an intimate connection between the statements about Jesus' sacrificial love in v. 1 and the introduction of the devil and Judas in v. 2, *Glory*, 12. Moloney then adds: "The narrator has set the scene by informing the reader of two designs: the design of God in and through Jesus' love for his own, and the design of Satan that one of these would betray Jesus," ibid., 13.

of sacrificial love, and then on the betrayal of Judas at the table (vv. 21–30), the opening deipnon sequence (13:1–20) swings to and fro between the love of Jesus and the hatred of Judas.

In this, the Johannine depiction of Judas may differ from that of the Synoptic Gospels, but it resembles the portrayal of similar figures in contemporary literature. Ancient literature abounds with scenes that highlight, and thereby condemn, betrayal and criminality in the context of a meal. As far back in Greek literature as the *Odyssey*, the customarily hospitable dinner table is turned into the site of deceit and intrigue when Circe prepares for the men of Odysseus " a mixture of cheese, barley-meal, and yellow honey flavoured with Pramnian wine" laced with "a powerful drug" (10.234–236).[19] Especially in Plutarch's *Lives*, symposia and deipna regularly serve as the likely setting of treachery – or else the means to avoid treachery. Recognizing the table as a dangerous place, Epaminondas boasts that the humble, brief meals he provides offered no opportunity for perfidious plans to be realized.[20]

Meal scenes in Josephus are especially relevant. The Hasmonean High Priest Simon dies at the hands of his son-in-law "after a plot against him in a symposium" (*BJ* 1.54; *AJ* 13.228; 20.240).[21] Malichus bribes Hyrcanus' wine-pourer to poison Herod's father, Antipater. Herod responds by having Malichus killed under cover of an invitation to a deipnon (*BJ* 1.233–34; *AJ* 14.291–92).[22] To these examples, which may reflect historical realities and not literary conventions, we can add the even more interesting cases where the tendentious hand of Josephus spices up meal scenes depicted differently elsewhere. For instance, the narrative of 2 Kings 15:23–26 describes the brief reign over Israel of Pekahiah (Phakeas in Greek), son of Menahem. The biblical version of 15:25 describes the betrayal in the following way:

---

[19] Cf. George Paul, "Symposia and Deipna in Plutarch's Lives and in Other Historical Writings," in *Dining in a Classical Context* (ed. William J. Slater; Ann Arbor: University of Michigan Press) 162.

[20] Plutarch, *Lycurgus*, 13.6. Also, Lucius Terentius (*Pompey* 3.2) is the tent-mate of Pompey, and is supposed to kill Pompey as the two share a meal. But while eating, Pompey gets wind of the plot, and then keeps eating, as though nothing has happened, but then sneaks out of the tent unperceived. In *Antony*, 32.2–5, Pompey himself almost uses a banquet as an opportunity for treachery. In *Pelopidas*, 9.2ff., the plan is hatched to overthrow tyrants at a party. Cf. Paul, "Symposia and Deipna," 163ff.

[21] Ibid., 164.

[22] Ibid., 164.

> Pekah son of Remaliah, his captain, conspired against him with fifty of the Gileadites, and attacked him in Samaria, in the citadel of the palace along with Argob and Arieh; he killed him, and reigned in place of him.

To the description of the attack in the citadel, however, Josephus adds " in a symposium with his friends" (ἐν συμποσίῳ μετὰ φίλων) to emphasize the underhandedness of the deed (*AJ* 9.233–234). The same occurs in Josephus' handling of Jeremiah 41:1–2, where Ishmael and ten assistants kill Gedaliah. Jeremiah depicts them eating bread together when the deed occurs, but Josephus specifically claims that the murder took place in a symposium, again adding the phrase ἐν τῷ συμποσίῳ (*AJ* 10.168–69).

Judas' treachery in the Last Supper, then, builds squarely on a solid foundation in ancient literature. But even more such evidence exists in the literary symposium tradition proper. Although the Johannine Last Supper only barely interacts with the constitutive elements of the literary symposium genre as Martin sees them, the one feature that the Johannine scene does share with the larger tradition is the early exit of Judas. The exit resembles the device that Martin dubs "Der Gekränkte geht," or "The Offended Guest Departs." The early exit of offended guests occurs rather frequently in sympotic texts, where a diner, somehow bothered by the behavior or conversation of the others, exits before the dinner is formally concluded.[23]

Plutarch, for instance, tells of Cleitomachus the athlete who removed himself from any dinner party where the guests' conversation became unseemly.[24] In Athenaeus, when Cynulcus asks for a drink by its Latin name *decocta*, Ulpian rails against him with the following rebuke (6.270b): "How long are you going to utter barbarisms

---

[23] The following discussion is indebted to Martin, *Symposion*, 101–106.

[24] The discussion occurs in Plutarch's *Table Talk*, a series of discourses, each one devoted to exploring the proper behavior among diners at a symposium. In 7.7 (710d–e), the question concerns whether or not flute-girls are appropriate after-dinner entertainment. For some ancient diners, the arrival of such entertainers was upsetting. But Plutarch does not support such a response. To defend his position, he recognizes that even Plato introduced a comedic speech of Aristophanes into his *Symposium*, and then asks the following question: ". . . are we to expel such pleasant entertainments from our dinners (συμποσίων), or retreat from them as though from the approach of Sirens? Cleitomachus the athlete was indeed admired for getting up and leaving a party if anyone mentioned sex; but is not a philosopher ridiculous if he runs from a party to escape a flute, or calls for his shoes and shouts to his boy to light the lantern when he hears a harp-girl tuning up? Is he to loathe the most innocent pleasures, as a dung-beetle loathes perfume?"

without ceasing? Must it be until I leave the symposium and go home, unable to stomach your words?" Later, Ulpian continues his assault on Cynulcus. After Cynulcus has indicated his desire to eat, Ulpian quotes a hexameter verse, responding, "'Full of greens is the market place, full of bread too.' But you, Cynic, are always famishing, and won't allow us to partake of good and ample discourse . . ." (6.270c) Cynulcus responds:

> If I had been invited to a feast of words (ἀκροάσεις λόγων) merely, I should have known enough to arrive at the hour of full market . . ., but if we have bathed only to come to a dinner of cheap talk, then, to quote Menander, 'I pay a contribution too high for the privilege of listening.' Wherefore, greedy, I yield to you the right to sate yourself on that kind of food . . ." [25]

After one last quip, Athenaeus adds, "With these words he made as if to get up to depart . . ." He decided to stay only when he saw huge platters of fish and other delicacies being brought into the room. The friendly character of the table is only barely preserved from a rude departure.[26]

Two other examples parallel Judas' exit somewhat more closely. First, in Xenophon's *Symposium*, a Syracusan is hired to entertain the symposiasts, and he resents that Socrates' conversation distracts attention from his dancers and gymnasts (6.6). He badgers and heckles Socrates as Socrates speaks, therefore, and offends the friendly feeling of the table. But his departure near the end of the party has the same effect as Judas' departure. Only after he leaves does Socrates offer his speech on love (8.1ff.).

A similarly disruptive guest leaves early from the table in Plutarch's *Dinner of the Seven Wise Men*. The character Alexidemus of Miletus encounters the other diners on their way to the table. He is agitated because he has been urged by his host Periander to dine, even though he preferred not to, and then has been placed in an ignominious place. He leaves in anger (149b). But not long after he departs, the guests begin to dine in friendly concord, delighted that their unpleas-

---

[25] Cynulcus here regrets that he has come to a "dinner of cheap talk," and that, instead of filling himself on the eating of food, he is burdened with the hearing of words. This alternation between food and speech will be important below.

[26] In Petronius' *Cena Trimalchionis*, 67.1ff., the guest Habinnas inquires why Trimalchio's wife does not dine with the guests at her husband's party. When he hears that she is busy tending to the slaves, he threatens to depart, miffed over her failure to appear before the guests.

ant companion is no longer in their midst.[27] The departure of the
cantankerous Alexidemus creates the kind of concord that Plutarch
believes should accompany the dinners of wise men. Thus, the exit
of an offensive figure is met in Xenophon with a speech on love,
and in Plutarch with a model scene of friendly interaction. Likewise,
only after Judas leaves in 13:30 does Jesus begin his intimate discourses to his disciples in 13:31, including the new commandment
in 13:34.

Emphasizing the structural significance of Judas' departure returns
attention to the discussion from chapter 1 of this study, where the
dramatic character of Judas' exit coincided with ancient dramatic
exits, especially where servants are ordered offstage (1) in order to
prepare for future turns in the plot and (2) in order to remove a
character whose presence interrupts the interaction of the other characters. This second aspect of the dramatic exit dovetails neatly with
the sympotic device surveyed here. Judas' exit prepares the way for
Jesus' conversations on love with his disciples. Sending Judas away
makes room for the intimacy of after-dinner conversation. John makes
this connection between Judas' departure and Jesus' speech explicit:
"When he had gone out, Jesus said . . ." (13:31). The connection
between Judas' departure and the commencement of Jesus' discourses
has been obscured by redaction theories that see the phrase "When
he had gone out" as a redactional link between two unrelated units.[28]
Dramatic and sympotic evidence, however, suggests a closer association between the exit and the discourses.

Martin, then, is correct to see Judas as an unfriendly guest whose
early departure introduces a more convivial spirit to a dinner, but

---

[27] After inspecting entrails that predict ill fortune, Thales ironically claims that
they need not worry, because they have already suffered the poor fortune of
Alexidemus' departure, indicating how little Alexidemus' presence, and how much
his departure, was appreciated by the fellow guests, 149c–f. See also Martin, *Symposion*,
315–16.

[28] For the structural significance of Judas' departure, see Moloney, *Glory not
Dishonor*, 23–4: "The author links Jesus' proclamation in vv. 31–32 with Judas'
departure: "when he went out" . . . This connection is generally ignored by commentators who read vv. 31–32 as the opening statement of the first discourse
(13:31–14:31) . . . As earlier the arrival of the Greeks led to Jesus' first announcement that the hour had come for the Son of Man to be glorified (see 12:20–33),
so now it is *because* Judas has been taken over by Satan after receiving the morsel,
in a radical rejection of the love of God revealed in and through Jesus' gift of the
morsel, that actions are in motion that will lead to Jesus' being lifted up
(v. 31a) . . . Judas' exit sets in motion the events promised by Jesus in vv. 18–20 . . ."

some qualification is in order. For, Judas departs from the scene not as a disaffected guest but as the betrayer of Jesus who leaves in order to accomplish his betrayal. Martin's designation of Judas as "Der Gekränkte" is, then, only partly accurate. Like other symposiasts, Judas departs early so that the friendly atmosphere can continue without him impeding it. But, more in keeping with the treachery of Circe and the stories in Josephus, Judas is a betrayer, not an unhappy guest. So the departure is motivated by reasons very different from those of the texts that Martin furnishes.[29] John's depiction of Judas is, rather, a combination of the trope "Der Gekränkte geht" and the trope of betrayal and intrigue in the supper.

And so, the first portion of the present chapter culminates in the exit of Judas. Focusing on this exit has stirred certain sympotic ingredients to the surface. Other connections are possible, but need not distract from the present argument.[30] Judas' exit is structurally very significant for John 13–17. Discovering how this is so, and why this matters, will expand the sympotic associations of the Johannine Last Supper scene.

---

[29] Bultmann notes this fact as well, *Gospel of John*, 483.

[30] Additional points can be made about the sympotic associations of the Farewell Discourses. For Martin, John's dinner concludes in a way reminiscent of sympotic scenes, *Symposion*, 316–17. When Jesus is finished speaking at the close of chapter 17, he and his disciples exit to the Kidron valley (18:1). Symposia often disband when the assembled guests take an after-dinner stroll, a peripatos, ibid., 147, 211; cf. Xenophon, *Symposium*, 9.7. The event at the start of the supper, the footwashing, is unique among the canonical Gospels, and also carries sympotic undertones. For a review of relevant texts, see John Christopher Thomas, *Footwashing in John 13 and the Johannine Community* (JSNTS 61; Sheffield: Sheffield Academic Press, 1991) 47–50. Plutarch, for instance, tells the story of a victorious athlete who attended a banquet where each guest was offered a foot basin of spiced wine upon entering the party. Similar events occur in several sympotic scenes. For footwashing as an act of hospitality in a variety of ancient settings, see ibid., 26–58. But the act generally receives minor attention, while for John the footwashing is an episode of immense theological import, Brown, *Gospel of John*, 2. 558–59. John's highly original presentation elevates an otherwise minor, though consistent, element of the symposium. Relihan, "Rethinking," 241, sees a further connection with the larger world of the literary symposia in that Jesus, like the enigmatic Socrates, speaks, "over the heads of the listeners . . ." Dennis Smith, *Symposium to Eucharist*, 222, adds the following parallels as well: the diners appear to lie down at the table (v. 23); they sit in a ranked order (v. 23); there is a discourse on a given topic (chaps 14–16); and the meal closes with a hymn (chap. 17). Cf. Coloe, "Welcome," 413. All of these features increase the sympotic feel of the Farewell Discourses, but discussing them in detail is not necessary here.

The Feast of Words

In literary symposia, the rough outline of the meal's development follows the basic progress of the symposium as a social phenomenon.[31] This is true for writers from Plato (c. 427–347 BC) to Athenaeus (fl. c. AD 200). In symposia, basically, people sit together in a set sequence of two parts. First, there is a meal, the deipnon. When the deipnon ends, the symposium begins. As its name implies, the symposium is at its core a party of communal drinking (σύν + πόσις). To mark the shift from the deipnon to the symposium proper, a number of things might occur. For instance, Athenaeus' *Deipnosophistae* contains a quotation of Xenophanes describing the ideal banquet, as well as the ideal way to transition from deipnon to symposium:[32]

> Now at last the floor is swept, and clean are the hands of all the guests, and their cups as well; one slave puts plaited wreaths on their heads, another offers sweet-smelling perfume in a saucer; the mixing bowl stands full of good cheer . . . (11.462c).

When the symposium commences, the evening's entertainment also begins, and this can include anything from dancers, gymnasts or musicians to poets and dramatic readings.[33] Or, the assembled guests might entertain one another with philosophical or clever conversation. As will be discussed later, philosophical conversation was the preferred form of entertainment in Plato's *Symposium*, as well as for authors writing under Plato's influence.

According to this formula, John's Last Supper scene is roughly modeled on the symposium format. It is a deipnon followed by a communal gathering. While the separation between the deipnon and the symposium is not marked in John in the same way that it is in standard literary symposia, it is clearly marked – by the departure of Judas at 13:31. Judas' exit distinctly separates the dinner and the conversation after the dinner. Until Judas goes from the scene, all

---

[31] For a nice summary of the Greek symposium as a social phenomenon, see F. Lissarrague, *The Aesthetics of the Greek Banquet: Images of Wine and Ritual* (trans. Andrew Szegedy-Maszak; Princeton: Princeton University Press, 1990), and Aune, "Septem," 70ff.

[32] Cf. Lissarague, *Aesthetics*, 26–27. A similar bridge occurs in Plato's *Symposium*: "Once [Socrates] and everyone else had finished eating, they performed all the traditional rites – the libations, the hymns to Zeus, and so on – and then they turned to drinking" (176a).

[33] For sympotic activity in general, see Lissarague, *Aesthetics*.

of the activity operates around the meal. Jesus rises from and returns to the deipnon (13:4; 12a) to wash the disciples' feet. After explaining the nature of the footwashing a second time (13:12b–17), Jesus predicts his betrayal, which returns attention to the meal, because food is the vehicle for identifying the betrayer (13:26a). Then, once Jesus has given Judas the morsel (13:26b), Satan enters into Judas. In 13:30, Judas accepts the morsel and departs. The meal, then, has been the center of attention until 13:30. The next line turns attention away from the meal: "Therefore, when he had departed, Jesus said . . ." And what Jesus begins to say at 13:31, he continues saying until the end of chapter 17, over four chapters later. Attention never returns to the meal setting. From 13:31 onward, the conversation, speeches and prayer of Jesus occupy the narrative. Judas' departure, then, is a major structural limit between the deipnon and the discourses. As was noted above, Judas must leave, because he is not one of the intimates. Judas may have participated in the banquet of food, but he cannot participate in the subsequent banquet of words. Clarifying the classical context of the banquet of words will help better to understand John's particular sympotic style.

This phrase "banquet of words" is a translation of the term λογόδειπνον from the opening lines of Athenaeus' *Deipnosophistae*. More precisely, it is a term found in the Epitomator's comments that open the *Deipnosophistae*. The *Deipnosophistae* does not survive intact and, even in the oldest manuscript, much of the text is represented solely by the summary comments of the book's Epitomator.[34] To start the work, the Epitomator offers a summary of the contents of the entire text. This epitome concludes with the following notice (1.1): "The wonderful Athenaeus, the manager of the discourse, offers the sweetest banquet of words (ἥδιστον λογόδειπνον)."[35] The Epitomator's comments, of course, are no more authoritative than those of any other reader of the text, and cannot be given too much control over interpretation. But at least one recent commentator has seen in these remarks a clue to the overall flow and plan of the book. This is a novel effort, since to see in Athenaeus a structure at all is a some-

---

[34] For the state of the text of Athenaeus, see Karl Mengis, *Die schriftstellenische Technik im Sophistenmahl des Athenaios* (Paderborn: F. Schöningh, 1920).

[35] This translation is a combination of the Loeb translation of Gulick and the translation of Luciana Romeri (trans. by Kerensa Pearson), "The λογόδειπνον: Athenaeus Between Banquet and Anti-banquet," in *Athenaeus and His World*, 257.

what under-appreciated enterprise. Very often, Athenaeus is mined more than he is read.[36] Because the *Deipnosophistae* refers to numerous authors, texts and social realities mentioned nowhere else in ancient literature, the work is treated as nothing more than a haphazard collection of conversations and episodes among a group of diners on one particular evening. The conversation is often vicarious, with each speech being in reality the quotation or paraphrase of other peoples' words. There seems to be no conclusion to which the text is directed. It is thought to have no center or literary plan.[37]

A more sophisticated plan arguably comes to the surface, however, when one enters the text through the Epitomator's term logodeipnon. The word implies an intimate connection between the banquet and the speeches that attend the banquet, between the logos and the deipnon. There is a harmonious interaction between the dishes served to the guests and the speeches that the guests deliver.[38] The cuisine and the speeches feed off of one another. Many times, when a new course is introduced, the guests break off into elaborate and learned discussion on that dish. They meet a serving of fish with a quotation from a venerable authority about fish, and the introduction of eggs with another quotation from another authority, etc.[39]

---

[36] Ibid., 256.

[37] The following excerpt demonstrates admirably why this opinion persists. After several pages of discussion on citrus fruit, the following transitional passage intervenes (3.85c–d):

> When Democritus had ended these remarks, most of the company expressed their wonder at the effects of the [citrus fruit], and ate it up as though they had not touched any food or drink before. Pamphilus, in the *Dialect Dictionary*, says that the Romans call it *citrus*. Following the dishes just described, there were brought in for us separately plates of oysters in quantity, as well as other testaceous foods. Most of them, practically, I find have been thought worthy of mention by Epicharmus in the Marriage of Hebe: 'He brings all sorts of shell-fish – limpets, lobsters . . .'

And so it continues even further.

[38] Ibid., 257ff.

[39] The summary of the first book contains the following description of one guest's behavior (1.4a5–b7):

> Clearchus says that Charmus of Syracuse met each new dish served at the meal with a proverbial quotation from Homer, Euripides or another ancient literary great. Thus, for fish: 'I come, having left the salty depths of the Aegean' [Euripides *Troaedes* 1]. For shellfish: 'Hail, whelks, the messengers of Zeus' [*Iliad* 1.334]. For intestines:'Twisting and in no way healthy' . . . [Euripides *Andromache* 448]. Ibid., 260.

"To each dish belongs its corresponding literary offering which, ultimately, only scholarly gourmets or gourmet scholars can truly
grasp . . . The food engenders the guests' conversation."[40] Conversely,
conversation about a certain animal or delicacy can inspire the introduction of the next course.[41] Sometimes, then, the discussion invites
a delicacy, and sometimes, the introduction of a certain delicacy
leads to a new turn in the conversation. Romeri writes,

> Food and erudition are, then, indissociably linked in the representa-
> tion of the deipnosophists: the former engenders the latter and recip-
> rocally the latter makes the former appear. The Deipnosophists always
> operate in both directions, as if their character (and their pleasure) as
> gourmets were not incompatible with their character (and their plea-
> sure) as scholars; or even better, as if their true pleasure were only in
> this union of understanding.[42]

Rather than being a disjointed collection of exotic foods and pedan-
tic conversation, the *Deipnosophistae* is oriented around the symphonic
interaction between dining and discourse. Hence, the Epitomator's
term logodeipnon is not to be ignored as a worthless comment by
a later reader. The term provides a nice summary of the connection between speech and feast in the *Deipnosophistae*.[43]

Such happy harmony between logos and deipnon is not shared
by all literary symposia. In other surviving texts, in fact, emphasis
falls either to the conversation shared by the guests, or to the food
consumed. To explain the nature of this dichotomy, it will be help-

---

[40] Ibid., 261.
[41] Ibid., 262. At 9.398b–c, the host Larensis speaks at length about an exotic
bird, the Asian sandgrouse. Even while he continues speaking, a sandgrouse is introduced for the admiration of the guests, but then removed to be prepared for a
later course in the meal, Ibid., 261.
[42] Ibid., 262.
[43] This point is made as well by Lukinovich, who laments that Martin (*Symposion*,
chapter 3) too sharply separates Athenaeus' work from non-sympotic deipna. The
Deipnosophistae spans the two literary forms. "In making this distinction, Martin does
an injustice to Athenaeus' work by annulling the precise feature which lends it originality: the fusion of *deipnon* and *symposion*." See Alessandra Lukinovich, "The Play
of Reflections between Literary Form and the Sympotic Theme in the *Deipnosophistae*
of Athenaeus," in *Sympotica: A Symposium on the Symposion* (ed. O. Murray; Oxford:
Oxford University Press, 1990) 263–4. The connection between dining and conversation are obvious, since the same mouth is responsible for both eating and
speaking. For a literary and cultural analysis of Renaissance banquets that capital-
izes on the connection between dining and discourse, see Michel Jeanneret, *A Feast
of Words: Banquets and Table-Talk in the Renaissance* (transl. Jeremy Whitely and Emma
Hughes; Cambridge: Polity, 1991).

ful to look to Plato. For, although the term logodeipnon comes from
Athenaeus' Epitomator, the concept of "a feast of words" is Platonic.

Several of Plato's dialogues make reference to the banquet of
words, even as Socrates and his interlocutors recline at the table.[44]
In the *Phaedrus*, there is the expression: "Lysias offered you a banquet of speeches."[45] Later, in the same text, the speeches between
Socrates and Phaedrus are referred to as "such a banquet."[46] In the
Republic, when Socrates urges the further exploration of a given topic
of conversation, he employs the image of the banquet: ". . . complete
for me the remains of the banquet."[47] Not far after this point, Socrates'
own speeches are referred to as a lexical meal in the repeated use
of the verb ἑστιάομαι.[48] In the opening lines of the *Timaeus*, Socrates
alludes to both the banquet that occupied the guests the day before,
and the one that they presently attend (17a–b). Finally, before the
beginning of Timaeus' speech, Socrates asks for a banquet of words
from Timaeus that will repay Socrates for the speech he himself had
offered on the previous day (27b):

> Bounteous and magnificent . . . is the feast of speech (τὴν τῶν λόγων
> ἑστίασιν) with which I am to be requited. So then, Timaeus, it will
> be your task, it seems, to speak next, when you have duly invoked the
> gods.

The concept of the banquet of words, then, originates with Plato,
and is taken up in Athenaeus. But the concept functions very differently
in the two authors. For Plato, the logodeipnon is not a union of the
logos and the deipnon, but a deipnon exclusively of logoi. The food
recedes into the background for Plato, and the diners feast not on
exotic birds like the Asian sandgrouse, but on one another's conversation. "Everything then happens as if, with Plato, the only possible banquet for good men was the banquet of words . . ."[49]

Indeed, the one text in the Platonic corpus specifically named after
a dinner party, the *Symposium*, has only the most cursory of references

---

[44] The discussion follows Romeri, "λογόδειπνον," 263–4, whence come the translations of classical texts employed in this paragraph.

[45] Λόγων ὑμᾶς Λυσίας εἱστία (227 b7).

[46] Τοιαύτη θοίνη (236 e8).

[47] Τὰ λοιπὰ μοι τῆς ἑστιάσεως ἀποπλήρωσον (1.352 b5–6).

[48] 1.354 a10–b3.

[49] Romeri, "λογόδειπνον," 263. In suppressing the normally raucous activities of
the symposium as a social ritual, Plato's *Symposium* is very unsympotic. For more
on this common insight, see Relihan, "Rethinking," 214–224.

to any food consumption.[50] Early on, the reader is told: "They then started dinner" (175c). Later, when Socrates has finally arrived, we see the notice:

> So Socrates lay down on the couch. Once he and everyone else had finished eating, they performed all the traditional rites – the libations, the hymns to Zeus and so on – and then they turned to drinking" (176a).

No attention is paid whatsoever to what was eaten, and nothing was said while eating. The meal quickly recedes into irrelevance. Xenophon's *Symposium* operates in very much the same mode. Socrates, who is the main character in the work, does not make conversation until the meal is concluded, as though the evening only really begins when he begins to speak. Those guests who do attend the meal eat in virtual silence (1.11), and the elaborate speeches that dominate the work begin only after the meal is concluded (Cf. 2.1). Plato and Xenophon, then, seem to reduce the meal portion of the sympotic feast to a position of less importance than the discussion that follows the meal.[51]

Not only does the disposition of the logodeipnon diminish the interest in the consumption of food in the deipnon, this same disposition also intrudes on the post-dinner revelry. While any number of excitements could pass the time in a symposium, more philosophical people would entertain themselves with learned conversation. This tradition begins with Plato's *Symposium*, where the following statement begins the entertainment part of the evening (176e):

> I [Erixymachus] next propose that the flute-girl who came in just now be dismissed . . . Let us seek our entertainment today in conversation.

For Plutarch, as well, the physical enjoyments of the table are mutually exclusive of the philosophical exchanges of good people. In a lengthy speech of Solon in *Dinner of the Seven Wise Men* (159d 4–9), the following model of behavior is established for the table:

---

[50] Romeri, "λογόδειπνον," 263.

[51] For the sake of balance, however, it needs to be emphasized that Xenophon's *Symposium* gives much more attention to entertainment and physical realities than the work of Plato. Xenophon permits in his *Symposium* features of the classical symposium that Plato excluded, i.e., dancers and more bawdy entertainment. "[In Xenophon's work, Socrates] is present at a symposium that is concerned with bodies much more than minds," Relihan, "Rethinking," 224. The present concern, however, is to demonstrate that the meal is marginal in Xenophon, as it is in Plato, regardless of after-dinner entertainment.

We, for example, just now did not look at each other or listen to each other. Each of us had his head down and was the slave of the need to eat. Now by contrast, the tables have been removed and we are free. As you see, we are garlanded and devote ourselves to conversation. We are in each other's company and we have plenty of time because we have reached the point where we are no longer hungry.

For Plutarch's Solon, food – deipnon – and philosophical discussion – logos – are mutually exclusive of one another. The guests at the table eat first, and only afterwards enjoy discussion. Where Athenaeus merges the logos and the deipnon, Plutarch maintains their separation and distinction. Only when the meal is over are the guests no longer focused on their food and themselves, but are joined to one another through discussion on a philosophical topic.

The distinction between the logos and the deipnon in authors like Plato and Plutarch is not universal. Lucian and Petronius directly oppose and parody the polite Platonic model of sympotic entertainment.[52] In the *Lexiphanes*, Lexiphanes presents to Lucian a text he has just written. It is a philosophical "anti-symposium" defined in relation to Plato's *Symposium* with the term ἀντισυμποσιάξω (*Lex.* 1).[53] Lexiphanes achieves his stated intention by detailing to the point of excess the food and drink enjoyed by the guests at his banquet. The following is a telling excerpt (6–8):

> Numerous and varied dishes were prepared: pig's trotters, sides of beef, tripe, the womb of a fertile sow, fried liver . . . Among the fish from the depths of the sea there were many cartilaginous and shelled species, and from those caught in nets slices of fish from the Black Sea and fish from Copais . . . The wine was not old but just out of the store. Certainly it was not yet sweet but still raw . . . So we drank without ever closing our mouths and we were soon overcome. We anointed ourselves with perfume and a dancer and triangle player moved among us.[54]

---

[52] See also Lucian's, *'Symposium,' or 'The Lapiths.'* Satirists often use the setting of a banquet for portrayals of excess and greed. See for instance, R. Bracht Branham, *Unruly Eloquence: Lucian and the Comedy of Traditions* (Cambridge, Mass.: Harvard University Press, 1989) 104–23; Niall Rudd, *The Satires of Horace* (2nd ed.; Berkeley: University of California Press, 1982) 213ff.; L.R. Shero, "The Cena in the Roman Satire," *CP* 18 (1923) 126–43. Cf. Smith, *Symposium to Eucharist*, 62–3, 315 n. 94, 315 n. 101. Relihan demonstrates nicely that Lucian and Petronius achieve their parody of the Platonic model by drawing in part on Platonic characters and themes, only to overturn them, "Rethinking," 226–7, 230–1. For Petronius' connections and allusions to Plato's *Symposium*, see also Edward Courtney, *A Companion to Petronius* (Oxford: Oxford University Press, 2001) 103–4, 109–10, 123, 194.

[53] Romeri, "λογόδειπνον," 268.

[54] Ibid., 268 for translation.

Instead of serving as a prelude to philosophical discussion, the food
and wine are celebrated in and for themselves. The convivial atmosphere does not inspire the exchange of the logos, of philosophical
discourse, but of pointless banter (*Lex.* 14): "After drinking we chat-
ted in our normal way, for it is certainly not out of place to chat
in one's cups." As Romeri notes,

> The pleasure is above all the pleasure of the stomach, a culinary cel-
> ebration which, far from inducing convivial speech-making that is use-
> ful to friendship and following the order of the banquet, generates
> instead noise and confusion, chatter and the mockery of an unbridled
> feast.[55]

The elements of the feast that are marginalized in Plato are celebrated in Lucian. Conversely, the philosophical speech that Plato
and Plutarch prize is peripheral in Lucian.

Petronius' *Cena Trimalchionis* is equally given to excessive indul-
gence, once again with no philosophical profit. The following passage demonstrates Petronius' tendency toward gastric excess in his
writing (49–50):[56]

> He had not finished all his blathering when a dish bearing an enor-
> mous pig took over the table ... Our surprise was all the greater
> because the pig seemed to be far bigger than the boar had been a lit-
> tle earlier. Then Trimalchio looked closer at it, and said, 'What's this?
> Has this pig not been gutted ... The cook got back his shirt, and
> seized a knife. Then with shaking hand he slit the pig's belly on each
> side. At once the slits widened with the pressure of the weight inside,
> and sausages and black puddings came tumbling out. The slaves clapped
> their hands at this trick, and cried in unison: 'Three cheers for Gaius!'
> The cook too was rewarded with a drink and a silver crown; he was
> handed a goblet on a tray of Corinthian ware.

Between Plato and Petronius, then, Athenaeus represents a third way.
His *Deipnosophistae* blends friendly conversation and food consumption. Athenaeus places equal emphasis on these two aspects of the
sympotic experience, and neither aspect is complete without the other.
His meal is equal parts logos and deipnon.

The term logodeipnon is equally apt for Plato's diners, but in a
different sense. For Plato, as well as for those who follow his model,
the true banquet is a banquet of words. The Fourth Gospel stands

---

[55] Ibid., 269.
[56] Petronius, *Satyricon* (transl. P.G. Walsh; Oxford: Oxford University Press, 1997).

in the line of Plato and Plutarch. John 13 is a deipnon, but appears only briefly and presents minimal detail about the dinner.[57] The meal is twice identified as a deipnon (13:2,4) and the meal setting comes to the fore in the betrayal of Judas, since his identity is revealed by his behavior at the table (13:23–30). From that point forward, however, the only banquet until 18:1 is the banquet of words. There is a discussion from 13:31 through 14:31 between Jesus and four disciples explicitly named. This leads into a monologue from chapters 15–16, which later again becomes a dialogue at the end of 16. The scene ends in a prayer with chapter 17. Thus, John's Last Supper at least loosely follows the Platonic recipe for the "banquet of words."

What, though, is the value of assigning this label to the Johannine meal? What new insights arise from reading John 13–17 as a logodeipnon? What, in the end, is the relation between form and function? To answer these questions will require investigating two ancient writers of symposia, Plutarch and Athenaeus. We will look first to Plutarch, and particularly his comments on Plato's *Symposium*.

Van Tilborg has noted that Platonic scholars have labored extensively to relate the content of the *Symposium* of Plato to the form in which it is expressed.[58] He urges Johannine students to find in this research new avenues of inquiry into the Gospel of John.[59] And, indeed, modern Platonic analysis might very well stimulate Johannine

---

[57] This is not to say that the meal is as irrelevant as the meals in testaments. Here, the meal provides the basic setting for the conversation. It provides a structure for the scene. The point being emphasized here is that the actual consumption of food in the meal scene is not the central narrative concern. The point of the meal is to highlight the discourses. But without the meal, there would be no setting for the discourses.

[58] Van Tilborg, *Imaginative Love*, 133.

[59] On the need to attend to the literary shape of the *Symposium*, and not merely its ideas abstracted from any context, Penwill writes, "[Plato] clearly intends the reader to respond to this work not as a philosophical treatise on the subject of Eros but as a work of literature which portrays a group of thinking human beings engaged in appraisal of an issue which is of fundamental importance in their lives," J.L. Penwill, "Men in Love: Aspects of Plato's *Symposium*," *Ramus* 7 (1978) 143. For additional efforts to relate the philosophy of Plato's Dialogues to the form in which they are presented, see Diskin Clay, *Platonic Questions: Dialogues with the Silent Philosopher* (University Park, Pennsylvania: Pennsylvania State University Press, 2000); Charles Kahn, *Plato and the Socratic Dialogue: The Philosophical Use of a Literary Form* (Cambridge: Cambridge University Press, 1996); Dorter, Kenneth. "The Significance of the Speeches in Plato's *Symposium*." *Philosophy and Rhetoric* 4 (1969): 215–234; Henry G. Wolz, "Philosophy as Drama: An Approach to Plato's *Symposium*," *Philosophy and Phenomenological Research* 30 (1970) 323–353.

scholarship. The following argument will rely, however, not on Plato's modern interpreters, but on one of his ancient interpreters, Plutarch (45–125 AD).

When he opens his several books of sympotic conversations, *Table Talks*, Plutarch justifies his literary effort by referring to the several grand old masters whom he follows. After recognizing that some people prefer to forget the goings-on at a symposium, Plutarch insists that (1.612E)

> ... to consign to utter oblivion all that occurs at a drinking-party is not only opposed to what we call the friend-making character of the dining-table, but also has the most famous of the philosophers to bear witness against it, – Plato, Xenophon, Aristotle, Speusippus, Epicurus, Prytanis, Hieronymous, and Dio of the Academy, who all considered the recording of conversations held at table a task worth some effort ... [60]

While this passage begins by referring to "all that occurs" at a symposium, the final emphasis of the passage falls particularly on the need to record the "conversations held at table" (ἀναγράψασθαι λόγους παρὰ πότον γινομένους). This deserves special emphasis, because later in the *Table Talk*, Plutarch adds further that Xenophon and Plato's use of the logodeipnon format makes their symposia more amenable to recollection and preservation. Plutarch's comments about Plato and Xenophon can easily apply as well to the Gospel of John so will be quoted here at length. After again urging the recollection of sympotic conversations, Plutarch praises the symposia written by Plato and Xenophon as follows:

> But a further advantage accrues to Plato's diners, namely the close examination of what was said while they drank. The pleasures of drinking and eating procure servile and faded memories, like the smell of last night or the fumes from roasting flesh. Discussion of philosophical problems and discourse by contrast is always present and fresh and makes those who recall it very happy. It also gives them the chance to offer a banquet just as good to those who were deprived of it. They, when they hear of it, have a part in it also. Hence today all the lovers of words participate and take pleasure from the Socratic banquets, just like the people who dined at that time. Now if bodily things provided pleasure, Xenophon and Plato should have left us a text not of dis-

---

[60] All of these symposia are lost, save those of Plato and Xenophon. This attempt to justify his literary effort by referring to a noted authority appears as well, for instance, in *How to Profit by One's Enemies*, 86c. Cf. S.-T. Teodorsson, *A Commentary on Plutarch's Table Talks* (Göteborg, Sweden: Acta Universitatis Gothoburgensis) 1.35.

courses given, but of dishes, cakes and desserts served by Callias and Agathon.[61] But things like that have never been judged worthy of discourse, even though they were in all probability the result of preparation and expense. In fact, however, in their writing they put serious philosophical questions linked to playful exchanges. They left models of how to be together, one and all, through the conversation at the symposia; and also of how to preserve the memory of the words that were said.[62]

Clearly, this passage is a polemic against the stomach-centered symposium represented by Lucian and Petronius, in favor of the logodeipna of Plato and Xenophon. But the polemic has to do with more than what is appropriate for philosophers at a symposium. By presenting a banquet, not of food, but of words, the discussions of Plato and Xenophon are "always present." This "also gives them the chance to offer a banquet just as good to those who were deprived of it." The later participants, "when they hear of it, have a part in it also. Hence today all the lovers of words participate and take pleasure from the Socratic banquets, just like the people who dined at that time." Plutarch desires to participate in Socrates' banquets centuries after the original events, and the way in which Plato and Xenophon recall the conversations allows him to do so. Socrates is lost, but attending to the writings of Plato and Xenophon recovers his lost presence, or rather puts the reader in the presence of Socrates.[63]

---

[61] Callias and Agathon were the hosts at Xenophon and Plato's symposia, respectively.

[62] *Table Talk*, 6.686b. Translation taken from Romeri, "λογόδειπνον," 270.

[63] This Plutarchan insight that Plato hopes to engage later generations, and not merely to chronicle a past event, accords with contemporary opinion about the form of Plato's dialogues, especially the *Symposium*. On the one hand, Plato strives to offer a realistic fifth-century historical framework for his Socratic dialogues. For example, Plato opens the *Republic* (1.327a) with Socrates announcing that he has just visited the Peiraeus to see the first festival for the new cult of the Thracian goddess Bendis in 430 BC. This places the dialogue in time and space. Other dialogues open with the mention of a particular battle or other monumental event. But, as Clay (23) writes:

> If Plato produces the illusion that his intellectual life remained fixed with Socrates in the fifth century, he also reminds us that his dialogues speak to another age – his own. The other Socratics evoked the memory of Socrates by bringing him into contact with the large and varied cast of his contemporaries. Plato did more. He not only provided his dialogues with recognizable historical settings, he also fashioned frame dialogues for the canvas of his dialogues that belong to another age.

The frame dialogues that appear in *Phaedo*, *Theatetus*, *Parmenides* and *Symposium* represent someone inquiring from a friend to hear of a decades-old conversation. The

Before applying these insights to the Gospel of John, one more
ancient symposium requires attention: the *Deipnosophistae* of Athenaeus.
To prepare to discuss Athenaeus, we must recognize that meals are
the primary vehicle for commemorating the dead in the ancient
Mediterranean. In Greek practices, for instance, several ritual meals
accompanied the burial and commemoration of the dead.[64] The
funerary banquet was a central element in Roman rites surrounding death as well.[65] For this reason, the tombs of the wealthy often
had chambers set aside for the regular celebration of a funerary meal
at the grave of the departed.

Beyond these customs, however, an elaborate association of death
and the banquet pervaded Mediterranean society.[66] Dining and death

---

Symposium opens with the frame to end all frames, in which the original events are
recorded through a series of reported conversations that recede ever further back,
like a set of Russian dolls or Chinese boxes. Apollodorus reports to unnamed friends
the conversations at the victory-party for Agathon. Apollodorus, however, was not
actually at the original party. He heard of it from Aristodemus, who can describe
Socrates' speech, but even Socrates' speech is a report of things that he heard from
Diotima. Plato never erases this character of the *Symposium*, never hides it, and,
indeed, actually emphasizes it with phrases like "he said that he said" (ἔφην φάναι).
We, the readers of Plato's dialogues, then, overhear a group of unnamed people
ask to hear a story told by Apollodorus, who was told by Aristodemus about a
speech delivered by Socrates, who quotes at length the comments of the priestess
Diotima. Cf. Clay, *Platonic Questions*, 23–31 and Halperin, "Erotics of Narrativity."

[64] Robert Garland, *The Greek Way of Death* (Ithaca: Cornell University Press, 1985),
passim. According to the testimony of Artemidorus (ca. 140 AD), the deceased person actually sat as host of the meal, thus reuniting the living with the dead, *Oneirokr.*
5.82. Cf. Garland, *Greek Way of Death*, 39.

[65] In addition to the celebration of a funereal feast (*silicernium*) on the day of a
burial, a meal on the ninth day after burial was also held at the tomb (*cena novien-
dialis*). Various days of the year served as additional opportunities for a feast at the
tomb of the deceased. The birthday of the dead was celebrated each year by a
meal at the gravesite, and, in addition to private observances by family or friends,
a public holiday, the *Parentalia*, in honor of dead family members, was observed by
the same type of meals in honor of the dead. See, for discussion, J.M.C. Toynbee,
Death and Burial in the Roman World (Ithaca, Cornell University Press, 1971) 50ff.,
63–4.

[66] Such commemorative meals, of course, represent only one way in which the
world of the Greek symposium and the Latin *convivium* interacted with the world
of the dead. In these cases, the meal enters the world of the dead. But, the world
of the dead also invaded the dining room. The music, poetry, and art prepared
for the dining table were riddled with references to death. A broad survey of evidence is collected in Grottanelli, "Wine and Death." Skeletons, for instance, appeared
regularly among the diners, either as drawings on cups and kraters, or as life-sized
models. For an exhaustive analysis of skeletons in sympotic decoration as well as
in broader contexts, see K. Dunbabin, "*Sic erimus cuncti* . . . The skeleton in Graeco-
Roman art," *JDAI* 101 (1986) 185–255.

were the opposite poles on a spectrum that measured the vitality of human experience. From the time of Homer onwards, the joys of the symposium were an expression of life; death signaled the absence of these joys.[67] This opposition between death and the delights of the table, however, does not separate the two worlds but, instead, causes them all the more to come together. The association of the two opposite realms is so total that, among the Romans, the term for dining room (*triclinium*) and the related term *triclia* come to be used in funerary inscriptions to refer to the tomb itself.[68]

It is no wonder, then, that commemoration of the dead is an occasion for a banquet. But there is another aspect to the interaction of death and the banquet. Not only did survivors eat memorial meals in honor of the dead, but tomb monuments often depicted the dead eating at a banquet. A prominent Greek example is the group of funerary reliefs that go by the collective name of *Totenmahl* ("death-feast").[69] "The principal compositional features of the series include a man reclining on a *kline* on the right, a table beside him laden with various kinds of food, including cakes, fruit, pomegranates and eggs, and a seated woman on his left."[70] The reliefs first appear in the Greek world at the close of the 6th century BC, and are last seen around 280 BC. Although they cease to be in production well before the rise of Christianity, when they are in production, they are widespread. They can be found throughout the Greek world – in several areas on the mainland, on several islands and in Greek settlements throughout Asia Minor and Italy.[71] The existence of the *Totenmahl* reliefs raises the question of whether or not these images reflect some vision of the afterlife as a perpetual celebration of the symposium.[72] The same question arises with Roman

---

[67] Oswyn Murray, "Death and the Symposium," *AION* (archeol) 10 (1988), 240. Cf. *Odyssey* 9.5ff.

[68] See Dunbabin, *Roman Banquet*, 128, 235 n. 63.

[69] On these reliefs, see Rhea N. Thönges-Stringaris, "Das griechische Totenmahl," *MDAI(A)* 80 (1965) 1–99, and, more recently, Johanna Fabricius. *Die hellenistischen Totenmahlreliefs: Grabrepräsentation und Wertvorstellungen in ostgriechischen Städten* (Studien zur antiken Stadt 3; München: F. Pfeil, 1999).

[70] Garland, *Greek Way of Death*, 70.

[71] Ibid., 70.

[72] Evidence suggesting that they do indicate such a view comes in Socrates' comments in the *Republic* (2.363D), where he mocks Orphic conceptions of the afterlife, in which the benefit of living a just life was "everlasting drunkenness." Ibid., 71. Murray opposes this interpretation in Murray, "Death and the Symposium."

grave decoration that also portrays the dead in a banquet setting.[73] It is not entirely clear what the sympotic monuments were meant to signify, and different people must certainly have intended different things by them. Three interpretations are reasonable. (1) Since by Roman times, it has become a cliché that the dead enjoy the funereal meal at the tomb together with their survivors, the grave monument depicts the dead person enjoying the memorial feast.[74] (2) The banquet represents a beatific vision of the happiness that the dead person enjoys in the afterlife. (3) The banquet evokes the life of the deceased. Since eating and drinking epitomize life, and death represents the absence of such delights, to depict someone in a dining scene is to recover something of the life that has been lost. Oswyn Murray expresses this last opinion in regard to the Greek world, but it can hold for all ancient evidence:

---

[73] See especially K. Dunbabin, *The Roman Banquet: Images of Conviviality* (Cambridge: Cambridge University Press, 2003), especially chapter 4 entitled "Drinking in the Tomb," as well as C. Grottanelli, "Wine and Death – East and West," in *In Vino Veritas* (ed. Oswyn Murray and Manuela Teçusan; London: British School at Rome, et al., 1995) 70–73. A 4th century AD mosaic from Antioch is especially instructive. The mosaic decorates a chamber surrounded by tombs, and within the chamber are stumps of what appear to be benches for dining. Cf. Richard Stillwell, ed. *Antioch-on-the-Orontes II: The Excavations of 1933–1936* (Princeton: Princeton University Press, 1938) Plate 55.76; C. Kondoleon, *Antioch the Lost Ancient City* (Princeton: Princeton University Press, 2000) 121. The central scene of the mosaic is a banquet in which several women sit around or serve at a sumptuous table. This central scene was originally surrounded by a variety of personified figures that recalled chronological and seasonal change. "The funerary banquet was framed by time – seasonal, calendrical and eternal." Ibid., 121. See also, for the significance of the iconography of the site, Doro Levi, *Antioch Mosaic Pavements* (2 vols.; Princeton: Princeton University Press, 1947) 1.291ff.; Sheila Campbell, *The Mosaics of Antioch* (Studia Mediaevallia 15; Toronto: Pontifical Institute of Mediaeval Studies, 1988) 77–78. Further, in the upper right corner of the scene, are two words: MNMO-ΣΥΝΗ (Mnemosyne, Memory) and ΑΙΩΧΙΑ, most probably a misspelling of ΕΥΩΧΙΑ (banquet). If Mnemosyne is a name, then it identifies the woman who owned the tomb. But, if Mnemosyne means "memory", then the pairing of the terms suggests that the room was used by a *collegium* of women for the regular commemoration of the dead at funeral banquets. Kondoleon, *Antioch*, 122. The definitive study of Roman *collegia* is J.P. Waltzing, *Étude historique sur les corporations professionelles chez les Romains depuis les origins jusqu'à la chute de l'Empire d'Occident* (4 vols.; Louvain: Peeters, 1895–1900).

[74] Dunbabin, *Roman Banquet*, 127. As for these three options, Dunbabin writes, "[O]n most examples, we probably draw a false distinction if we ask whether the scene is meant to be read as the banquet at the tomb, as that in the next world, or as one from the deceased's past life. All these senses may be implicit together, or one or another may be emphasized; all are linked by the common idea of the banquet as the ideal metaphor for happy existence," ibid., 132.

> The occasional evidences of the sympotic lifestyle in death . . . are to be explained not as a part of a systematic vision of the afterlife, but as a pale echo of life itself, a symbol perhaps of the status of the dead man, a defiant gesture by an individual protesting against death . . .[75]

To depict a dead person at the table was somehow to protest against his or her death and to recover, in some pale echo, the life that was lost.

James Davidson's recent interpretation of the *Deipnosophistae* sees precisely this effort behind Athenaeus' massive work, and specifically uses Murray's quotation as its starting point.[76] But, in the case of Athenaeus, the monument that protests against death and loss is not made of stone and paint. The monument is the very words in the text of the *Deipnosophistae*. For whose death, however, is the text a verbal grave monument? To answer this question, we will need to recognize that the entire discourse takes place under the shadow of death.[77] From the very beginning, the work evokes a funerary context, by paraphrasing Plato's *Phaedo*. *Phaedo* 57a reads as follows:

> Were you Phaedo, present in person with Socrates on that day on which he drank poison in the prison, or did you hear from someone else?

The *Deipnosophistae* (1.2) alludes to this phrase when it begins as follows, with a brief dialogue:

> Athenaeus, were you yourself present in the splendid gathering of the people now known as Deiposophists, which became the talk of the town? Or was the account you gave of it to your friends derived from someone else?[78]

---

[75] Murray, "Death and the Symposium, 254–5. Dunbabin nuances some of Murray's claims, but then writes in regard to the Roman world, "In the Roman world, the confrontation between death and the symposium (or better, the *convivium*), which Murray defines as an attempt to come to terms with mortality, is undoubtedly still valid; it resulted in powerful and expressive imagery in both art and epigram," *Roman Banquet*, 140.

[76] James Davidson, "Pleasure and Pedantry in Athenaeus," in *Athenaeus and his World: Reading Greek Culture in the Roman Empire* (eds. David Braund and John Wilkins; Exeter: University of Exeter Press, 2000) 294.

[77] Davidson, "Pleasure and Pedantry," 293, writes, "We do not need to read death into the *Deipnosophistae*. It is already clearly present."

[78] The translation of Athenaeus is taken from Michael Trapp, "Plato in the Deipnosophistae," in *Athenaeus and his World: Reading Greek Culture in the Roman Empire* (eds. David Braund and John Wilkins; Exeter: University of Exeter Press, 2000) 353.

Obvious allusion in Greek to the *Phaedo* is limited.[79] But there are several verbal and situational allusions to other Platonic texts, especially the *Symposium*.[80] Thus, the *Deipnosophistae* at its very inception joins the first and model literary symposium, Plato's *Symposium*, with the dialogue in which Socrates dies, the *Phaedo*. Death, then, will play no small role in this sympotic text. But the work not only begins with an allusion to death. It concludes in the same way. As we have already seen at the start of this chapter, the symposium draws to a close soon after the death of Ulpian (15.686b–c), who dies after his final speech in the symposium. And his death is described as a silence: "Not many days after that, as if he himself had had a premonition of the silence that was to be his, he died happily . . ." (15.686c).[81]

---

[79] The relevant texts of the *Phaedo* and the *Deipnosophistae* read as follows, where the opening address is the closest connection between the two texts:

αὐτός, ὦ, Φαίδων, παρεγένου Σωκράτει ἐκείνῃ τῇ ἡμέρᾳ ᾗ τὸ φάρμακον ἔπιεν τῷ δεσμητηρίῳ, ἢ ἄλλου του ἤκουσας (*Phaedo* 57a).

αὐτός, ὦ, Ἀθήναιε, μετειληφὼς τῆς καλῆς ἐκείνης συνουσίας τῶν νῦν ἐπικληθέντων δειπνοσοφιστῶν, ἥτις ἀνὰ τὴν πόλιν πολυθρύλητος ἐγένετο, ἢ παρ' ἄλλου μαθὼν τοῖς ἑταίποις διεξήσεις (*Deipnosophistae* 1.2).

[80] The Epitomator is again here insightful, when he opens the dialogue with the phrase, "Athenaeus imitates Plato in the composition of his dialogue," 1f. Several terms in this brief introductory section correspond to Platonic terms as well, such as, πολυθρύλητος (*Phaedo* 100b; *Republic* 8.566b); συνουσία (*Symposium* 172b, 172c). That the inquiry concerns a dinner party (συνουσία), now well known, and which has been told to others (*Deipnosophistae* 1.2a–b) especially evokes Plato's *Symposium* 172a–c. See Trapp, "Plato," 363–4, 577 n.1ff., who analyzes at length Plato's importance to Athenaeus.

[81] Relihan, "Rethinking," 215, views the preoccupation with death as a definitive characteristic of the literary symposium, and includes the Gospel of John in his comment: "What is crucial to a literary symposium is the anticipated death of its main character." This is only implicit in Plato and Xenophon, where subtle allusions to the death of Socrates can be detected, i.e., Lycon, one of Socrates' principle accusers (Cf. Plato, Apology, 23 E, 36 A), praises him generously near the end of Xenophon's *Symposium* (9.1). Several Platonic dialogues allude much more explicitly to the death of Socrates, though, than the *Symposium*, cf. Clay, *Platonic Questions*, 33–40. Even so, an obvious preoccupation with the coming demise of all of the characters in Plato's *Symposium* deserves notice. See especially Halperin, "Erotics of Narrativity," 100, and John Brentlinger, "The Cycle of Becoming in the *Symposium*," in Suzy Q. Groden (trans.), *The* Symposium *of Plato* (Massachusetts: University of Massachusetts Press, 1970) 2 and passim. As for later symposia, the texts of Petronius and Athenaeus most clearly demonstrate that literary symposia follow the symposium as a social institution in injecting death into the meal setting. For Athenaeus, see, for instance, Davidson, "Pleasure and Pedantry." For Petronius, see William Arrowsmith, "Luxury and Death in the Satyricon," *ARION* 5 (1966) 304–31. For additional texts, see Relihan, "Rethinking, 215–216.

But Ulpian's death, and its attending silence, is symbolic of a larger death, that of the classical Greek past. Perhaps influenced by the concerns of the orators of the Second Sophistic, Athenaeus sought to revive the virtues of classical Greek *paideia* in the Roman Empire.[82] Modern scholars debate whether this nostalgia for the Greek past was a retreat from the oppressive Roman present by Greeks who hoped to set themselves apart, or, rather, an effort by all upper class people, Roman and Greek, to distinguish themselves from their less sophisticated contemporaries.[83] Whatever the case, their nostalgia took the form of an attempt to restore and memorialize the habits, and especially the language, of classical Greece. Athenaeus' text brims with so-called Atticist debates about proper Greek usage.[84] Further antiquarianism appears in the elaborate quotations of the great thinkers and writers of the past, an exercise that Athenaeus takes to the extreme degree.[85]

---

[82] The Second Sophistic, technically speaking, defines the activity of a series of Greek orators who lived from the middle of the 1st century to the middle of the 3rd century AD. Philostratus' *Lives of the Sophists* honors these orators and gives them their name. The movement is defined by an overarching interest in the culture and language of classical Athens, and was so influential that figures other than Philostratus' orators reflect the movement's preoccupations. It is in this sense that the label is used here, to indicate that Athenaeus reflects the basic concerns of the Second Sophistic, as do other prose authors. For more on Athenaeus' nostalgic interest in the Greek past, see Laura K. McClure, *Courtesans at Table: Gender and Greek Literary Culture in Athenaeus* (New York: Routledge, 2003).

[83] For the opinion that the effort was largely ethnic, see E.L. Bowie, "Greeks and their Past in the Second Sophistic," in *Studies in Ancient Society* (ed. M.I. Finley; Boston: Routledge, 1974) 166–209; repr. from *Past and Present* 46 (1970) 3–41 and Simon Swain, *Hellenism and Empire: language, classicism and power in the Greek world AD 50–250* (Oxford: Clarendon Press, 1996), especially pp. 17–63. For one representative of the opinion that this nostalgia was not as ethnic as it was just generally elitist, see McClure, *Courtesans*, 27ff.

[84] "Athenaeus is using his text to revivify dead words and lost usages." Recall the example cited earlier in the chapter, where Ulpian almost leaves the symposium because the Latin term *decocta* is used in asking for boiled wine (3.121e–122a). Ulpian responds to Cynulcus' request, with the rebuke (6.270b): "How long are you going to utter barbarisms without ceasing?" Cf. Davidson, "Pleasure and Pedantry," 295. As one example of trends related to Second Sophistic obsession with language, Lucian humorously presents the attempt to recover purer Greek in his *Judgement of the Vowels*, which is a debate between the latters Tau and Sigma. The use of the double Tau was an Attic means for expressing the Ionic double Sigma. Koine Greek lost entirely the double Tau, opting for the double Sigma exclusively. The Atticists, of course, revive the double Tau, which is the background of Lucian's courtroom drama.

[85] For the kind of antiquarianism reflected in writers of the time, note that the traveler Pausanias mentions almost no monuments later than 150 BC in his *Description*

Thus, nostalgia inspired Athenaeus' elaborate symposium, which is a memorial to a time when such symposia were common. In the last few books of the work, this nostalgia is most obvious, where the perspective turns back to a time when Hellenic symposia abounded: "Rhapsodes were not missing from our symposia . . . and those called hilarodes often performed for us" (14.620b). Therefore, as the book draws to a close, Ulpian's death comes to represent not only the conclusion of the work, but the end of such discourses as well. In this way, Athenaeus' sympotic monument memorializes the Greek past, and provides a textual grave relief that protests against the loss of a culture in which such symposia were commonplace.

Davidson's interpretation of Athenaeus is somewhat speculative.[86] But, at a certain level of abstraction, it is suggestive for the Gospel of John. Most especially, Davidson provides an interesting link between a written text and the broader social realities in which the dead are memorialized and commemorated in banquets, whether actual or artistic. If Davidson is right, then a sympotic text is just as much a protest against the death of someone, or something, as a sympotic grave monument. That John's Gospel presents Jesus in a sympotic scene suggests that the Gospel could operate in the same way, using this scene to commemorate Jesus, and thereby recover some pale echo of his earthly existence. Further, Davidson remarks in regard to the death of Ulpian, "His death is described as a falling

---

of Greece. Cf. Bowie, "Greeks and Their Past," 22. As for the desire to quote venerable authorities, McClure writes, "Nowhere is this process more evident than in the text of Athenaeus, which overwhelms the reader with hundreds of disembodied quotations from the Greek literary tradition," *Courtesans,* 28. Almost any page of the *Deipnosophistae* reads like the response of the diner Plutarch to Ulpian's request to know what ancient author speaks of "the fatted goose," (ὁ σιτευτὸς χήν). Plutarch responds to the question as follows:

> Theopompus of Chios, in his *History of Greece,* and in the thirteenth book of his *History of Philip,* said that when Agesilaus of Lacedaemon arrived in Egypt, the Egyptians sent him fatted geese and calves. And the comic poet Epigenes says in *The Bacchae*: 'But supposing that someone took and stuffed him up for me like a fatted goose.' And Archestratus in his famous poem: 'And dress the fatted young of a goose with it, roasting that also simply' (9.384a).

[86] In the first place, he may make too much of the association with the *Phaedo.* Cf. Trapp, "Plato in the Deipnosophistae," 354–55 and 577 n. 7. Second, many contemporary writers indulge in this nostalgic attempt to recover the Greek past. That Athenaeus chose to do so in a sympotic scene may very well be incidental and irrelevant, and may not be based on cultural assumptions about memorial meals and death.

silent . . ., so how appropriate to commemorate him in a discourse."[87] The same can be very understandably applied to Jesus, where one might say, somewhat differently, because he is The Word, how appropriate to commemorate him in a feast of words.

But this is precisely where the similarities cease. For, the *Deipnosophistae* is as much concerned with food, and the other physical delights of the table, as it is with discourses. Athenaeus commemorates both logos and deipnon. But, the Johannine logodeipnon seems quite distant from this form of commemoration. The eating and drinking found on grave decorations, in funereal meals and in Athenaeus is precisely the thing that the Fourth Gospel avoids.[88] For Plutarch, Socrates is not accessible to future generations who want to share his bread and wine. Quite the opposite, it is Socrates' philosophical discourse that later pupils are able to share and enjoy. Not Socrates the diner, but Socrates the teacher is always available to those who want to learn from him. Thus, this interpretation of Athenaeus provides a suggestive way to interact with the broader cultural assumptions about the interaction between death and the banquet. But, it also does not address the specific evidence of the Gospel of John.

The quotation of Plutarch cited earlier provides a much more likely expression of what we have in the Gospel of John. And so it is appropriate to wonder, If John uses the same form that Plutarch praises in Plato, might John also intend the same function that Plutarch sees? Jesus' own comments in the Farewell Discourses suggest that this might be so. The remainder of the chapter will review the relevant evidence in John 13–17.

---

[87] Davidson, "Pleasure and Pedantry," 294.

[88] By stressing that John does not concern himself with the deipnon part of the symposium, I do not mean to draw attention to the removal as well of the institution of the Eucharist from the Last Supper, in contrast to the Synoptic and Pauline presentations of Jesus' final meal with his disciples. It is beyond the scope of the present inquiry to determine precisely why John has transposed the Eucharistic passage to chapter 6, but this study is less concerned with what the Fourth Gospel has removed from the supper, and more concerned with what it has included: various sympotic characteristics. For a review of the relevant issues in regard to the Sacraments in the Fourth Gospel, see Brown, *Gospel of John*, 1.CXI, 281ff.; 2.573ff. It bears mentioning here, however, that scholars have endeavored to connect the Synoptic and Pauline presentations of Jesus' institution of the Eucharist to ancient commemorative meals of many different types. See especially H.-J. Klauck, *Herrenmahl und Hellenistischer Kult: Eine religiongeschichtliche Untersuchung zum ersten Korintherbrief* (Aschendorff: Münster, 1982).

"I Did Not Say These Things . . ."

The entire Fourth Gospel is a story about the past written for the benefit of later believers.[89] The comment at 20:29 – "Blessed are those who have not seen and yet have come to believe" – emphasizes that the Gospel intends not merely to record the past, but to influence future generations. This same concern is prominent in the Farewell Discourses.

Jesus' admonition at 16:4b insists that the sole purpose of his entire set of discourses is to allow his followers to hear his voice when they can no longer see his countenance. Jesus says, "I did not say these things to you from the beginning because I was with you. But now I am going to him who sent me . . ." (16:4b) Where Plutarch claims that Socrates' dinner conversations are a feast for later generations not originally present with Socrates, Jesus similarly insists that his words from the Last Supper are spoken for a time when he is no longer present. Preserved as they are in a logodeipnon, later generations can share in the feast long after Jesus departs. "I did not say these things (ταῦτα) to you from the beginning because I was with you. But now I am going to him who sent me . . ." Indeed, with this comment, Jesus is already partially being displaced by his words. His earthly presence in his *flesh* is already becoming a presence in his *words*, ταῦτα.

Determining the precise content of the ταῦτα in this verse has generated some controversy.[90] Do "these things" refer solely to the

---

[89] Margaret Daly-Denton, *David in the Fourth Gospel: The Johannine Reception of the Psalms* (Leiden: Brill, 2000) 119. Daly-Denton connects the role of memory in 2:22 to an interest in preserving the words of the Gospel for those mentioned in 20:29.

[90] The term ταῦτα appears in 16:1, 4a, where Jesus discusses persecution, but also appears later in 16:6, where Jesus discusses his impending departure: "But because I have said these things (ταῦτα) to you, sorrow has filled your hearts. Nevertheless, I tell you the truth: it is to your advantage that I go away . . ." (16:6–7). Do "these things," then, resume the earlier use of the term in 16:1,4a, or look forward to the later usage in 16:6. To Brown, 16:4b should be understood with what comes before it. The dominant theme of 15:18–16:4a is the hatred of the world toward the followers of Jesus. The description of hatred comes to a head in 16:1ff., where the disciples are told that they will be thrown out of the synagogue. In 16:1 and 16:4a, Jesus refers to the message about persecution as "these things" (ταῦτα). Therefore, when he repeats ταῦτα again in 16:4b, Brown assumes that he again refers solely to the themes of persecution. For Brown, the fact that Jesus uses the phrase "from the beginning" in a persecution context in 15:27 suggests that the same concern is at issue in 16:4 when he uses the same phrase. Thus, Jesus did not tell the disciples about persecution "from the beginning," i.e., at the start of

predictions about persecution in 15:18–16:4a, or solely to the mention of Jesus' departure in 16:5? Poised directly between the two sections, ταῦτα could point either forward or backward, to one theme or the other. This suggests that "these things" refer not to one or the other, but to both. Even further, and perhaps more correctly, Moloney and Segovia view "these things" as a reference to the entire set of discourses.[91] Thus, when Jesus says, "I would have said these things to you from the beginning, but I was with you," he is defining the place of the Farewell Discourses in the wake of his departure. While he is present, there is no need for him to say ταῦτα. The words are necessary for a time when Jesus is no longer with his followers. As is true of the philosopher Nigrinus or the Apostle Paul (see chapter 3), Jesus' presence is valuable to his disciples and his absence is distressing. The disciples need their teacher and Lord. The Paraclete softens this distress, making Jesus present even in his absence. The banquet of words accomplishes the same thing, rendering Jesus present. Or, somewhat differently but more accurately, the banquet of words invites Jesus' later disciples into *his* presence, drawing them into the feast of words that Jesus shared with his original followers on the night before his death. The Johannine logodeipnon, therefore, functions somewhat analogously to a philosopher's instructional letter to his pupils, bridging the gap between

---

his earthly ministry, because he did not want to frighten them prematurely ("ἐξ ἀρχῆς" appears as well in 6:64 and 15:27, and refers to beginning of the earthly ministry.). "Perhaps the idea is that as long as he was with them, all persecution was directed against him. Only when he departs is there a problem for his disciples, who will become the chief spokesmen of the word of God." Ibid., 2.704. For the same opinion, see also Schnackenburg, *Gospel of John*, 3.126. But this reading is confusing in light of the traditional manner in which commentators separate the different sections of the Farewell Discourses. Almost all commentators divide the first several verses in chapter 16, so that 16:4a closes the previous section and 16:4b opens a new section (cf. Segovia, *Farewell*, 174–178 for a review of the options in dividing this section). 16:4b, then, is better understood in light of what comes after it, not what comes before it. This fact makes it all the more puzzling that Brown reads the ταῦτα in connection solely to the ταῦτα of 16:1,4a. Such a reading, as noted above, confines Jesus' comments to the need to explain persecution as a result of his impending departure, and ignores the possibility that the disciples are distressed at the departure of Jesus *per se*. It also ignores the fact that ταῦτα appears not only in 16:1 and 4, but also in 16:6. And in 16:6, ταῦτα refers not to persecution, but to the general anguish surrounding Jesus' departure: "But because I have said these things (ταῦτα) to you, sorrow has filled your hearts. Nevertheless, I tell you the truth: it is to your advantage that I go away . . ." (16:6–7).

[91] Segovia, *Farewell*, 225; Moloney, *Glory*, 77–78.

teacher and student.[92] The logodeipnon draws the disciples into Jesus'
feast, just as Plato's logodeipnon draws later devotees of Socrates
into his feast.

Furthermore, an intense interest in the later life of the Johannine
community shines through the entire set of discourses. Within the
narrative, Jesus speaks to the disciples gathered with him on the
night when he was betrayed, but he also speaks as one who has
already triumphed over that betrayal (16:33).[93] And since he stands
on the victorious side of the Resurrection, his discourses are aimed
particularly toward those disciples who share this same perspective,
and not only those assembled with him at the deipnon.

An insight from narrative criticism extends this proposal. The
Farewell Discourses are unique in the Fourth Gospel in giving very
little space to interpretive comments from the narrator. Throughout
the Gospel, the narrator is the authoritative interpreter of Jesus' words,
and the narrator alone shares Jesus' post-Resurrection perspective.[94]
But when the narrator all but disappears in the Farewell Discourses,
the post-Resurrection message remains – in the teaching of Jesus.[95]

---

[92] See chapter 3, note 104.

[93] See Dodd, *Interpretation*, 397f., who writes eloquently on the post-Resurrection
perspective: "Thus the whole series of discourses, including dialogues, monologues
and the prayer in which it all culminates, is conceived as taking place within the
moment of fulfillment. It is true that the dramatic setting is that of 'the night in
which he was betrayed,' with the crucifixion in prospect. Yet in a real sense it is
the risen and glorified Christ who speaks." See also Schnackenburg, *Gospel of John*,
3.80, where in regard to verse 14:21 he writes, "The whole verse confirms that the
evangelist has the post-paschal period, in other words, the existence on earth of
Jesus' disciples, in mind." For the blending of time periods in the Farewell Discourses,
see Frey, *Eschatologie II*, 252ff. and passim.

[94] To demonstrate the value of the narrator for the Gospel, Culpepper cites for
special emphasis the conversation between Jesus and his disciples at 11:11–14,
Anatomy, 35. The narrator's intrusion at 11:13 clarifies the disciples' misunderstanding
of Jesus. Jesus had told the disciples that they were going to visit Lazarus because
he had "fallen asleep" (11:11). Jesus' phrase "Lazarus has fallen asleep" encouraged
the disciples, because if he was only sleeping, he was surely still healthy. Then, the
narrator intrudes with the comment, "Jesus, however, had been speaking about his
death, but they thought that he was referring merely to sleep" (11:13). After this
narrator's comment, Jesus adds, "Lazarus is dead" (11:14). Without the narrator's
comment, the difference between what Jesus said at 11:11 and what he said at
11:14 makes no sense in the narrative. The narrator's comment is essential to the
proper understanding of the conversation. As Culpepper writes, "Without the narration, the dialogue in this passage loses most of its significance," ibid., 35.

[95] Jesus knows that "the Father has given all things into his hands" (13:3); that
the Father has "given him authority over all people" (17:2); that he is going to
God (13:3; 17:13). Further, Jesus already has been glorified (13:31), already has

Jesus now speaks in an unmediated directness to his followers at the dinner, and to those who share in the dinner later. The disappearance of the narrator, together with the assumption of the post-Resurrection message by Jesus, diminishes the boundary between the reader and the discourses. The readers share more directly and immediately in the feast of words. They sit alongside the disciples who share Jesus' original logodeipnon.

Jesus orients the words of his Farewell Discourses toward the future in several other ways as well. He urges his followers, for instance, to remember and to keep his words. He twice commands them to remember what he says to them:[96]

> 15:20 Remember (μνημονεύετε) the word that I said to you . . .
> 16:4a But I have said these things to you so that when their hour comes you may remember (μνημονεύητε) that I told you about them.

These injunctions only confirm the high status accorded to Jesus' words throughout the Fourth Gospel. In 2:19–22, for instance, the Gospel equates Jesus' words with the words of Scripture. When Jesus confronts his opponents after cleansing the Temple, the following exchange occurs, with a critical explanation from the narrator:

> Jesus answered them, 'Destroy this temple and in three days I will raise it up.' The Jews then said, 'This temple has been under construction for forty-six years, and will you raise it up in three days?' But he was speaking of the temple of his body. After he was raised from the dead, his disciples remembered that he had said this; and they believed the scripture and the word that Jesus had spoken.[97]

The episode demonstrates the hermeneutical impact of the Resurrection on the ability to understand Jesus' words.[98] But, more to the pre-

---

overcome the world (16:33) and already has finished his work (17:4). Dodd, *Interpretation*, 398.

[96] In addition to these two examples, see also Jesus' promise that the Paraclete will remind (ὑπομνήσει) the disciples of Jesus' words (14:26).

[97] It is not exactly clear what scripture is in mind here. See Daly-Denton, *David*, 121f., for a review of options.

[98] Ashton, *Understanding*, 415. For Ashton, the words and actions of Jesus, such as the temple episode and the entry into Jerusalem, are riddles, Ibid., 415. As riddles, they have both a plain and an esoteric meaning. Only the first level of significance, the plain, is available to Jesus' hearers. But the esoteric level is reserved for the readers of John's Gospel, who have been given the key to understand the deeper meaning of Jesus' words. Daly-Denton applies a narrative orientation to this dichotomy and refers to the plain meaning as the level of "story" and the esoteric meaning as the level of "discourse." The characters in the story understand Jesus'

sent point, Jesus' words are equal to the words of Scripture: ". . . they believed the scripture and the word which Jesus had spoken" (2:22). Later, in chapter 18, the Gospel twice quotes the words of Jesus with the same formula used to invoke the Old Testament.[99] The words of Jesus are thus canonized alongside the words of Scripture. Jesus speaks God's words.[100]

Because Jesus' words are so valuable, the disciples must not only remember them. They must also "keep" them.[101] But, what does it

---

words in one sense, but the discourse of the Gospel communicates a deeper significance that can only be unlocked with a special key, *David*, 119. An episode similar to the Temple scene occurs when Jesus enters Jerusalem on a donkey in chapter 12. The narrator explains, "His disciples did not understand these things at first; but when Jesus was glorified, then they remembered that these things had been written of him and had been done to him" (12:16).

[99] John several times opens Old Testament quotations with some variation of the phrase "ἵνα ἡ γραφὴ πληρωθῇ" (12:38; 13:18; 15:25; 17:12; 19:24; 19:36). In 18:9, when Jesus refers back to his prayer at 17:12 (cf. 6:39; 10:28) about not losing any of those entrusted to his care, the quotation opens with a variation on this phrase "ἵνα πληρωθῇ ὁ λόγος ὅν εἶπεν . . ." Similarly, when 18:32 refers back to Jesus' claim at 12:32 about his death (cf. 3:14; 8:28), the statement opens with the phrase "ἵνα ὁ λόγος τοῦ Ἰνσοῦ πληρωθῇ," Wayne Meeks, *The Prophet King: Moses Traditions and the Johannine Christology* (Leiden: E.J. Brill, 1967) 289.

[100] Aune, *Cultic Setting*, 70–71. "[The] words of Jesus are uttered on the authority of God, and can only be disregarded with the gravest of consequences (John 12:47–50; 5:30–32; 7:16–18; 8:14–16, 38, 40)," ibid., 70. His final prayer at the close of the farewell discourses opens, "the words (ῥήματα) that you gave to me I have given to them . . . " (17:8).

[101] Immediately prior to the promise that the Spirit will remind the disciples of Jesus words (14:26), Jesus announces (14:21), "They who have my commandments and keep them are those who love me . . ." In 14:23–24, the following warning is given: "Those who love me will keep (τηρήσει) my word." Similarly, following immediately on the command to remember his words, Jesus gives the following warning about keeping his words in 15:20: "'Servants are not greater than their master.' If they persecute me, they will persecute you; if they kept (ἐτήρησαν) my word, they will keep (τηρήσουσιν) yours also. A particular problem presents itself in reconciling the various injunctions to keep Jesus' words, however. Jesus' admonishes the disciples to keep his word (14:23) and words (14:24) in chapter 14. These statements are often connected to the commandments of Jesus in 14:15, 21. To keep the words of Jesus (14:23–24) and to keep his commandments (14:15, 21) are "alternative ways of referring to the demand for faith that pervades the whole Gospel." Cf. Ashton, *Understanding*, 458. The questions begin, however, when one attempts to reconcile the plural "commandments" in 14:15 with the first announcement of Jesus' singular "commandment" to love one another in 13:34 and the subsequent expansion on this commandment in 15:12–17. The shift from singular to plural suggests to some that these admonitions refer to different objects, that the "commandments" of chapter 14 and the "commandment" of chapters 13 and 15 are not the same thing. But the problem is easily reconciled when one recognizes that the Father's commandments are also spoken of in both the singular and the plural.

mean to "keep" the word(s) of Jesus? In the most obvious sense, one keeps the word of Jesus by performing the acts that he prescribes. At another level, the disciples must keep Jesus' word by transmitting his message (15:20) and by testifying on his behalf (15:26). But, even more basically, the disciples "keep" the word of Jesus by enshrining it in the Gospel of John.[102] Ashton writes:

> He asks only that they should 'keep his word'. To do this they must literally keep a record of his *words*, which means in practice keeping a copy of the Gospel. The actual composition of the Gospel is part, and an essential part at that, of the carrying-out of Jesus' last commission to his disciples.[103]

The very production of the Gospel, then, is a response to Jesus' injunction to keep his words. In the Farewell Discourses, the preservation of Jesus' words receives particular emphasis through the utilization of the logodeipnon format. For the Gospel does not preserve Jesus' words in just any random format. Jesus' words are preserved as a series of sympotic conversations. The decision, conscious or not, to portray Jesus' discourses in this way can reasonably be explained in two ways. First, we have seen that Greco-Roman funereal art often portrays a dead person enjoying a banquet. One of the explanations for this convention is that it recovers something of the departed person's life. Such art is a way of coming to terms with death, and of maintaining some vestige, however slight, of the dead person's former existence. Since eating and drinking are the most vital of life's experiences, to depict the dead person in this way is like depicting him or her in the prime of life, as opposed to the decrepit or ill stage that often accompanies death. The Farewell Discourses, however, present not a stone monument to Jesus, but a

---

They are plural in 15:10, singular in 14:31. The change in noun number, then, presents no difficulty. Brown, *Gospel of John*, 2. 663.

[102] "The recipients of the commission to "keep my commandments" are Jesus' disciples, who will carry out this command simply by keeping his *word*, a charge that may have been thought to have been partly fulfilled by their preservation of the very Gospel which has been composed to promote faith in Jesus' words among its readers," Ashton, *Understanding*, 474.

[103] Ibid., 459. Ashton recognizes that several testaments also place great concern on the preservation of the book in which the testament is contained. A sterling example is 4 Ezra 14. See ibid., 474–75. However true this is, John has presented these discourses, as well as the injunction to preserve them, in the context of a meal. This, too, serves as a vehicle to preserve Jesus' words. Davies "bilingualism" is here again evident, "Reflections," 44.

verbal one. The pale echo of his life takes the form of his words, reverberating through the centuries.

And yet the very fact that Jesus is depicted as speaking, not eating and drinking, also distances him from this memorial function of the meal. Here, the quotation of Plutarch is instructive. For, Plutarch emphasizes that Plato and Xenophon's diners are always fresh and present to later generations precisely because they eschew food and excessive, drink, consuming instead the words of their conversation. This is especially true of Plato, who removes the physical delights of the symposium even more thoroughly than Xenophon. That John so closely follows the form that Plutarch praises in Plato suggests that he also understands why Plutarch praises the form. In the same way that later followers of Socrates will always be able to sit in the presence of the master and dine on his words, so too, Jesus' disciples will be ever able to sit in the presence of their Lord and be nourished by his feast of words.

This chapter began with Ulpian departing from the table as in a play after his final speech (15:686b–c). Immediately after he departs, the following notice intervenes:

> Not many days after that, as if he himself had had a premonition of the silence that was to be his, he died happily . . . (15:686c).

Ulpian's death signals the silent close of his loquacious participation in the world of the symposium. Jesus, too, speaks under the shadow of death during his final meal, a circumstance that evokes all of the cultural tropes that connect death and the dinner setting, as noted above. Like Ulpian as well, Jesus leaves the symposium bound for a death that will grieve his companions. But here the similarities with Ulpian end. For, in the same way that Jesus' tragic exit to death is no tragedy at all when understood properly, so, too, his departure from the supper does not end in silence. For his words have been kept and preserved. Through the medium of the logodeipnon, Jesus continues to speak to all generations of believers.

A summary of the preceding argument can now conclude this chapter. As other scholars have demonstrated, the Farewell Discourses variously resemble the literary symposium tradition, and share certain of the cultural attitudes and practices of Greco-Roman meals. The behavior of Judas sets the stage for the argument, because Judas serves as a flashpoint for several sympotic themes. As a character that opposes the love and friendship of the table, Judas in the first place accentuates the intimacy that Jesus shares with his disciples, an intimacy similar to that in other literary symposia. Judas' early departure from the table is no less sympotic, and parallels the similar activity in the literary symposium tradition of characters who upset the concord for which the symposium strives. Further, Judas' exit neatly divides the deipnon in chapter 13 from the discourses that dominate the scene until 18:1. Indeed, Judas' exit instigates the discourses, since Jesus only begins speaking after Judas leaves, and ceases to offend the atmosphere of loyal friendship. But, even though Judas' activity circulates around the deipnon, the meal itself receives little attention, and is soon dwarfed and overwhelmed completely by the discourses of Jesus. The feast is a feast of words.

A quotation from Plutarch suggests that this form has a particular function. Plutarch praises Plato for ignoring the food and entertainments common to the symposium, and depicting Socrates in a way that focuses on the speeches offered around the table. This format allows later generations to share bounteously in the feast of words. John, too, emphasizes that his discourses are designed to include believers who no longer stand in the presence of Jesus. 16:4b is particularly meaningful: "I would have said these things to you from the beginning, but I was with you." This rich statement suggests that Jesus' discourses are to serve his disciples when he is no longer among them. In a sense he is already somewhat displaced in this comment, since he already speaks of a time when he is no longer present. Because his words are the words of God, they must be remembered and kept. The very writing of the Gospel – and especially of the Farewell Discourses – serves as a basic way in which the keeping of his words is accomplished. Consequently, Jesus continues to speak even after he has returned to the Father. His fleshly presence is replaced by his *logic* presence. The Word who became flesh is now present in his words.

CHAPTER FIVE

SUMMARY AND CONCLUSION

This study has argued that the Johannine Farewell Discourses are both more, and less, unified than traditional scholarship has seen them. They are more unified, in that the troubling departure of Jesus at 14:31 can actually support a synchronic interpretation. This huge obstacle in the middle of the discourses has been smoothed over by recourse to ancient tragedy. But this very recourse to a new literary genre suggests that the single mind, or set of minds, that produced the Gospel occupied a far more varied literary world than previous scholarship has suggested. The Farewell Discourses are not merely one more example of the biblical testament. They also resonate with Greek tragedy, ancient consolation literature and the literary symposium.

Now, how consciously the authors(s) moved from one genre to the next, how consciously they mimicked this or that venerable figure or common trope is difficult to determine for certain. For instance, the exit of Judas from the Last Supper demonstrates the difficulty in even distinguishing one genre from the other. The Farewell Discourses only begin when Judas departs: "Therefore, *when he left*, Jesus said . . ." Because scholars have assumed that the phrase "when he left" is a redactional gloss, they have not adequately recognized the connection between Judas' departure and Jesus' speech. When chapter 1 compares this exit to the exits of servants in Greek and Roman drama, the relevance of the exit clearly appears. Judas is ordered offstage in order to prepare for future action, in this case the betrayal of Jesus. And his departure removes from the scene a character whose continuing presence would prevent an important conversation among other characters, in this case Jesus' discourses with his disciples. But, is this a stage borrowing, and nothing else? In the literary symposium, guests commonly depart from the intimacy of the supper because their continuing presence would intrude on the conviviality of the table. Disaffected diners often depart just before the customary sympotic discussion on love. Judas' exit, then, is both dramatic and sympotic. Thus, to wonder which genre was more on the mind of the composer(s) of the Gospel is unhelpful. The discourses clearly resonate with several different literary styles. This is so because the author(s) of the Gospel sought, not to be true to a given literary form, but to be true to a particular portrait of Jesus and his work. To this end, various literary forms were bent and twisted as needed. Attending to this variety has been the object of the present study. The single scene speaks simultaneously in several generic idioms. Far from being merely an example of the testament, the Farewell Discourses reflect generic polyphony.

To be sure, there are certain and clear connections between the Farewell Discourses and the testament form, but to view these discourses only as a testament far too tightly confines the interpretive possibilities. Such things as the exit of Judas do not receive their due significance. Even more important, it is impossible to see how John has modified the testament form in his unique presentation.

On a general level, John deviates from the standard expectations of the testament by emphasizing Jesus' continuing presence with his disciples, and not merely Jesus' impending absence. This shift in emphasis is achieved by forging the testament together with other literary styles. While the theme of departure/absence is supported by recourse to the dramatic exit to death, consolation literature and the literary symposium emphasize Jesus' continuing presence. On a more specific level, aspects of the Farewell Discourses that seem at first to coincide with the testament form begin to look very different after closer inspection. A summary of each chapter will demonstrate how John's testament is no ordinary testament.

Chapter 2 emphasizes the dramatic action of Jesus' exit, which is nothing like what one sees in the testament form. The departure of Jesus is a critical theological and narrative concern in the Fourth Gospel. Because Jesus is the Ascending and Descending Redeemer, whose purpose culminates in a return to the Father, and because Jesus is the one who gives his life for his friends, culminating in his death on the cross, Jesus' exit from the Farewell Discourses is the completion of his life and work. Greek tragic exits provide a ready literary form to emphasize and dramatize Jesus' departure and return to the Father.

The exit movement of Jesus further evokes tragic exits when Jesus pauses his departure at 14:31. He engages in a series of discourses that reflect on the nature of his coming exit. Recognizing that Jesus' delay is similar in many ways to the delay of tragic figures helps to come to grips with the methodological divide that now separates Johannine scholars. Narrative critics seek to trace the synchronic flow of the narrative's plot, but they struggle to interpret the delay at 14:31 without recourse to diachronic and redaction theories. Historians, therefore, reject synchronic literary arguments because such readings assume the unity of the text without proving it or arguing for it. The delayed exit provides a means to argue for, not merely assume, the unity of the text.

Quite apart from these notorious methodological issues, Jesus' exit sequence generates a context and setting in which to deliver his testamentary farewell. Jesus' "Big Speech" evokes the tragic practice of reflecting on an exit to death before carrying through with it. Like other such speeches in exits to death, the setting of the speech is somewhat unclear. Has Jesus left the room? Does he speak along the way? Where is the way? In the tragic last speech, the speaking figure is abstracted from his or her immediate surroundings, in order to place absolute focus on the speaker and the speech. In the Gospel of John, this abstraction from the immediate surroundings is accomplished by the confusing delay at 14:31. Jesus transcends his immediate surroundings as he prepares to return above to the Father. But, in highlighting Jesus' departure and his absence, the tragic form supports the general character of the testament, which also emphasizes departure.

Chapters 3 and 4, however, emphasize presence, not absence. More specifically, chapter 3 argues that Jesus' Farewell Discourses include themes and techniques of classical consolation to soften the disciples' grief. To counter the dread and sadness that will accompany Jesus' absence, the Paraclete-Spirit will serve as a token of Jesus' continuing presence. More important, the Paraclete will remind the disciples of all that Jesus has said. Because consolation is a form of moral exhortation, and not merely the expression of sympathy, Jesus' concern is not simply to cheer the disciples in the face of his departure, but rather to provide for their continuing association with him, and their continued instruction. The Paraclete accomplishes both tasks, by making Jesus and his words of instruction present to the disciples. Arguments in favor of the testament character of the discourses emphasize that the Paraclete is Jesus' successor just as Joshua is the successor of Moses. This is certainly accurate, but incomplete. The Paraclete is more than a successor, and the Paraclete's role as Jesus' double stands out clearly in light of ancient consolation.

Until the teacher and Lord can be with the disciples again, the
Paraclete serves as a token of the Lord's presence.

This insight leads to the literary symposium, discussed in chapter 4. For, Jesus' discourses are not only delivered in the setting of
his exit to death. They are delivered in the setting of an after-dinner
conversation. The exit *to* death is simultaneously an exit *from* a deipnon. Therefore, Jesus' testament is a tragic "Big Speech" delivered
in the context of sympotic discourse. Jesus' banquet, however, is not
a deipnon of debauchery and excess, but rather a banquet of words
in which Jesus lovingly prepares his disciples for his departure. Or,
perhaps it is better to say that he speaks to his disciples from the
perspective of one who has already gone, from the post-Resurrection
perspective. Because of this perspective, his banquet of words is as
nourishing for later generations as it is for those who heard it in his
earthly life. The relevance of this is not at all clear when one notes
merely that the testament can occasionally include a brief meal.
John's intentions become most clear in light of the classical logodeipnon, in which Jesus announces, "I would have said these things
to you from the beginning, but I was with you."

To conclude, the Gospel of John is not a drama, the Farewell
Discourses are not a treatise on consolation, nor is the Last Supper
a symposium. But, each of these three literary forms bears close
resemblance to aspects of the Farewell Discourses, and attending to
these additional forms clarifies the unique shape of the testament of
Jesus in the Gospel of John. Such a literary-historical exercise also
lays bare the overarching concern of the discourses to render Jesus
present in his absence, to bring future generations into the presence
of their Lord. To paraphrase Plutarch: "Hence today all the lovers
of *The Word* participate and take pleasure from the banquet, just like
the people who dined at that time."

BIBLIOGRAPHY

Editions and Translations of Greek and Latin authors are from the Loeb Classical Library unless otherwise indicated. All translations of biblical texts are taken from the New Revised Standard Version. Translations of Old Testament apocryphal and pseudepigraphic texts, unless noted otherwise, are derived from James H. Charlesworth, ed. *The Old Testament Pseudepigrapha. 2 Vols.* (New York: Doubleday, 1983–5).

Arnott, W.G. *Menander, Plautus and Terence.* Clarendon Press: Oxford, 1975.

Arrowsmith, William. "Luxury and Death in the Satyricon." *ARION* 5 (1966): 304–331.

Ashton, John. *Studying John.* Oxford: Clarendon Press, 1994.

———. *Understanding the Fourth Gospel.* Oxford: Clarendon Press, 1991.

Ashton, John, ed. *The Interpretation of John.* Issues in Religion and Theology 9. Philadephia: Fortress, 1986.

Atkinson, J.E. "Seneca's *Consolatio Ad Polybium.*" *ANRW* 32.2 860–884. Part 2, Principat, 32.2. Edited by W. Haase. New York: de Gruyter, 1984.

Attridge, Harold. "Genre Bending in the Fourth Gospel." *JBL* 121 (2002): 3–21.

Aune, David. *The Cultic Setting of Realized Eschatology in Early Christianity.* Supplements to Novum Testamentum 28. Leiden: E.J. Brill, 1972.

———. *The New Testament in its Literary Environment.* Philadelphia: Westminster, 1987.

———. "The Phenomenon of Early Christian 'Anti-Sacramentalism'." Pages 194–214 in *Studies in New Testament and Early Christian Literature: Essays in Honor of Allen P. Wikgren.* Edited by David Aune. Leiden: Brill, 1972.

———. "Septem Sapientium Convivium (Moralia 146B–164D)." Pages 51–105 in *Plutarch's Ethical Writings and Early Christian Literature.* Edited by Hans Dieter Betz. Leiden: E.J. Brill, 1978.

Bain, David. *Masters, Servants and Orders in Greek Tragedy: Some Aspects of Dramatic Technique and Convention.* Publications of the Faculty of Arts of the University of Manchester 26. Manchester: Manchester University Press, 1981.

Balch, David L. "Political Friendship in the Historian Dionysius of Halicarnassus, *Roman Antiquities,*" Pages 123–44 in *Greco-Roman Perspectives on Friendship.* Edited by John T. Fitzgerald. Leiden: E.J. Brill, 1996.

Bammel, E. "The Farewell Discourse of the Evangelist John and its Jewish Heritage." *Tyndale Bulletin* (1993): 103–116.

Becker, J. "Das Johannesevangelium im Streit der Methoden (1980–1984)." *TRu* 51 (1986): 1–78.

Bennet, Kathryn. *The Motivation of Exits in Greek and Latin Comedy.* Ann Arbor: University of Michigan Press, 1932.

Berger, K. "Hellenistische Gattungen im Neuen Testament." *ANRW* 25:2: 1031–1432. Part 2, Principat, 25.2. Edited by W. Haase. New York: de Gruyter, 1984.

Bettini, Maurizio. *The Portrait of the Lover.* Translated by Laura Gibbs. Berkeley: University of California, 1999.

———. "Litterarische Gattungen im Johannesevangelium: Ein Forschungsbericht 1919–1980." *ANRW* 25:3: 2506–2568. Part 2, Principat, 25.3. Edited by W. Haase. New York: de Gruyter, 1984.

Bilezikian, Gilbert G. *The Liberated Gospel: A Comparison of the Gospel of Mark and Greek Tragedy.* Grand Rapids: Baker, 1987.

Black, C. Clifton. "The Words That You Have Given to Me I Have Given to Them: The Grandeur of Johannine Rhetoric." Pages 220–39 in *Exploring the Gospel of John in Honor of D. Moody Smith*. Edited by R. Alan Culpepper and C. Clifton Black. Louisville: Westminster John Knox Press, 1996.

Blundell, Mary Whitlock. *Helping Friends and Harming Enemies*. Cambridge: Cambridge University Press, 1989.

Boegehold, Alan L. *When a Gesture Was Expected: A Selection of Examples from Archaic and Classical Greek Literature*. Princeton: Princeton University Press, 1999.

Bornkamm, G. *Geschichte und Glaube*. Gesammelte Aufsätze. 3 vols. München: Kaiser, 1968–1971.

Bowie E.L. "Greeks and their Past in the Second Sophistic." Pages 166–209 in *Studies in Ancient Society*. Edited by M.I. Finley. Boston: Routledge, 1974. Repr. from *Past and Present* 46 (1970): 3–41.

Branham, R. Bracht. *Unruly Eloquence: Lucian and the Comedy of Traditions*. Cambridge, Mass.: Harvard, 1989.

Brentlinger, John. "The Cycle of Becoming in the *Symposium*." Pages 1–31 in *The Symposium of Plato*. Translated by Suzy Q. Groden. Massachusetts: University of Massachusetts Press, 1970.

Braund, D. and John Wilkins, eds. *Athenaeus and His World: Reading Greek Culture in the Roman Empire*. Exeter: University of Exeter, 2000.

Brown, R. *The Community of the Beloved Disciple*. New York: Paulist Press, 1979.

———. *The Gospel According to John*. Anchor Bible. 2 vols. Garden City, NY: Doubleday, 1966–1970.

———. "The Paraclete in the Fourth Gospel." *NTS* 13 (1996–67): 113–132.

Bultmann, R. "Die Bedeutung der neuerschlossenen mandäischen und manichäischen Quellen fur das Verständnis des Johannesevangeliums." *ZNW* 24 (1925): 100–146.

———. *The Gospel of John: A Commentary*. Translated by G.R. Beasley Murray, et al. Philadelphia: Westminster Press, 1971.

Buresch, C. "Consolationum a Graecis Romanisque scriptarum historia critica." *Leipziger Studien zur classischen Philologie* 9 (1886): 1–170.

Burge, Gary. *The Anointed Community: The Holy Spirit in the Johannine Tradition*. Grand Rapids: Eerdmans, 1987.

Burnett, Anne Pippin. "The Virtues of Admetus." *CP* 60 (1965): 240–55.

Burridge, Richard. *What are the Gospels?* SNTSMS 70. Cambridge: Cambridge University Press, 1992.

Campbell, Sheila. *The Mosaics of Antioch*. Studia Mediaevalia 15; Toronto: Pontifical Institute of Mediaeval Studies, 1988.

Chapa, Juan. *Letters of Condolence in Greek Papyri*. Papyrologia Florentina 29. Florence: Edizioni Gonnelli, 1998.

Charlesworth, James. "A Critical Comparison of the Dualism in 1QS 3:13–4:26 and the Dualism Contained in the Gospel of John." Pages 76–106 in *John and Qumran*. Edited by James Charlesworth. London, Geoffrey Chapman, 1972.

Christenson, David M. *Plautus, Amphitruo*. Cambridge: Cambridge University Press, 2000.

Clark-Soles, Jaime. *Scripture cannot Be Broken: The Social Function of the Use of Scripture in the Fourth Gospel*. Leiden: Brill, 2003.

Clay, Diskin. Atkinson, J.E. "Lucian of Samosata: Four Philosophical Lives (Nigrinus, Demonax, Peregrinus, Alexander Pseudomantis)." *ANRW* 36.5 3406–3450. Part 2, Principat, 36.5. Edited by W. Haase and Hildegard Temporini. New York: de Gruyter, 1992.

———. *Platonic Questions: Dialogues with the Silent Philosopher*. University Park, Pennsylvania: Pennsylvania State University Press, 2000.

Coleman, K.M. "Fatal Charades: Roman Executions Staged as Mythological Enactments." *JRS* 80 (1990): 44–73.

Coloe, Mary L. "Welcome into the Household of God: The Footwashing in John 13." *CBQ* 66 (2004): 400–415.

Connick, C. Milo. "The Dramatic Character of the Fourth Gospel." *JBL* 67 (1948): 159–169.

Conway, Colleen. "The Production of the Johannine Community: A New Historicist Perspective." *JBL* 121 (2002): 479–95.

Cortés, E. *Los Discursos de adiós de Gn 49 a Jn 13–17: Pistas para la historia de un género literario en la antigua literatura judía*. Barcelona, 1976.

Counet, Patrick Chatelion. *John, A Postmodern Gospel: Introduction to Deconstructive Exegesis Applied to the Fourth Gospel*. Biblical Interpretation Series 44. Leiden: E.J. Brill, 2000.

Courtney, Edward. *A Companion to Petronius*. Oxford: Oxford University Press, 2001.

Culpepper, R. Alan. *The Anatomy of the Fourth Gospel: A Study in Literary Design*. Philadelphia: Fortress, 1983.

Dahl, Nils. "Anamnesis: Memory and Commemoration in Early Christianity." Pages 11 29 in *Jesus in the Memory of the Early Church*. Minneapolis: Augsburg, 1976.

Daly-Denton, Margaret. *David in the Fourth Gospel: The Johannine Reception of the Psalms*. Leiden: E.J. Brill, 2000.

Davidson, James. "Pleasure and Pedantry in Athenaeus." Pages 292–303 in *Athenaeus and his World: Reading Greek Culture in the Roman Empire*. Edited by David Braund and John Wilkins. Exeter: University of Exeter Press, 2000.

Davies, J.G. "The Primary Meaning of ΠΑΡΑΚΛΗΤΟΣ." *JTS* n.s. 4 (1953): 35–38

Davies, W.D. "Reflections on Aspects of the Jewish Background of the Gospel of John." Pages 43–64 in *Exploring the Gospel of John in Honor of D. Moody Smith*. Edited by R. Alan Culpepper and C. Clifton Black. Louisville: Westminster John Knox Press, 1996.

De Boer, M.C. "Narrative Criticism, Historical Criticism, and the Gospel of John." *JSNT* 47 (1992): 35–48.

De Jonge, M. *Jesus: Stranger from Heaven and Son of God*. Edited and Translated by John E. Steely. SBLSBS 11. Missoula, Montana: Scholars Press, 1977.

De La Potterie, Ignace. "The Paraclete." Pages 57–76 in idem, *The Christian Lives by the Spirit*. Translated by John Morris. New York: Alba House, 1971.

De Lacy, Phillip. "Biography and Tragedy in Plutarch." *AJP* 73 (1952): 159–71.

Dettwiler, Andreas. *Die Gegenwart des Erhöhten: Eine exegetische Studie zu den johanneischen Abschiedsreden (Joh 13,31–16,33) unter besonderer Berücksichtigung ihres Relectur-Charakters*. FRLANT 169. Göttingen: Vandenhoeck and Ruprecht, 1995.

Dodd, C.H. *The Interpretation of the Fourth Gospel*. Cambridge: Cambridge University Press, 1968.

Domeris, William. "The Johannine Drama." *Journal for Theology for Southern Africa* 42 (1983): 29–35.

Dorter, Kenneth. "The Significance of the Speeches in Plato's Symposium." *Philosophy and Rhetoric* 4 (1969): 215–234.

Dover, Kenneth. *Plato, Symposium*. Cambridge: Cambridge University Press, 1980.

Duckworth, G.E. *The Nature of Roman Comedy*. Princeton: Princeton University Press, 1952. Repr., London: Bristol Classical Press, 1994.

Duke, Paul D. *Irony in the Fourth Gospel*. Atlanta: John Knox Press, 1985.

Dunbabin, K. *The Roman Banquet: Images of Conviviality*. Cambridge: Cambridge University Press, 2003.

———. "*Sic erimus cuncti* . . . The Skeleton in Graeco-Roman Art." *JDAI* 101 (1986): 185–255.

Easterling, P.E. "From Repertoire to Canon." Pages 211–227 in *The Cambridge Companion to Greek Tragedy*. Edited by P.E. Easterling. Cambridge: Cambridge University Press, 1997.

Easterling, P.E., ed. *The Cambridge Companion to Greek Tragedy*. Cambridge. Cambridge University Press, 1997.

Engberg-Pedersen, Troels, ed. *Paul Beyond the Judaism/Hellenism Divide*. Louisville: Westminster/John Knox, 2001.

Fabricius, Johanna. *Die hellenistischen Totenmahlreliefs: Grabrepräsentation und Wertvorstellungen in ostgriechischen Städten*. Studien zur antiken Stadt 3. München: F. Pfeil, 1999.

Fagles, Robert, transl. *Aeschylus: The Oresteia*. New York: Penguin, 1984.

Feldman, Louis. "The Influence of the Greek Tragedians on Josephus." Pages 51–80 in *Hellenic and Jewish Arts: Interaction, Tradition and Renewal*. Edited by A. Ovadiah. Tel Aviv: Ramot Publ. House, Tel Aviv University, 1998.

Fitzgerald, John T. *Jesus' Last Will and Testament: Wills, Friendship and the Fourth Gospel*. Atlanta: Scholars Press, forthcoming.

Fitzgerald, John T., ed. *Greco-Roman Perspectives on Friendship*. Leiden: E.J. Brill, 1996.

Fornara, Charles. *The Nature of History in Ancient Greece and Rome*. Berkeley: University of California Press, 1983.

Fortna, R.T. *The Fourth Gospel and its Predecessor*. Philadelphia: Fortress, 1988.

Fraenkel, E. *Agamemnon*. 3 vols. Oxford: Clarendon Press, 1950.

Frey, Jörg. *Die johanneische Eschatologie. Band II: Das johanneische Zeitverständnis*. WUNT 110. Tübingen, Mohr Siebeck, 1998.

Frost, K.B. *Exits and Entrances in Menander*. Oxford: Clarendon Press, 1988.

Garland, R. *The Greek Way of Death*. Ithaca: Cornell University Press, 1985.

Goodwin, Sarah Webster and Elisabeth Bronfen. *Death and Representation*. Baltimore: Johns Hopkins University Press, 1993.

Graver, Margaret. *Cicero on the Emotions: Tusculan Disputations 3 and 4*. Chicago: University of Chicago Press, 2002.

Grayston, K. "The Meaning of PARAKLĒTOS." *JSNT* 13 (1981): 67–82.

Gregg, Robert C. *Consolation Philosophy: Greek and Christian Paideia in Basil and the Two Gregories*. Patristic Monograph Series 3. Cambridge, MA: Philadelphia Patristic Foundation, 1975.

Gregory, J.W. "Euripides' Alcestis." *Hermes* 107 (1979): 259–70.

Griffith, Mark. *Sophocles, Antigone*. Cambridge: Cambridge University Press, 1999.

Grollios, C. *Seneca's 'Ad Marciam.'* Athens: G.S. Christou and Son, 1956.

Grottanelli, C. "Wine and Death – East and West." Pages 62–87 in *In Vino Veritas*. Edited by Oswyn Murray and Manuela Tecuşan. London: British School at Rome, et al., 1995.

Hägerland, Tobias. "John's Gospel: A Two-Level Drama?" *JSNT* 25 (2003): 309–22.

Halleran, Michael R. *Stagecraft in Euripides*. Totowa, New Jersey: Barnes and Noble, 1985.

Halperin, David. "Plato and the the Erotics of Narrativity," Pages 93–129 in *Oxford Studies in Ancient Philosophy*. Supplementary volume: *Methods of Interpreting Plato and His Dialogues*. Edited by J.C. Klagge and N.D. Smith. Oxford: Oxford University Press, 1992.

Hamilton, R. "Announced Entrances in Greek Tragedy." *HSCP* 82 (1978): 63–82.

Hani, Jean. *Plutarque: Consolation a Apollonios* Etudes et Commentaires 78. Paris: Klincksieck, 1972.

Harrill, J. Albert. "The Dramatic Function of the Running Slave Rhoda (Acts 12:13–16): A Piece of Greco-Roman Comedy." *NTS* 46 (2000): 150–57.

Harris, Elizabeth. *Prologue and Gospel: The Theology of the Fourth Evangelist*. JSNTSS 107. Sheffield: Sheffield Academic Press, 1994.

Harrison, S. J., ed. *Oxford Readings in the Roman Novel*. Oxford: Oxford University Press, 1999.

Hengel, Martin. *Studies in the Gospel of Mark*. Translated by John Bowden. Philadelphia: Fortress, 1985.

Hitchcock, F.R.M. "Is the Fourth Gospel a Drama?" Pages 15–24 in *The Gospel of John as Literature: An Anthology of Twentieth Century Perspectives*. Edited by Mark Stibbe. Leiden: E.J. Brill, 1993. Repr. from *Theology* 7 (1923): 307–17.

Hock, Ronald F. "An Extraordinary Friend in Chariton's *Callirhoe*: The Importance of Friendship in the Greek Romances," Pages 145–162 in *Greco-Roman Perspectives on Friendship* (ed. John T. Fitzgerald; Atlanta: Scholars Press, 1997).

Holloway, Paul. *Consolation in Philippians: Philosophical Sources and Rhetorical Strategy.* SNTSMS 112. Cambridge: Cambridge University Press, 2001.

———. "Left Behind: Jesus' Consolation of His Disciples in John 13,31–17,26." *ZNW* (forthcoming: January, 2005).

———. "*Nihil inopinati accidisse*: A Cyrenaic Consolatory *Topos* in 1 Peter 4:12." *NTS* 48 (2002): 433–48.

Hoskyns, Edwyn Clement. *The Fourth Gospel.* Edited by F.N. Davey. Rev. ed. London: Faber and Faber, 1947.

Hough, John. "Plautine Technique in Delayed Exits." *CP* 35 (1940): 39–48.

———. "The Structure of the *Asinaria.*" *AJP* 58 (1937): 19–37.

———. "The Structure of the *Captivi.*" *AJP* 63 (1942): 26–37.

Hutchinson, G.O. *Aeschylus' 'Septem Contra Thebas.'* Oxford: Clarendon Press, 1985.

Jacobson, H. *The Exagoge of Ezekiel.* Cambridge: Cambridge University Press, 1983.

Jeanneret, Michel. *A Feast of Words: Banquets and Table-Talk in the Renaissance.* Translated by Jeremy Whitely and Emma Hughes. Cambridge: Polity, 1991.

John Chrysostom. *Commentary on Saint John the Apostle and Evangelist.* Translated by Sister Thomas Aquinas Goggin, S.C.H.: New York; Fathers of the Church, 1960.

Johnston, George. *The Spirit-Paraclete in the Gospel of John.* SNTSMS 12. Cambridge: Cambridge University Press, 1970.

Jones, Christopher P. "Dinner Theatre." Pages 185–198 in *Dining in a Classical Context.* Edited by William J. Slater. Ann Arbor: University of Michigan Press, 1991.

Kahn, Charles. *Plato and the Socratic Dialogue: The Philosophical Use of a Literary Form.* Cambridge: Cambridge University Press, 1996.

Kassel, R. *Untersuchungen zur griechischen und römischen Konsolationsliteratur.* Zetemata 18; Munich, 1958.

Kennedy, George. *New Testament Interpretation through Rhetorical Criticism.* Chapel Hill: University of North Carolina Press, 1984.

Klauck, H.-J. *Herrenmahl und Hellenistischer Kult: Eine religiongeschichtliche Untersuchung zum ersten Korintherbrief.* Aschendorff: Münster, 1982.

Kokolakis, M. "Lucian and the Tragic Performances in his Time," *Platon* 12 (1960) 67–106.

———. "Pantomimus and the treatise περὶ ὀρχήσεως." *Platon* 11 (1959) 1–56.

Kondoleon, C. *Antioch: The Lost Ancient City.* Princeton: Princeton University Press and the Worcester Art Museum, 2000.

Konstan, David. *Friendship in the Classical World.* Cambridge: Cambridge University Press, 1997.

Kurz, W.S. "Luke 22:14–38 and Greco-Roman and Biblical Farewell Addresses," *JBL* 104 (1985): 251–68.

Lacomara, A. "Deuteronomy and the Farewell Discourse (Jn 13:31–16:33)." *CBQ* 36 (1974): 65–84.

Lattimore, Richmond. *The Complete Greek Tragedies.* 3 vols.; Chicago: University of Chicago Press, 1955.

Lee, E.K. "The Drama of the Fourth Gospel." *ET* 65 (1953): 173–6.

Levi, Doro. *Antioch Mosaic Pavements.* 2 vols. Princeton: Princeton University Press, 1947.

Lissarrague, F. *The Aesthetics of the Greek Banquet: images of wine and ritual.* Translated by Andrew Szegedy-Maszak. Princeton: Princeton University Press, 1990.

Lohfink, N. "Die deuteronomistische Darstellung des Übergangs der Führung Israels von Mose auf Josue." *Scholastik* 37 (1962): 32–44.

Lowe, J.C.B. "Aspects of Plautus' Originality in the *Asinaria.*" 42 (1992): 152–175.

Lukinovich, Alessandra. "The Play of Reflections between Literary Form and the Sympotic Theme in the *Deipnosophistae* of Athenaeus." Pages 263–71 in *Sympotica: A Symposium on the Symposion*. Edited by Oswyn Murray. Oxford: Oxford University Press, 1990.

Macintosh, Fiona. *Dying Acts: Death in Ancient Greek and Modern Irish Tragic Drama*. Cork: Cork University Press, 1994.

———. "Tragic Last Words: The Big Speech and the Lament in Ancient Greek and Modern Irish Tragic Drama." Pages 414–25 in *Tragedy and the Tragic*. Edited by M.S. Silk. Oxford: Clarendon Press, 1996.

MacRae, George W. "Theology and Irony in the Fourth Gospel." Pages 103–13 in *The Gospel of John as Literature*. Edited by M. Stibbe. Leiden: E.J. Brill, 1993. Repr. from Clifford, R.J. and MacRae, G.W. *The Word in the World: Essays in Honour of F.L. Moriarty*. Cambridge, Mass.: Weston College, 1973. 83–96.

Malherbe, A. *Ancient Epistolary Theorists*. SBLSBS 19. Atlanta: Scholars Press, 1988.

———. "Exhortation in 1 Thessalonians." *NovT* 25 (1983): 238–56. Repr. in *idem, Paul and the Popular Philosophers*. Minneapolis: Fortress, Press, 1989, 49–66.

———. *Paul and the Popular Philosophers*. Minneapolis: Fortress Press, 1989.

———. *Paul and the Thessalonians*. Philadelphia: Fortress Press, 1987.

Malina, Bruce and Richard Rohrbaugh. *Social Science Commentary on the Gospel of John*. Minneapolis: Fortress Press, 1998.

Manning, C. E. *On Seneca's 'Ad Marciam.'* Mnemosyne Supplement 69. Leiden: Brill, 1981.

Marrow, Stanley B. "Κόσμος in John," CBQ 64 (2002): 90–102.

Martin, J. "Deipnonliteratur." *RAC* 3 (1950): 658–66.

———. *Symposion: Die Geschichte einer literarischen Form*. SGKA 17 ½. Paderborn: Ferdinand Schöningh, 1931.

Martyn, J.L. *History and Theology in the Fourth Gospel*. Rev. ed. New York: Harper and Row, 1979.

Mastronarde, Donald J. *Contact and Discontinuity*. University of California Publications in Classical Studies 21. Berkeley and Los Angeles: University of California, 1979.

McClure, Laura. *Courtesans at Table: Gender and Greek Literary Culture in Athenaeus*. New York: Routledge, 2003.

Meeks, Wayne. "Galilee and Judea in the Fourth Gospel," *JBL* 85 (1966): 159–69.

———. "The Man from Heaven in Johannine Sectarianism." Pages 141–73 in *The Interpretation of John*. Edited by John Ashton. Philadelphia: Fortress Press, 1986. Repr. from *JBL* (1972): 44–72.

———. *The Prophet King: Moses Traditions and the Johannine Christology*. Leiden: E.J. Brill, 1967.

Menander: The Plays and Fragments. Translated by Maurice Balme. Intro. by Peter Brown. Oxford: Oxford University Press, 2001.

Menander Rhetor. Edited with translation and commentary by D.A. Russell and N.G. Wilson. Oxford: Clarendon Press, 1981.

Mengis, Karl. *Die schriftstellenische Technik im Sophistenmahl des Athenaios*. Paderborn: F. Schöningh, 1920.

Mitchell, Margaret M. *Paul and the Rhetoric of Reconciliation: An Exegetical Investigation of the Language and Composition of 1 Corinthians*. Tubingen: Mohr (Siebeck), 1991. Repr. Louisville: Westminster/John Knox, 1993.

Mlakuzhyil, George. *The Christocentric Literary Structure of the Fourth Gospel*. Analecta Biblica 117. Rome: Pontificio Istituto Biblico, 1987.

Moloney, F. *Belief in the Word: Reading the Fourth Gospel: John 1–4*. Minneapolis: Fortress Press, 1993.

———. *The Gospel of John*. Sacra Pagina 4. Collegeville, MN: Liturgical Press, 1998.

———. *Glory Not Dishonor: Reading John 13–21*. Minneapolis: Fortress Press, 1998.

Moore, Stephen D. *Literary Criticism and the Gospels*. New Haven: Yale University Press, 1989.

Mossman, J.M. "Tragedy and Epic in Plutarch's *Alexander*." Pages 209–228 in *Essays on Plutarch's Lives*. Edited by Barbara Scardigli; Oxford: Clarendon Press, 1995.

Motyer, Steve. "Method in Fourth Gospel Studies: A Way out of the Impasse?" *JSNT* 66 (1997): 27–44.

Muilenberg, J. "Literary Form in the Fourth Gospel." *JBL* 51 (1932): 40–3.

Munck, J. "Discours d'Adieu dans le Nouveau Testament et dans la literature biblique." Pages 155–70 in *Aux sources de la tradition chrétienne: Mélanges offerts à M. Maurice Goguel*. Bibliothèque théologique. Neuchatel and Paris: Delachaux and Nestlé, 1950.

Murray, O. "Death and the Symposium." *AION* (archeol) 10 (1988): 239–55.

Murray, O, ed. *Sympotica: A Symposium on the Symposion*. Oxford: Clarendon Press, 1990.

C. Musonius Rufus. Reliquiae. Edited by Otto Hense. Leipzig: Teubner, 1905.

Musurillo, Herbert. *The Light and the Darkness*. Leiden: Brill, 1967.

Nauck, A. *De Tragicorum Graecorum Fragmentis Observationes Criticae*. Berlin, 1855.

Neyrey, Jerome. "The 'Noble Shepherd' in John 10: Cultural and Rhetorical Background." *JBL* 120 (2001): 267–91.

Nicholson, Godfrey C. *Death as Departure: The Johannine Descent-Ascent Schema*. SBLDS 63. Chico, California: Scholar's Press, 1983.

O'Day, Gail. "'I Have Overcome the World' (John 16:33): Narrative Time in John 13 17." *Semeia* 53 (1991): 153–166.

Origen. *The Ante-Nicene Fathers*. Volume 4. Ed. Alexander Roberts and James Donaldson. 1885. Repr. Grand Rapids, MI: Eerdmans, 1951–53.

Painter, John. "The Farewell Discourses and the History of Johannine Christianity." *NTS* 27 (1981): 525–543.

Parsenios, George. "Παραμυθητικὸς Χριστός: John Chrysostom interprets the Johannine Farewell Discourses." *GOTR* (forthcoming).

Paul, George. "Symposia and Deipna in Plutarch's Lives and in Other Historical Writings." Pages 157–70 in *Dining in a Classical Context*. Edited by William Slater. Ann Arbor: University of Michigan Press, 1991.

Penwill, J.L. "Men in Love: Aspects of Plato's Symposium." *Ramus* 7 (1978): 143–175.

Petronius. *Cena Trimalchionis*. Edited with notes, introduction by Martin S. Smith. Oxford: Clarendon Press, 1975.

———. *Satyricon*. Translated with notes, intro. By P.G. Walsh. Oxford: Oxford University Press, 1997.

Poe, Joe Park. "The Determination of Episodes in Greek Tragedy." *AJP* 114 (1993): 343 396.

Porsch, F. *Pneuma und Wort. Ein Exegetischer Beitrag zur Pneumatologie des Johannesevangeliums*. Frankfurter Theologische Studien 16. Frankfurt: Knecht, 1974.

Price, Jonathan. "Drama and History in Josephus' *BJ*." Paper presented at the annual meeting of the Society of Biblical Literature Josephus Seminar, Boston, MA, November, 1999.

Relihan, Joel C., et al. "Rethinking the History of the Literary Symposium." *ICS* 17 (1992): 213–44.

Rehm, Rush. *The Play of Space: Spatial Transformation in Greek Tragedy* (Princeton: Princeton University Press, 2002).

Ringe, Sharon. *Wisdom's Friends: Community and Christology in the Fourth Gospel*. Louisville, Kentucky: Westminster John Knox Press, 1999.

Romeri, Luciana. Translated by Kerensa Pearson. "The λογόδειπνον: Athenaeus Between Banquet and Anti-banquet," in *Athenaeus and His World: Reading Greek*

Culture in the Roman Empire. Edited by David Braund and John Wilkins. Exeter: University of Exeter Press, 2000.

Rosati, Gianpiero. "Trimalchio on Stage." Pages 85–104. in *Oxford Readings in the Roman Novel.* Edited by S.J. Harrison. Oxford: Oxford University Press, 1999.

Rose, V. *Aristotelis Fragmenta.* Leipzig, 1886.

Rudd, Niall. *The Satires of Horace.* 2nd ed. Berkeley: University of California Press, 1982.

Sandy, Gerald N. "Scaenica Petroniana" in *TAPA* 104 (1974): 329–46.

Scafuro, Adele C. *The Forensic Stage: Settling Disputes in Graeco-Roman New Comedy.* Cambridge: Cambridge University Press, 1997.

Schenke, Ludger. "Joh 7–10: Eine dramatische Szene." *ZNW* 80 (1989): 172–192.

———. *Das Johannesevangelium: Einführung, Text, dramatische Gestalt.* Stuttgart: Verlag W. Kohlhammer, 1992.

———. *Johannes Kommentar.* Dusseldorf: Patmos, 1998.

Schmeling, G., ed. *The Novel in the Ancient World.* E.J. Brill, Leiden, 1996.

Schnackenburg, R. *The Gospel According to St. John.* 3 volumes. Translated by Cecily Hastings, et al. Second Edition. London: Burns and Oates. 1980.

Scholtissek, K. "Abschied und neue Gegenwart: Exegetische und theologische Reflexionen zur johanneischen Abshiedsrede 13,31–17,26." *EphTheolLov* 75 (1999): 332–58.

———. "Das hohepriesterliche Gebet Jesu. Exegetische-theologische Beobachtungen zu Joh 17, 1–26," *TrierTheolZeit* 109 (2000): 199–218.

Scourfield, J.H.D. *Consoling Heliodorus. A Commentary on Jerome "Letter 60."* Oxford: Clarendon Press, 1993.

Segal, Arthur. *Theatres in Roman Palestine and Provincia Arabia.* Mnemosyne Supplements 140. Translated by N.H. Reisner. Leiden: E.J. Brill, 1995.

Segal, Charles. "Euripides' *Alcestis*: How to Die a Normal Death in Greek Tragedy." Pages 213–241 in *Death and Representation.* Edited by Sarah Webster Goodwin and Elisabeth Bronfen. Baltimore: Johns Hopkins University Press, 1993.

Segovia, F. *The Farewell of the Word: The Johannine Call to Abide.* Minneapolis: Fortress, 1991.

———. "John 15:18–16:4a: A First Addition to the Original Farewell Discourse?" *CBQ* 45 (1983): 210–30.

———. *Love Relationships in the Johannine Tradition.* SBLDS 58. Atlanta: Scholars Press, 1982.

Shero L.R. "The *Cena* in the Roman Satire." *CP* 18 (1923): 126–43.

Sifakis, G.M. *Studies in the History of Hellenistic Drama.* London: University of London, Athlone Press, 1967.

Slater, William J. "Pantomime Riots." *Classical Antiquity* 13 (1994): 120–144.

Slater, William J, ed. *Dining in a Classical Context.* Ann Arbor: University of Michigan Press, 1991.

Smith, Dennis. *From Symposium to Eucharist: The Banquet in the Early Christian World.* Minneapolis: Fortress, 2003.

———. "Table Fellowship as a Literary Motif in the Gospel of Luke". *JBL* 106 (1987): 613–638.

Smith, D. Moody. *John.* Abingdon New Testament Commentaries. Nashville: Abingdon, 1999.

———. *John Among the Gospels.* Philadelphia: Fortress, 1992. Repr. Columbia, SC: University of South Carolina Press, 2001.

Smith, Wesley D. "The Ironic Structure in *Alcestis.*" *Phoenix* 14 (1960): 127–45.

Staley, Jeffrey Lloyd. *The Print's First Kiss: A Rhetorical Investigation of the Implied Reader in the Fourth Gospel.* SBLDS 82. Atlanta, Georgia: Scholars Press, 1988.

Stauffer, E. "Abschiedsreden." *RAC* 1 (1950): 29–35.

——. *New Testament Theology*. Translated by John Marsh. London, SCM Press, 1955.

Stibbe, M. *John's Gospel*. New York: Routledge, 1994.

——. *John as Storyteller: Narrative Criticism and the Fourth Gospel*. SNTSMS 73. Cambridge: Cambridge University Press, 1992.

Stibbe. M., ed. *The Gospel of John as Literature*. Leiden: E.J. Brill, 1993.

Stillwell, Richard, ed. *Antioch-on-the-Orontes II: The Excavations of 1933–1936*. Princeton: Princeton University Press, 1938.

Stowers, Stanley. *Letter Writing in Greco-Roman Antiquity*. Philadelphia: Westminster, 1989.

Strachan, R.H. *The Fourth Evangelist: Dramatist or Historian?* London: Hodder and Stoughton, 1925.

Swain, Simon. *Hellenism and Empire: language, classicism and power in the Greek world AD 50 250*. Oxford: Clarendon Press, 1996.

Talbert, C.H. "The Myth of a Descending-Ascending Redeemer in Mediterranean Antiquity." *NTS* 22 (1975/76): 418–43.

Taplin Oliver. *Stagecraft in Aeschylus: The Dramatic Use of Exits and Entrances in Greek Tragedy*. Oxford: Clarendon Press, 1977.

——. "Significant Actions in Sophocles' *Philoctetes*." *GRBS* 12 (1971): 25–44.

Tarrant, R.J. "Greek and Roman in Seneca's Tragedies," *HSCP* 97 (1995): 215–230.

——. "Senecan Drama and its Antecedents," *HSCP* 82 (1978): 213–63.

Teodorsson, Sven-Tage. *A Commentary on Plutarch's Table Talks*. 3 volumes. Göteborg, Sweden: Acta Universitatis Gothoburgensis, 1989–1996.

Thalmann, William G. *Dramatic Art in Aeschylus' Seven Against Thebes*. Yale Classical Monographs 1. New Haven: Yale University Press, 1978.

Thom, Johan C. "'Harmonious Equality': The *Topos* of Friendship in Neopythagorean Writings." Pages 77–103 in *Greco-Roman Perspectives on Friendship*. Edited by John T. Fitzgerald. Leiden: E.J. Brill, 1996.

Thomas, John Christopher. *Footwashing in John 13 and the Johannine Community*. JSNTSS 61. Sheffield: Sheffield Academic Press, 1991.

Thönges-Stringaris, Rhea N. "Das griechische Totenmahl." *MDAI(A)* 80 (1965): 1–99.

Tolmie, D. *Jesus' Farewell to the Disciples*. Leiden: E.J. Brill, 1995.

Toynbee, J.M.C. *Death and Burial in the Roman World*. Ithaca: Cornell University Press, 1971.

Tilborg, S. van. *Imaginative Love in John*. Leiden: E.J. Brill, 1993.

Trapp, Michael. "Plato in the Deipnosophistae." Pages 353–363 in *Athenaeus and his World: Reading Greek Culture in the Roman Empire* (eds. David Braund and John Wilkins; Exeter: University of Exeter Press, 2000).

Usener, H. *Epicurea*. Leipzig: Teubner, 1887.

Vernant, J.P. "Figuration de l'invisible et catégorie psychologique du double: Le colossus," Pages 325–338 in *Mythe et pensée chez les grecs*. Paris, 1966. English translation: "The Representation of the Invisible and the Psychological Category of the Double: The Colossos," Pages 305–320 in *Myth and Thought among the Greeks* (London, 1983).

Walbank, F.W. "History and Tragedy." *Historia* 9 (1960): 216–34.

Walsh, P.G. *The Roman Novel: The Satyricon of Petronius and the Metamorphoses of Apuleius*. Cambridge: Cambridge University Press, 1970.

Waltzing, J.P. *Étude historique sur les corporations professionelles chez les Romains depuis les origins jusqu'à la chute de l'Empire d'Occident*. 4 vols.; Louvain: Peeters, 1895 1900.

Westcott, B.F. *The Gospel According to Saint John*. Rev. and enl. ed. James Clarke and Co. London. 1958.

Wilkins, John. "Dialogue and Comedy: The Structure of the *Deipnosophistae*." Pages 23–37 in *Athenaeus and His World: Reading Greek Culture in the Roman Empire*. Edited by David Braund and John Wilkins. Exeter: University of Exeter Press, 2000.

Windisch, Hans. Die fünf johanneischen Parakletsprüche. Pp. 110–137 in *Festgabe für Adolf Jülicher*. Tübingen, 1927. Repr. in *The Spirit-Paraclete in the Fourth Gospel*. Translated by James W. Cox. Philadelphia: Fortress, 1968, 1–26.

Winter, Martin. *Das Vermächtnis Jesu und die Abschiedsworte der Väter. Gattungsgeschichtliche Untersuchung der Vermächtnisrede im Blick auf Joh. 13–17*. FRLANT 161. Göttingen: Vandenhoeck and Ruprecht, 1994.

Witherington, Ben. *John's Wisdom: A Commentary on the Fourth Gospel*. Cambridge: Lutterworth Press, 1995.

Wolz, Henry G. "Philosophy as Drama: An Approach to Plato's Symposium," *Philosophy and Phenomenological Research* 30 (1970): 323–353.

Zeitlin, Froma. *Under the Sign of the Shield: Semiotics and Aeschylus' Seven Against Thebes*. Rome: Edizioni dell' Ateneo, 1982.

Zumstein, J. "Le processus de relecture dans la littérature johannique." *EtudTheolRel.* 73 (1998): 161–76.

INDEX OF MODERN AUTHORS

INDEX OF ANCIENT SOURCES

DEUTEROCANONICAL BOOKS

OLD TESTAMENT PSEUDEPIGRAPHA

ANCIENT CHRISTIAN WRITINGS

CLASSICAL GREEK AND LATIN WRITINGS

SUPPLEMENTS TO NOVUM TESTAMENTUM

ISSN 0167-9732

2. Strobel, A. *Untersuchungen zum eschatologischen Verzögerungsproblem auf Grund der spätjüdi-sche-urchristlichen Geschichte von Habakuk 2,2 ff.* 1961. ISBN 90 04 01582 5

16. Pfitzner, V.C. *Paul and the Agon Motif.* 1967. ISBN 90 04 01596 5

27. Mussies, G. *The Morphology of Koine Greek As Used in the Apocalypse of St. John.* A Study in Bilingualism. 1971. ISBN 90 04 02656 8

28. Aune, D.E. *The Cultic Setting of Realized Eschatology in Early Christianity.* 1972. ISBN 90 04 03341 6

29. Unnik, W.C. van. *Sparsa Collecta.* The Collected Essays of W.C. van Unnik Part 1. Evangelia, Paulina, Acta. 1973. ISBN 90 04 03660 1

31. Unnik, W.C. van. *Sparsa Collecta.* The Collected Essays of W.C. van Unnik Part 3. Patristica, Gnostica, Liturgica. 1983. ISBN 90 04 06262 9

34. Hagner, D.A. *The Use of the Old and New Testaments in Clement of Rome.* 1973. ISBN 90 04 03636 9

37. Reiling, J. *Hermas and Christian Prophecy.* A Study of The Eleventh Mandate. 1973. ISBN 90 04 03771 3

43. Clavier, H. *Les variétés de la pensée biblique et le problème de son unité.* Esquisse d'une théologie de la Bible sur les textes originaux et dans leur contexte historique. 1976. ISBN 90 04 04465 5

47. Baarda, T., A.F.J. Klijn & W.C. van Unnik (eds.) *Miscellanea Neotestamentica.* I. Studia ad Novum Testamentum Praesertim Pertinentia a Sociis Sodalicii Batavi c.n. Studiosorum Novi Testamenti Conventus Anno MCMLXXVI Quintum Lustrum Feliciter Complentis Suscepta. 1978. ISBN 90 04 05685 8

48. Baarda, T., A.F.J. Klijn & W.C. van Unnik (eds.) *Miscellanea Neotestamentica.* II. 1978. ISBN 90 04 05686 6

50. Bousset, D.W. *Religionsgeschichtliche Studien.* Aufsätze zur Religionsgeschichte des hellenistischen Zeitalters. Hrsg. von A.F. Verheule. 1979. ISBN 90 04 05845 1

52. Garland, D.E. *The Intention of Matthew 23.* 1979. ISBN 90 04 05912 1

53. Moxnes, H. *Theology in Conflict.* Studies in Paul's Understanding of God in Romans. 1980. ISBN 90 04 06140 1

56. Skarsaune, O. *The Proof From Prophecy.* A Study in Justin Martyr's Proof-Text Tradition: Text-type, Provenance, Theological Profile. 1987. ISBN 90 04 07468 6

59. Wilkins, M.J. *The Concept of Disciple in Matthew's Gospel, as Reflected in the Use of the Term 'Mathetes'.* 1988. ISBN 90 04 08689 7

64. Sterling, G.E. *Historiography and Self-Definition.* Josephos, Luke-Acts and Apologetic Historiography. 1992. ISBN 90 04 09501 2

65. Botha, J.E. *Jesus and the Samaritan Woman.* A Speech Act Reading of John 4:1-42. 1991. ISBN 90 04 09505 5

66. Kuck, D.W. *Judgment and Community Conflict.* Paul's Use of Apologetic Judgment Language in 1 Corinthians 3:5-4:5. 1992. ISBN 90 04 09510 1

67. Schneider, G. *Jesusüberlieferung und Christologie.* Neutestamentliche Aufsätze 1970-1990. 1992. ISBN 90 04 09555 1

68. Seifrid, M.A. *Justification by Faith.* The Origin and Development of a Central Pauline Theme. 1992. ISBN 90 04 09521 7

69. Newman, C.C. *Paul's Glory-Christology*. Tradition and Rhetoric. 1992.
    ISBN 90 04 09463 6
70. Ireland, D.J. *Stewardship and the Kingdom of God*. An Historical, Exegetical, and
    Contextual Study of the Parable of the Unjust Steward in Luke 16: 1-13. 1992.
    ISBN 90 04 09600 0
71. Elliott, J.K. *The Language and Style of the Gospel of Mark*. An Edition of C.H. Turner's
    "Notes on Marcan Usage" together with other comparable studies. 1993.
    ISBN 90 04 09767 8
72. Chilton, B. *A Feast of Meanings*. Eucharistic Theologies from Jesus through Johannine
    Circles. 1994. ISBN 90 04 09949 2
73. Guthrie, G.H. *The Structure of Hebrews*. A Text-Linguistic Analysis. 1994.
    ISBN 90 04 09866 6
74. Bormann, L., K. Del Tredici & A. Standhartinger (eds.) *Religious Propaganda and
    Missionary Competition in the New Testament World*. Essays Honoring Dieter Georgi.
    1994. ISBN 90 04 10049 0
75. Piper, R.A. (ed.) *The Gospel Behind the Gospels*. Current Studies on Q. 1995.
    ISBN 90 04 09737 6
76. Pedersen, S. (ed.) *New Directions in Biblical Theology*. Papers of the Aarhus Conference,
    16-19 September 1992. 1994. ISBN 90 04 10120 9
77. Jefford, C.N. (ed.) *The* Didache *in Context*. Essays on Its Text, History and Trans-
    mission. 1995. ISBN 90 04 10045 8
78. Bormann, L. *Philippi – Stadt und Christengemeinde zur Zeit des Paulus*. 1995.
    ISBN 90 04 10232 9
79. Peterlin, D. *Paul's Letter to the Philippians in the Light of Disunity in the Church*. 1995.
    ISBN 90 04 10305 8
80. Jones, I.H. *The Matthean Parables*. A Literary and Historical Commentary. 1995.
    ISBN 90 04 10181 0
81. Glad, C.E. *Paul and Philodemus*. Adaptability in Epicurean and Early Christian
    Psychagogy. 1995. ISBN 90 04 10067 9
82. Fitzgerald, J.T. (ed.) *Friendship, Flattery, and Frankness of Speech*. Studies on Friend-ship
    in the New Testament World. 1996. ISBN 90 04 10454 2
83. Tilborg, S. van. *Reading John in Ephesus*. 1996. 90 04 10530 1
84. Holleman, J. *Resurrection and Parousia*. A Traditio-Historical Study of Paul's Escha-
    tology in 1 Corinthians 15. 1996. ISBN 90 04 10597 2
85. Moritz, T. *A Profound Mystery*. The Use of the Old Testament in Ephesians. 1996.
    ISBN 90 04 10556 5
86. Borgen, P. *Philo of Alexandria - An Exegete for His Time*.1997. ISBN 90 04 10388 0
87. Zwiep, A.W. *The Ascension of the Messiah in Lukan Christology*. 1997.
    ISBN 90 04 10897 1
88. Wilson, W.T. *The Hope of Glory*. Education and Exhortation in the Epistle to the
    Colossians. 1997. ISBN 90 04 10937 4
89. Peterson, W.L., J.S. Vos & H.J. de Jonge (eds.) *Sayings of Jesus: Canonical and Non-
    Canonical*. Essays in Honour of Tjitze Baarda. 1997. ISBN 90 04 10380 5
90. Malherbe, A.J., F.W. Norris & J.W. Thompson (eds.) *The Early Church in Its Context*.
    Essays in Honor of Everett Ferguson. 1998. ISBN 90 04 10832 7
91. Kirk, A. *The Composition of the Sayings Source*. Genre, Synchrony, and Wisdom
    Redaction in Q. 1998. ISBN 90 04 11085 2
92. Vorster, W.S. *Speaking of Jesus*. Essays on Biblical Language, Gospel Narrative and
    the Historical Jesus. Edited by J. E. Botha. 1999. ISBN 90 04 10779 7
93. Bauckham, R. *The Fate of Dead*. Studies on the Jewish and Christian Apocalypses.
    1998. ISBN 90 04 11203 0

94. Standhartinger, A. *Studien zur Entstehungsgeschichte und Intention des Kolosserbriefs.* 1998. ISBN 90 04 11286 3

95. Oegema, G.S. *Für Israel und die Völker.* Studien zum alttestamentlich-jüdischen Hintergrund der paulinischen Theologie. 1999. ISBN 90 04 11297 9

96. Albl, M.C. *"And Scripture Cannot Be Broken".* The Form and Function of the Early Christian *Testimonia* Collections. 1999. ISBN 90 04 11417 3

97. Ellis, E.E. *Christ and the Future in New Testament History.* 1999. ISBN 90 04 11533 1

98. Chilton, B. & C.A. Evans, (eds.) *James the Just and Christian Origins.* 1999. ISBN 90 04 11550 1

99. Horrell, D.G. & C.M. Tuckett (eds.) *Christology, Controversy and Community.* New Testament Essays in Honour of David R. Catchpole. 2000. ISBN 90 04 11679 6

100. Jackson-McCabe, M.A. *Logos and Law in the Letter of James.* The Law of Nature, the Law of Moses and the Law of Freedom. 2001. ISBN 90 04 11994 9

101. Wagner, J.R. *Heralds of the Good News.* Isaiah and Paul "In Concert" in the Letter to the Romans. 2002. ISBN 90 04 11691 5

102. Cousland, J.R.C. *The Crowds in the Gospel of Matthew.* 2002. ISBN 90 04 12177 3

103. Dunderberg, I., C. Tuckett and K. Syreeni. *Fair Play: Diversity and Conflicts in Early Christianity.* Essays in Honour of Heikki Räisänen. 2002. ISBN 90 04 12359 8

104. Mount, C. *Pauline Christianity.* Luke-Acts and the Legacy of Paul. 2002. ISBN 90 04 12472 1

105. Matthews, C.R. *Philip: Apostle and Evangelist.* Configurations of a Tradition. 2002. ISBN 90 04 12054 8

106. Aune, D.E., T. Seland, J.H. Ulrichsen (eds.) *Neotestamentica et Philonica.* Studies in Honor of Peder Borgen. 2002. ISBN 90 04 126104

107. Talbert, C.H. *Reading Luke-Acts in its Mediterranean Milieu.* 2003. ISBN 90 04 12964 2

108. Klijn, A.F.J. *The Acts of Thomas.* Introduction, Text, and Commentary. Second Revised Edition. 2003. ISBN 90 04 12937 5

109. Burke, T.J. & J.K. Elliott (eds.) *Paul and the Corinthians.* Studies on a Community in Conflict. Essays in Honour of Margaret Thrall. 2003. ISBN 90 04 12920 0

110. Fitzgerald, J.T., T.H. Olbricht & L.M. White (eds.) *Early Christianity and Classical Culture.* Comparative Studies in Honor of Abraham J. Malherbe. 2003. ISBN 90 04 13022 5

111. Fitzgerald, J.T., D. Obbink & G.S. Holland (eds.) *Philodemus and the New Testament World.* 2004. ISBN 90 04 11460 2

112. Lührmann, D. *Die Apokryph gewordenen Evangelien.* Studien zu neuen Texten und zu neuen Fragen. 2004. ISBN 90 04 12867 0

113. Elliott, J.K. (ed.) *The Collected Biblical Writings of T.C. Skeat.* 2004. ISBN 90 04 13920 6

114. Roskam, H.N. *The Purpose of the Gospel of Mark in its Historical and Social Context.* 2004. ISBN 90 04 14052 2

115. Chilton, B. & C. Evans (eds.) *The Missions of James, Peter, and Paul.* Tensions in Early Christianity. 2005. ISBN 90 04 14161 8

117. Parsenios, G.L. *Departure and Consolation.* The Johannine Farewell Discourses in Light of Greco-Roman Literature. 2005. ISBN 90 04 14278 9